MW01461460

TEACHING EXCELLENCE

THE DEFINITIVE GUIDE TO NLP FOR TEACHING AND LEARNING

© 2016

Richard Bandler

Kate Benson

ISBN 978-0-9987167-1-8

1st edition UK
Artwork by Frank Zuithof of Logoshop
Copy editing by Jane Pikett of The Creation Group
Typesetting by Frank Zuithof of Logoshop
2nd edition
Typesetting by Juan Gabriel Díaz R.
djuangabriel.myportfolio.com
Printed by New Thinking Publications

NEW THINKING
PUBLICATIONS

© 2016 Richard Bandler and Kate Benson

All rights reserved.
No part of this publication may be reproduced, stored in a retrieval system, or transmitted in any form or by any means, electronic, mechanical, photocopying, recording or otherwise, without the written permission of the publishers.

DISCLAIMER

Please note that all information in this book is provided for educational purposes only and should not be construed as, nor replace medical or psychiatric advice. If you wish to use Teaching Excellence in the teaching of others you are required to undergo the appropriate training. See www.teachingexcellencebook.com for details

*For our children, Elizabeth, Jay, Keir and Tom
and for all the children who teach us so much
about love and learning*

Publishers Notes

Welcome and thank you for purchasing Teaching Excellence.

Bring your reading, learning experience to life. We have some members only content available at https://teachingexcellencebook.com.
As an owner of this book you are entitled to a free membership.
That membership entitles you access to interviews, chapter intros and outros.

Interlaced throughout our print publications are QR codes. Simply scan and visit. (free membership required)

Enjoy your learning...

Table of Contents

Acknowledgements X

Preface: A revolutionary new educational technology XI

Introduction XIV
The Challenge of Education Today
The Solution to Successful Teaching
The Educational Model of NLP
How the Brain Learns
How to be a Highly Effective Teacher
How to use this book

PART 1 THE BUILDING BLOCKS OF NLP APPLIED TO LEARNING 23

Chapter 1 How Learning Works 24
Discover the fundamentals of NLP which underpin learning strategies
Learn the basics of NLP used in teaching
Explore the tools for Thinking on Purpose
Learning on Purpose – the secrets of how learning works

Chapter 2 Building Strategies 36
How to drive learning with good feelings
A step-by-step guide to Learning Strategies
The secrets of building motivation and propulsion for learning
The benefits of Assessment FOR not OF Learning

PART 2 STRATEGIES FOR LEARNING 49

Chapter 3 How to teach anyone to spell 50
Learn the secrets of how to spell well
Discover the steps to teaching spelling from scratch
Identify the steps to improve poor spelling
Make spelling great for the whole class

Chapter 4 How to teach anyone to read – the mechanics and beyond 61
Discover how to create pleasure in reading
Identify the strategies to master the mechanics of reading
Explore the difference between learning to read and reading to learn
Learn the strategies for reading for meaning and reading quickly

Chapter 5 How to teach anyone to remember - Memory Strategies 74
How to build a great memory
Remembering names
Remembering lists and facts
Making remembering fun and rewarding

Chapter 6 How to teach anyone to calculate: Strategies for Mathematics 86
Developing your 'Mathematical Mind'
Counting and Skip Counting
Attractive Addition
Sublime Subtraction

Chapter 7 Mathematical Magic 98
Mastering Multiplication
Fast and effective Division
Geometry made easy
Engineering successful strategies

Chapter 8 How to nurture Creativity and Talent 116
Strategies for Music
Strategies for Art
Strategies for Creative Writing

PART 3 HIGHLY EFFECTIVE CLASSROOM TEACHING 130

Chapter 9 What makes a Highly Effective Teacher? 131
Discover the core beliefs that highly effective teachers hold true
Translate these beliefs into effective behaviours in the classroom
Develop the 7 habits of Highly Effective Teachers

Chapter 10 The Mind of a Highly Effective Teacher - The Art of the State — 145
Choose success ahead of time
Be ready for any challenge
Control the variables in the class
Drive your own neurology
Optimise your pleasure in teaching

Chapter 11 Winning your class over — 155
Discover the secret of super-fast rapport
Create powerful learning states with your students
Control the variables in the classroom
Learn how to anchor great learning states
Chain states together to lead students into resourceful learning states

Chapter 12 Building an Effective Learning Environment — 170
The success focus attitude
The keys to engagement and motivation in the classroom
Building exciting learning outcomes
Removing barriers to success

Chapter 13 Keeping the lesson on track — 186
Spinning the prayer wheel
Building Confidence with Competence
How to praise effectively
Giving feedback for great results

Chapter 14 Ending with new beginnings — 199
Creating the desire for more learning
Taking the learning beyond the classroom
Stretch and Challenge through questioning
Storytelling and Nesting learning

PART 4 TROUBLESHOOTING AND CHALLENGE — 213

Chapter 15 Changing unhelpful beliefsand attitudes — 214
Learn how to shrink a BIG problem down to size
Discover what is really being said
Use effective questions for change

Chapter 16 Timelines and other techniques for Motivation and Success — 229
Timelines in the classroom – preparing for exams
Bringing success into the present
Spinning bad feelings into good feelings
From stuck to motivated with a Visual Squash
Swish for a change
Visual Squash for a whole class

Chapter 17 Strategies for Learning Difference — 241
Learning difference not difficulty
Working with ADHD, Dyspraxia, Dyslexia, Autism and OCD
How to teach to the symptom not the syndrome
Explore neurological diversity

PART 5 NLP FUN IN SCHOOLS — 257

Chapter 18 Early Years: Under 5-years-old — 259
Changing submodalities to overcome anxiety and create happy states
Small changes in language create a big impact on an under 5
Language patterns with children with little English language
How to use music for state management
Creative use of spatial anchoring in the classroom

Chapter 19 Primary and Elementary School, 5 to 11-year-olds — 270
Subject-specific teaching strategies
Whole-class Spelling strategy
Spelling success in the Netherlands
Spreading the strategy across the school
Comfort and fun to improve reading
Eye accessing study of different reading strategies
Creativity and confidence in French language teaching
Creative use of NLP for creative writing

Chapter 20 Primary and Elementary School, 5-11-year-olds — 292
Creating positive learning states and overcoming challenges
Milton Language patterns with a hearing impaired learner
Creating happiness and harmony for a child with multiple challenges

Working with a child displaying severe anxiety
Simple language changes for big impact
Spatial classroom anchors for quiet attention.
Readiness to learn – metaphors and stories

Chapter 21 Secondary and High School 11-to-15 year olds 307
Creating enthusiasm for French grammar
Moving from a child who does not write to a writing enthusiast.
It's good to talk in Science teaching
State and language to build confidence in outdoor pursuits
Revision and recall in Science
Voice tone and body language in Food Technology

Chapter 22 Post-compulsory education, 16 years and over 327
Preparation for success
Memory strategy research
States for Learning Excellence, observation and Leadership for undergraduates
Academic coaching and mentoring

Chapter 23 Education Management 346
Challenging self-limiting beliefs in school
Disseminating NLP across the whole school
Supporting change in a school in Special Measures

Conclusion 362

Appendix A	Submodality checklist	364
Appendix B	Questions to calibrate eye-accessing cues	366
Appendix C	The Meta Model and Blooms Taxonomy	367
Appendix D	Transcript to use with students	370
Appendix E	Glossary of terms	372
Bibliography		376
Index		379
The authors		387
Testimonials		388

Acknowledgements

Our great appreciation goes to those teachers and students whose work contributed to this book. Whether your case studies made it into the final manuscript or not, we admire your enthusiasm for taking NLP into your classrooms. You are the ones who change lives, educate the next generation and install hope in the future. Our very warm thanks go to the many people who helped to bring this book to publication. In particular, Kay Cooke for her unswerving enthusiasm and practical support in the early drafts, Paul Boross for his pragmatic advice and Owen Fitzpatrick for his knowledge and valuable suggestions in the final stages of writing.

Our thanks go to Hugh Street, Julie Olsson and Joost van de Leij and the Meta Education team for supporting and promoting NLP Teaching Excellence training for teachers across the world.

A particular mention must go to our copy editor Jane Pikett. Thank you for believing in this book, and for your thorough approach and good humour throughout.

TEACHING EXCELLENCE

The definitive guide to NLP for Teaching and Learning

PREFACE

We live in a time of unprecedented opportunity. More children have access to more teaching and learning than ever before in history. New advancements in technology are placing a vast world of information at the touch of a button, the click of a mouse. The Neuro-Sciences are providing more and more information about how we learn and how we remember. The challenges facing teachers every day are greater than they have ever been. Curriculum changes, the expectations of parents, more and more administration. All this combined with the growing competition of social media leaves teachers with less time for delivery. We believe it is a wonder that people still enter the teaching profession. Yet it is for most of them, not just a job, but a mission. A mission to spread enthusiasm and joy for learning. The sense of achievement helping those hard to reach students to learn more.

JUST IMAGINE

You could radically transform how quickly and easily your students could learn.

JUST IMAGINE

You were equipped with the tools to entertain and captivate the attention of your students, so they were able to reach a greater potential.

JUST IMAGINE

You had the secret of teaching excellence!

Neuro-Linguistic Programming (NLP) is a set of skills, behaviours, and beliefs which enable people to think in much the same way as a successful expert thinks. Whether it is spelling, basketball, art, music or maths, NLP finds the structure and teaches it to those already so gifted.

NLP was created by Dr. Richard Bandler and Dr. John Grinder in the 1970s, to study excellence, and replicate it. In the field of Education, NLP furnishes the teacher, or parent, with a way to change how a student learns. NLP can create a paradigm shift in every learner, in every classroom, in every school, in every college. Our action-based research, published in the Durham Report, as well as other project reports, demonstrates stunning results.

THE UNIQUENESS OF THIS BOOK is that it does what no other book can. This book gets right into the heart of how learning works with the collaboration of Dr. Richard Bandler and the Director of Education for the Society of Neuro-Linguistic Programming™, Kate Benson. This collaboration of two people with such a deep and abiding passion for learning is the result of decades of relentless work.

Dr. Richard Bandler has spent the last 45 years developing elegant and swift ways to help people to think on purpose. To think more successfully, in a special way for each task. To motivate, decide and remember in new ways that make life easier and more effective.

Kate Benson has taught thousands of teachers to utilise NLP in teaching and learning to create happy and successful learners.

This book provides precise guidance that will enable every teacher to teach effectively to learners of every age, in every context. Whether you are new to teaching or very experienced, you can systematically improve your skills using the powerful technology of NLP. Those who train teachers will find strategies to train teachers. Ensuring the next generation of teachers gain the attitude, skills and behaviours that go into making great teachers great. So their students become tenacious learners.

This book shows you how to design and teach for learning, from memorising facts to magical mathematics, effective spelling, reading, creative writing, and so much more.

To survive and thrive in this world, learning itself is an essential skill set. Everything is changing faster than ever before. Learning to learn thus becomes, itself, a skill set. With this book everybody can become a more effective learner, and teach others along the way.

This book was written for you the teacher. We are very certain, since you are reading this book, you want to be the best teacher you can be. This book is designed to inspire and provide a step-by-step approach to mastering the art and science of learning. By the end of this book you will have the secrets of how to captivate your students and create exquisite learning effortlessly. Our mission is to share with you an exciting set of tools that can transform the impact you have in your classroom.

INTRODUCTION

Scan this to see the videos

"It is the supreme art of the teacher to awaken joy in creative expression and knowledge."

Albert Einstein

The children couldn't believe their ears. Here was a teacher telling them to cheat! When people hear the word 'cheat' they are shocked. We are taught from an early age that cheating is wrong, and indeed it is. But this teacher was not talking about cheating the way we normally understand the term. He was talking about using your mind in a way that you never did before. The teacher (Richard Bandler) was talking about organising and driving your brain so that it helps you to spell consistently, speak fluently, calculate effectively, read efficiently, remember consistently and learn easily. When learners are taught the quick and easy steps to learning it does seem that they have an unfair advantage, unless or until of course all children are taught the same processes. So some people may think this is cheating, while learners today might use the term 'learning hacks'. We prefer the terms **learning on purpose** and **thinking on purpose**

LEARNING ON PURPOSE
This book explores some vital questions:
Why do some students learn more easily than others? What makes

some teachers more effective than others? What are the keys to effective learning, remembering and thinking? The answers to these questions are surprising. The answers reveal that it is less a matter of intelligence and far more a matter of teaching teachers how to teach powerfully and teaching learners how to learn effectively. We can do this by understanding the mechanics of how teaching and learning happens in the brain. The training of teachers often pays scant regard for the tools of the teacher's trade - communication skills. Teachers learn about lesson plans, preparation of materials, pedagogic theory, but there is little or no input on how the brain works, how learning happens and how to effectively communicate these skills to learners. This is where our book fills the gap. The reason why we have helped thousands of teachers to improve how they teach is because the technology you are about to learn in this book looks at learning in a dramatically different way than ever before. Rather than talking about what students learn, we will explore exactly how they learn. More importantly, we reveal how you can help them to master learning.

A LEARNING REVOLUTION
The reality is that in the world we live in today, there are teachers of different standards and skill levels. The fact that you are reading this book suggests that you are one of those people who are truly interested in becoming terrific at what you do and making the lives of your students so much better. Perhaps you know intuitively that you can do even more and you are looking for the tools that can help you improve.

Addressing the failure of students to learn effectively is urgent. Across Europe, 1 in 5 people are functionally illiterate. In the UK, only 25% of the population have a reading level of a good GCSE and 44% have a similarly low level of numeracy.[1] 1 in 3 people in the USA cannot write a letter or use a calculator to determine a 10% discount. [2] The lack of basic skills costs the UK economy £81.312 billion and the cost to the US economy is $300.80 billion.[3] The problem is not simply economic or confined to basic skills. Many studies show happiness, wellbeing, health and crime rates all correlate to the level of educational attainment.[4]

The situation may also be critical as we find ourselves in the 21st Century with an outdated education system and training programmes for teachers that were designed for the 19th Century. The challenge educators now face is how to equip the next generations for a world where the job for life has disappeared. Today there is a need for flexibility and adaptability in working life and there is a dominant need for continual re-skilling. In fact, the pace of change is so rapid that almost every subject children learn as a 'truth' now will be irrelevant, out of date or 'untrue' in 10 years.(5)

MAKE THE DIFFERENCE

The solution to improve an outdated system, we believe, does not lie merely in a change to the structure or management of the education systems, but **with teachers themselves**. The good news is that teachers have the power to influence young minds and learners of all ages. You have the capacity to inspire, motivate, engage and create voracious, tenacious and enthusiastic learners every day of your life. Are you a teacher or do you simply care enough to want smarter solutions for the education of our next and future generations?

If you are a teacher you may well be thinking 'yes, but what about the pressures to deliver results, grades and league tables?' Of course you are right, there are many pressures on teachers to deliver and a great deal of bureaucracy to contend with. Also, some of you may be working in institutions that do not always support you in the way that you may wish. However, waiting for 'the authorities' to make your life easier just doesn't seem to work somehow. There are some really great teacher-led initiatives emerging in the field of Education and we know that they are gradually working into mainstream education.(6)

NLP IS AN EDUCATIONAL MODEL

The introduction of NLP into education by teachers trained by us means the system is beginning to benefit from well-documented, proven strategies for effective teaching and learning. The success of an excellent teacher is often attributed to qualities such as being charismatic, inspiring, energetic etc. However, NLP enables us to elicit the beliefs, attitudes and behaviours of such teachers and teach them to others. Whilst we can each claim our own individual pockets of excellence, we can all do more. You are one of the most important people in the lives of your learners. It is in learning from what has worked in this field that we can powerfully and practically improve the standards of teaching in every classroom and educational establishment. Here is our claim: By eliciting the strategies of the greatest geniuses of our time - excellent artists, magnificent mathematicians and exquisite experts in any field - and teaching these strategies to your students, you can ensure that they learn the thought processes and behaviours to successfully learn any subject. We believe that anyone can learn these apparently innate skills and become an inspiration to others and even more is possible as NLP provides the steps and strategies for how learning works.

As a teacher (and/or parent, carer and mentor) you have an unprecedented opportunity to teach the ability to think on purpose right from the beginning of a child's life or at least during their formative years. This means that rather than having to build on rocky foundations, you lay the foundations of healthy and happy values, beliefs and attitudes and teach children to drive their own brains so they become lifelong learners.

NEURO LINGUISTIC PROGRAMMING: THE STUDY OF EXCELLENCE
One of the most frequently asked questions is 'what is NLP'? In the 1970s Richard Bandler and John Grinder asked a different but very important question: *'How come some people go into a room and affect change in others whilst others don't?'*

By studying people who were actually succeeding in change work, looking at their behaviour and verbal/non-verbal communication, Bandler and Grinder systematically identified the factors that lead to change in clients. Interestingly, despite the very different approaches and theoretical models used by the therapists, they found that they had many of the actual behaviours in common. The behaviours and communication patterns used by the therapists were mostly unconscious or outside of their awareness. Bandler and Grinder paid very little attention to what the therapists *said* they were doing, and paid a great deal of attention to what they were actually *doing*.

To test their observations, Bandler and Grinder set out to replicate the behaviours of well-known experts in the field of psychotherapy such as Milton Erickson (a prominent hypnotherapist), Virginia Satir (a renowned family therapist) and Fritz Perls (a well-known gestalt therapist) and found that they could achieve amazing results despite lacking the vast experience of these leading figures.(7) The field of NLP began to grow at a rapid rate as the co-founders began to explore how the same methodology could identify the structure of excellence in other industries and areas such as medicine, business and, crucially, learning.

Similar questions can be asked of the teaching profession. How come some teachers are highly effective at enabling students to learn and others are not? Assuming that most teachers are experts in their subject, how come students are enthused and learn easily in the company of some teachers and not in the company of others?

We have been lucky enough to get an opportunity to study highly effective teachers on a mass scale. We have noticed that although each person has a unique style, there are common characteristics that they all share:

- They are systematic in their behaviours
- They are proactive and outcome-orientated
- They take notice, watch and listen (using all their senses)
- They are flexible in their behaviour, so students learn by example
- They are process rather than content-driven
- They see problems as challenges and opportunities to learn
- They endeavour to like their students

These characteristics are not innate, which means they can be learned. In this book we teach you how to adopt a mindset that enables you to be the best teacher you can be. As you begin to learn NLP and move through the chapters of this book, be aware that there is a significant side effect.

As you begin to apply the principles to your teaching, you may notice that the strategies can be used to make yourself happier, more effective and fulfilled, not just as a teacher but as a person! NLP isn't about 'fixing people' because they are not broken. NLP is about **optimisation**, so that you can make the most of the brain and body you have, free yourself from your personal fears, enjoy your loved ones and find pleasure and satisfaction in your life.

THINKING ON PURPOSE

An easy way to think of NLP is as **thinking on purpose**. Neuro Linguistic Programming is a set of behaviours, skills and attitudes that enable us to understand how we organise information and communicate with others. Put simply, your nervous system **(Neuro)** is directly affected at all levels by the way you communicate with yourself **(Linguistic)**. The interplay between your neurology and your language sets up patterns of behaviour **(Programming)**.

We learn how to communicate with ourselves through the way other significant people in our lives communicate with us as we grow and learn. Children learn through 'modelling' the adults around them. They learn the verbal and non-verbal ways to communicate with themselves through the way adults respond to them. Many people who discover NLP for the first time as adults find that they have the ability to choose their thought processes. This is often a huge revelation to them.

As NLP continues to develop and be applied to areas of medicine, sport and business, in this book we also draw on other technologies created by Richard Bandler. We make use of the three main technologies that produce the best results:

NLP: A model based on elegance; what is the minimum change we can make to get the maximum results?

Design Human Engineering® (DHE®): Enables us to design perfect strategies from scratch rather than elicit and install another person's strategy. So, instead of just learning from what someone else does, we can create new ways of getting even better results.

Neuro-Hypnotic Repatterning® (NHR®): Teaches people to lead with their feelings and create exquisite states of pleasure and enjoyment so that learning is not unpleasant and a struggle, but delightful, easy and fun. Much evidence points to the neurological benefits of learning whilst having fun!

For the first time, the co-founder of NLP reveals his discoveries of teaching and learning over more than 45 years of studying human behaviour through the NLP methodology. Finally, you hold in your hand the cutting-edge secrets of transforming how you teach and of using a technology that has begun to revolutionise the educational system.

When NLP was originally developed, advances in neuroscience, Magnetic Resonance Imaging, and the understanding of the enteric nervous system had yet to be discovered. NLP was perceived as a useful model. Over the past few years more and more scientific research has become available to support the model and our understanding of teaching learning.

Advances in the neurosciences and biochemistry have much to teach us about how people learn, however this forms little part of the teacher education curriculum. For example, we know that the most effective learning takes place when we are having fun because laughter releases endorphins into the bloodstream and smiling releases serotonin. Both of these neurotransmitters help us to feel good, and as these two chemicals react on the neural pathways, they aid in the creation of new synaptic links.[8] This short cuts the development of new neural pathways. So, rather than thinking about being a 'nice' teacher, it really is about generating smarter, more effective brain activity for learning.

We live in exciting times and we hope that you will join us on a journey of discovery for yourselves, your students and the future.

Here is the challenge we set out to address. We have yet to meet a teacher who doesn't want their students to learn and succeed. However, although there are many resources relating to teaching specific subjects, there has been very little attention paid to how people actually learn something new. The verb 'to learn' is very non-specific. The instructions given to a student often relate to the external behaviours they are expected to engage in, such as take notes, draw a diagram, read aloud. The students are not given the details of the steps they need to go through inside their mind to learn something new. Learning something new involves what you do on the outside and the inside of your mind and body.

It is now time to re-evaluate our teaching processes, focusing not just on content but on process, and learn to learn for life. The focus in many classrooms is 80% content and 20% process. We would reverse this and propose that good learning is 20% content and 80% process. What if the lesson content was merely the Trojan horse for the skills and processes of learning to learn so that we equip the next generations for the 21st Century and beyond? What if you could teach in such a way that would allow your learners to learn quickly and easily and to 'cheat' fairly? What if you could help give them a wonderful advantage that would last them the rest of their lives?

This book has its origins many years ago with a question on a seminar. Kate asked, 'How come you can teach NLP quickly and easily because you use NLP to teach NLP, but we are not using NLP to teach all the other subjects taught in schools and colleges?' Richard's answer was, 'that is a very good question – off you go and figure it out!' This conversation began a long collaboration between the two of us to combine our deep and abiding passion for teaching people to create exquisite learning through the technologies of NLP. This book is an outcome of our collaboration and we want to share our experience and understandings with you – the teachers of the next generation.

REFERENCES

1. Europe together against Functional Illiteracy www.literacy –and-vocation.eu
2. US Department of Labor Future work Trends and Challenges for work in 21st Century www.dol.gov
3. Final report of World Literacy Foundation April 2012 www.worldliteracyfoundation.org/The_Economic_&_Social_Cost_of_Illiteracy.pdf
4. The Social Benefits of Education, Behrman JR and Stacey N (eds). Ann Arbor, MI: University of Michigan Press, 1997
5. See: Sir Ken Robinson Changing Educational Paradigms www.thersa.org/events/rsaanimate/animate/rsa-animate-changing-paradigms
6. See the Durham report and Section 5 of this book for teacher led case studies http://www.teachinginfluence.com/resources/files/DurhamNLP_Report.pdf
7. Richard Bandler and John Grinder Frogs into Princes, 1979
8. Sue Perry Neurotransmitters: How Brain Cells Use Chemicals to Communicate http://www.brainfacts.org/

HOW TO USE THIS BOOK

This book is designed as a learning tool. There are bullet points at the beginning of each chapter to give you the main messages and 'big picture' and a summary at the end to consolidate your learning. Each chapter has accompanying activities to apply your new knowledge. Some activities are designed to enrich your own learning and others are designed to use and adapt in your own classes and with learners. NLP is a practical set of skills and 'knowing' about NLP is not 'utilising' NLP. The menu is not the same as the meal, so we strongly advise you to use the activities to practise and gain experience for yourself. If you are new to the field of NLP you will do well to read Part 1 thoroughly, as these chapters lay the foundations for understanding how to teach effective learning strategies and underpin all the later chapters. Once you have explored all the strategies for learning in Part 2, move on to discover more of how NLP applies to teaching and learning with the whole group and classroom context in Part 3. Part 4 examines ways to further support your learners and Part 5 hands over to teachers who have learned to use NLP in their classrooms so you can explore their applications and case studies. If you have some experience of NLP you may wish to skim over Part 1, which covers the elementary principles of NLP which form the foundation of strategies. We advise you to skim rather than skip these chapters because all the examples given are applied to the teaching and learning environment, so even if you are a Master Practitioner there will be new applications to learn. However you choose to experience this book, relax and enjoy!

PART 1

THE BUILDING BLOCKS OF NLP APPLIED TO LEARNING

Scan this to see the videos

CHAPTER 1

How Learning Works

'The aim of education should be to teach us rather how to think, than what to think.'[1]

Bill Beattie

In this chapter

- Discover the fundamentals of NLP which underpin learning strategies
- Learn the basics of NLP used in teaching
- Explore the tools for Thinking on Purpose
- Learning on Purpose – the secrets of how learning works

"Thursday is the only evening she has free. There is extra Maths on Monday, Literature on Tuesday, and karate on Wednesday - it's important she learns to stand up for herself! - Friday is Music, and Saturday its exam preparation." These words, spoken by a regular mum, are typical of the scheduling of children's time after school. Most teachers would agree that children are not in fact the *'empty vessels waiting to be filled with knowledge'* that the 19th Century philosopher John Locke claimed they were.[2]

Yet these days, far too often, we constantly try to cram more and more information into children's minds without considering how to promote thinking and use methods for learning that actually work. Teaching and learning are about the wonderful mysteries of the universe, and one of the biggest mysteries of all is exactly how to use your mind and your feelings. Simply transferring information isn't enough. We have to give people the mental tools to be able to know how to think for themselves, and we don't think that the ability to systematically give people these tools has ever existed before. Maybe we had one or two inspiring teachers, but they didn't consciously know what they were doing, and since they didn't know, they couldn't teach other teachers the tools. Now at last, NLP provides us all with the tools to do this.

THINKING ON PURPOSE
Take a moment to join us in an experiment. What is your immediate thought when you hear the word 'DOG'? Now ask a few other people for their responses when you say the word 'DOG' to them. What you may notice is that some people will see mental pictures of their dog, others will remember a bark, someone else may get a warm feeling, and another person may come out in a rash!

Next, select only the people who had a similar representation of the word 'dog' to you and ask them to describe the details or draw a picture. How many similarities/differences would you expect? Who is right and holds the master definition of the word 'dog'? Each person's dog reference is unique to them, yet we can all agree that these representations relate to a fairly uniform definition:
Dog: A domesticated descendent of wolf, generally 4 legs and a tail, variable size, colour and disposition.

As humans we experience the world through our five senses by seeing, hearing, touching, tasting and smelling our environment. This sensory input is filtered, coded and stored, and later recalled. To do this we create representations of the five senses with which we experience the world. In effect, we think through re-presenting to ourselves an interpretation of our senses. In NLP, we call this re-presenting of the senses of sight, sound, touch, taste and smell **the representational systems**, and we refer to each of these as visual, auditory, kinaesthetic, olfactory and gustatory.

When we ask you to think of your favourite teacher, how do you do this? Are you now aware of re-creating and accessing your experience as a picture, and/or sound, and/or feeling, and/or smell, and/or taste? Your **representation** of your experience is unique to you.

When your brain takes in your external experience through one (or a combination) of the sensory channels, you then code and store this data for later recall as a memory. Of course this retrieval (image, sound, etc.) is not actually the original perception, but your unique representation of it. Each representation has certain qualities, such as the size of the image, how loud or soft the sound is, where the feeling is located in your body, the type of smell or taste - sweet, sour, pungent etc. The qualities of these representations are called the **submodalities**. They are the distinctions between one representation and another.

Think again of your favourite teacher and compare this representation with one of a teacher you didn't like very much. In order to distinguish between the two teachers in your memory notice the differences in the submodalities of your recall. One picture you might have in your mind's eye may be still or moving, in colour or black and white, bordered or panoramic. Similarly, you may hear sounds such as the teacher's voice or some other sound, and this may be a surround sound or from a particular direction, high or low pitch, fast or slow beat. You might notice feelings in specific parts of your body or all over, you might feel a temperature change or a sense of lightness or heaviness. Perhaps there is even a taste or smell associated with the representations. So each experience has distinctions and there is a range of submodalities within the representation, which are not the same as reality. The map is not the territory!

To teach a learner to learn something new, it is crucial to identify their learning strategy. A learning strategy is the sequence of things a person does on the inside and the outside of their head, and the submodalities or qualities of these thoughts. We pay attention to these internal and external behaviours so we can determine precisely the sequence of the representational systems and the associated submodalities and this gives us the information to teach it to other learners. The instructions you give to a learner should be equally precise - when to make a picture, when to say something inside their head, when to feel a particular feeling. We want the strategy to have precise behaviours - both the ones we can see on the outside and the behaviours on the inside. (A full list of the submodalities to use for practice can be found in Appendix A.)

There are some abiding myths and mistaken assumptions about how skilled people are able to do wonderful things. For example, the assumption that musicians only use their (inherent) strong auditory representational system to compose or play great music. Similarly, that painters must have a 'good eye'. This is not necessarily the case. For example, one famous musician was asked on the radio how he composed music. He said: *'I wait until I can see it all out there in a big space in front of me and then I play the images!'* A friend who played in an orchestra was asked after a concert what she had been playing. She said, *'Oh, I don't know - I just play the dots'.* She saw the dots and her hands and bow moved to the correct position, then she heard the notes and made sure the sound matched the dots on the page.

All strategies in a kinaesthetic have a sequence of representations and most begin and end with a kinaesthetic representation - a feeling that tells you that you haven't done it yet and one that tells you that you have finished.

At this point, you may be reminded of a commonly held misconception in education - the idea that we each have a visual, auditory or kinaesthetic (VAK) learning style. Many schools and colleges use questionnaires to assess their students' learning styles, and while understanding individual **learning preferences** may be useful, it is a serious mistake to limit a person's chance of learning as a result of the idea that there is only one channel and one fixed way through which that person can learn.

The visual, auditory and kinaesthetic (VAK) learning style questionnaires used in many schools may have taken as their starting point the NLP representational systems described by Bandler and Grinder[3] but the use of VAK learning styles are reductionist - a gross oversimplification which falls short of supporting fast and easy learning. Instead, we need to be paying real attention to the **learning strategy** a person uses. Why? Because strategies can be identified, modelled and taught to others, quickly and effectively, using NLP.

LEARNING ON PURPOSE

Learning something new, remembering it and recalling it are process skills which involve a series of steps that utilise the representational systems. People don't use just one representational system all the time, although they may have context-related preferences. Furthermore, the more fully the representational systems are engaged and overlap, the more powerful the learning. The useful process of overlapping representational systems is known as synaesthesia, which is a good thing! As we learn something new, the more the representational systems are engaged, the more powerful and memorable the learning becomes. So, in short, a learning strategy is the sequence of mental and behavioural steps a person uses to install and encode the learning.

People are rarely aware of the process they are going through inside their minds because this process takes place unconsciously unless or until they become aware of it. Were you aware of how you thought about your teachers before you read the paragraphs above?

Even if we could make a learning styles questionnaire sophisticated enough to reflect the processes we have discussed, it still wouldn't be accurate because what people think they do and what they actually do can be very different. Take for example the (incorrect) assumption that people who like sport must be kinaesthetic and then look closely at the strategies used to score goals in the case of someone like David Beckham. Amazing players like Beckham need to be able to calculate distance, speed, velocity, and angles in addition to the kinaesthetic ability to kick the ball well. This involves a complex sequence using imagery, sounds and feelings.

Watching an 11-year-old playing very good football on the field, we observed him talking to himself the whole time, running through what he was doing, saying things like, *'Yes! He scores a goal! Back of the net'*. He was running his own personal coaching commentary. He was also visualising and calculating how the ball would go in the net with good kinaesthetic coordination in using his leg and foot to hit the ball. It is not surprising that sports coaches have made excellent and high profile use of NLP, using representational systems to bring about peak performance.

There is a trend in some schools of 'learning by doing' - or learning kinaesthetically - as a primary way of teaching. Although it is true that learning through doing can be a great way to learn, the problem with this approach is that it confines everyone to only one choice of how to learn. Worse, it also leads students to believe that this is the only way. The children who can learn with this type of teaching either make sense of it directly through the kinaesthetic channel, or they are able to translate it through their representational systems, which is how they manage to make it work for them. So they may talk to themselves about it as they do it, or they may make pictures of themselves doing the activity. The important thing is not what they do on the outside, but what they do on the inside. The teacher's job is to find the fastest, easiest and best way to encode the learning inside the learner and to limit their strategy to one method hinders learning.

Many students who are deemed to be 'slow learners' do not somehow have brains that work more slowly - they are just poor translators. This means they find it difficult to translate the teacher's teaching strategy into their learning strategy. Approximately 30% of children today are deemed to be 'academic' and may go on to higher education. However, what this more accurately reflects is their ability to translate information presented to them in a relatively limited way, through their own representational systems. Some have more flexibility in their internal behaviour, others process information in a similar way to the teacher, making it easier for them to learn. As Ignacio Estrada said, *'if a child can't learn the way we teach, maybe we should teach the way they learn'*.[4]

Sadly, it seems the input channels for learning offered to children become increasingly restricted as a child grows. There are interactive and sensory-rich experiences offered in early years, whilst at around the age of 7 or 8 there is generally a move to visual and auditory input, which then reduces to mainly auditory input for teenagers. Adult education takes a further turn to favour visual channels. This is one way people are restricted when they find it difficult to translate the input channel into their chosen representations. As one American teenager commented, *'when I am in school I have to power down'* (5) because his brain works faster than the speed of the teaching.

A research project undertaken by Frank Coffield evaluated 13 learning style models including the VAK questionnaire and concluded that, *'all but one of the learning style instruments were unreliable and invalid and had a negligible impact on the teaching of staff and the learning of students'*(6). The 'one' was not the VAK questionnaire! The only one given any validity was Howard Gardner's theory of Multiple Intelligences, which proposes that people are 'intelligent' in a variety of different ways. People may ask, *'if I can't use a questionnaire how can I find out how my students learn?'* Our answer is simple - **watch them** and **listen to them**.

People will show you or tell you how they are learning, or not learning, and give you all the clues you need to elicit their strategy. By watching and listening to a person, you can learn to read a learner's unconscious, non-verbal responses by matching external behavioural cues with a specific internal response. In this way, you can start to understand how they are thinking. This process is called **calibration**. The calibration tool we call **eye accessing cues** is one of the best-known discoveries of NLP. This easy-to-understand model enables you to notice and calibrate a person's eye movements. By observing a person's eye patterns, we can see where s/he accesses information, as follows:

- Looking up, left or right = accessing visual information
- Eyes to either side, level with ears = accessing auditory information
- Eyes down and to their right = accessing kinaesthetic information
- Eyes down to their left = talking to themselves

The direction of the eyes, left or right, depends on whether they are recalling/remembering information, or constructing/creating new information. Calibration is essential as these are generalised patterns, and it is important not to assume everyone has the same pattern.

See the chart below to see how this works in more detail. Imagine this illustration superimposed on the face of someone you are looking at:

```
Visually Constructed                    Visually Remembered
Auditory Constructed                    Auditory Remembered
Kinaesthetic                            Auditory Digital
                                        Talking to yourself
```

This is not new information; it's just that nobody noticed it before. You can test this for yourself. Notice what happens when you ask someone what colour are their child's eyes. Or what are the last words of the National Anthem. Ask them what temperature their toes are at the moment. Be careful not to make assumptions and pay attention to the way you ask the question. The response you get will be different depending on what and how you ask. One mother told us, *'I knew he was lying because he looked up and to the left'* (his right, indicating a constructed picture). But it is not necessarily the case that he lied at all - all we can say is that he created something visual. Perhaps it was an image of himself getting into trouble if he told a lie!

Attention to non-verbal cues from body language and eye accessing cues, combined with verbal feedback from a person, provides most of the information you need to elicit their strategy for learning. Hopefully you are even more aware now of how much information is available to you as you pay more and more attention to the clues, both verbal and non-verbal, of how a person processes information. Other cues to pay attention to are breathing rates, changes in the colour of a person's face, and the evenness of skin tone, to name a few. The important skill to develop is your ability to notice – your sensory acuity.

Now you could elicit a brilliant learning strategy, or one that doesn't work so well, or even one that is a disaster! What is really important is for you to become aware of the sequence in the way someone encodes and decodes information. This is the basis of their strategy for learning in that particular context.

THE EMOTIONAL STATE OF LEARNING

Effectively teaching a new strategy for learning involves more than merely knowing the steps to take. We don't want any key factors to be left to chance in the learning process and we want to take account of as many of the variables involved in effective learning as possible. A crucial variable is the feeling or feelings that learners experience when they are learning. This is not just about feeling good all the time. The way we feel enables a person to want to start learning, provides the motivation to continue, and to know when they are finished.

Take a moment to think about something that you were brilliant at and really enjoyed learning when you were at school. You probably knew you were good at it because you got feedback. You enjoyed it because your teacher was enthusiastic, fascinated, and nice to you. Your teacher created in you some of the key factors in learning well - a sense of security and being cared for, curiosity, enthusiasm, and motivation. Unfortunately, as teachers we often leave these key factors to chance rather than controlling them as variables.

When a person learns something new, the chemical and neurological conditions which exist at that time are directly connected to the learning. Any new learning is effectively 'glued' to the specific state you are in at the time you are learning. Many of us are aware that learning is an emotional process and it can be a great experience or, sadly, a fearful one. The term **'state'** in NLP means the total on-going mental, emotional and physical conditions that a person is experiencing at that moment in time, and from which a person acts. State is the totality of what you are thinking and feeling. For example:

- Remembering the past
- Imagining the future
- Referencing facts
- Hallucinating fiction
- Making pictures and movies in your mind's eye
- Making sound tracks of internal dialogue
- Feeling internal feelings like butterflies, excitement, calm, tenacity,
- Experiencing bio-chemical changes triggered by fight, flight or freeze

Your ability to enthuse your students, convince them that they can learn, it's worth doing and they want to learn, is a variable that is within your control to manage. So it's essential that you as a teacher find the state of enthusiasm for yourself first, and then convey that through your voice tone and language to the learner. So in the next chapter you will discover more about creating great states in your learners to ensure that they are motivated to learn and have fun doing so.

SUMMARY

During this chapter you have discovered how the representational systems work to encode and decode learning, and how we make use of this process to elicit and install simple strategies. You have increased your knowledge of sensory acuity so you can start to notice more and more about how your students learn and alter your language to communicate more effectively. You have considered current practice regarding learning styles and how NLP provides a much more effective way to elicit and install exquisite learning. Some of these fundamentals are re-visited in later chapters in relation to group and classroom work. Now you have some of the building blocks of learning strategies, go ahead, stay curious and have fun!

REFERENCES

1. Antonia and Bill Beattie, author, I Ching or Book of Changes
2. Locke, John. Some Thoughts Concerning Education and of the Conduct of the Understanding. Eds. Ruth W. Grant and Nathan Tarcov. (1996) Indianapolis: Hackett Publishing Co., Inc.
3. Bandler, Richard; Grinder, John (1976). The Structure of Magic II.Palo Alto: Science and behavior Books Inc.
4. Ignacio Estrada Director, Grants and Administration, Gordon and Betty Moore Foundation.
5. David Puttnam, www.theguardian.com/education/2007/may/08/elearning.schools
6. Frank Coffield et al 2008 Just suppose teaching and learning became the first Priority: Learning and Skills Network

ACTIVITIES

Activity 1

Ask a friend or colleague to spend a few minutes with you while you study their eye accessing cues.

Use an image such as this to draw arrows to indicate which way they look when you ask him/her questions. There is a list of questions in Appendix B to get you started, then be creative and start asking your own questions and notice the results.

Activity 2

Build some of the questions from the list and some of the ones you have created yourself into questions you can ask in class and start to notice where your students look and how they respond. Notice that how you frame your questions has an impact on the way your students represent the answer to themselves. Introduce your students to eye accessing with a pairs activity based on your own list.

Extension activity

Spend a day paying attention to how you give instructions. Record yourself for an hour and listen to how you phrase your questions and instructions. Ask your family, friends and colleagues too. Your children will tell you the truth! Do you use some phrases more habitually than others?

- Look this way
- Listen up
- Show me
- Tell me
- Follow these instructions
- Get on with it
- Notice how to do this
- Do you see what I mean?

- Do you understand what I am saying?
- Does it make sense to you?

All of these statements give a person a suggestion as to how to act on the inside. Evaluate your list and decide if the meaning of your communication is conveyed through the specific use of the words you choose.

CHAPTER 2

Building Strategies

Scan this to see the videos

'The illiterate of the 21st Century will not be those who cannot read and write, but those who cannot learn, unlearn, and relearn.' (1)

Alvin Toffler

In this chapter

- How to drive learning with good feelings
- A step-by-step guide to Learning Strategies
- The secrets of building motivation and propulsion for learning
- The benefits of Assessment FOR not OF Learning

Una, a Teaching Excellence student, was one of the best readers we have ever encountered. Una could read anything effectively and efficiently and enjoy the process. This is her strategy: As she begins to think about reading something she has a warm and light feeling of excitement and confidence, she smells a faint smell of pipe tobacco and Old Spice aftershave, and starts to imagine her 'reading room'. She studies the reading matter and decides what sort of reading room would be best for this particular literature. If it is a technical report, she might decide that a high stool with a stainless steel desk and a bright lamp would be good. Or if it is a novel she might decide that a big comfy armchair by a fire would be nice. When she has created her room she enters it in her imagination and begins to read. She can do this anywhere. It doesn't matter if she is on the Underground or standing at a windy bus stop because when she reads she is undisturbed in her reading room.

Eliciting her strategy was fun and illuminating. Asked how she learned to read, she said her father would come home from the city and sit her on his lap. He would read The Financial Times to her, moving his finger along the words as he read them out loud. Do you notice the sensory richness of her experience? She didn't need a special reading scheme and her experience shows that the context and process of learning is far more important than the content.

A huge amount of a child's learning takes place at home and is, for the most part, a matter of trial and error because parents have little access to understanding learning processes. Parents naturally have an expectation that schools and colleges have the best teaching strategies in place and use them at all times with their children. Yet one of the things we notice time and time again is how few teachers and parents understand the significance of knowing what a learning strategy actually is, when a strategy really works, and how to test that it works. Even fewer teachers and parents know how to build self-propelling systems for motivation to learn, despite understanding the importance of these processes.

DRIVING LEARNING WITH GOOD FEELINGS
The ability to merely learn to play music isn't enough. You want to have a self-propelling system to motivate yourself to enjoy learning and enjoy practising. Rather than just teaching children the dates on which a President was born, we want to teach them how to be motivated enough to pick up a book and discover information, to become interested in what that person offered to history and to think about how his part in history may affect the future.

Learning a new strategy is not only about the learning state you start with, but how to connect each step with the best state, in sequence, until you finish and feel great. Whatever the activity - whether it's a sport, art, music, geometry or spelling - if you are terrified you just won't do something as well as when you feel good. Doing a scientific experiment in chemistry in a state of curiosity and inquisitiveness leads to you watching carefully, making clear notes, and noticing what happens.

To install a good strategy we want to teach people what to feel just before they do something new, what to feel as they do it, and what feeling to have that tells them they have done it correctly - and stop! The key is to constantly attach the right state to the activity at the right moment, so that the activity itself triggers the internal feeling and provides the propulsion to complete it.

Think for a moment of the typical objections you may have heard from learners about learning something new. *'I want to do it, but I just can't seem to get around to it'*. What is lacking is the feeling of excitement about beginning something new. How about later in the process? *'I'm stuck and can't get back into it'*. This learner needs the state of tenacity and determination to push through to the end. Then of course there is the student who just drafts and redrafts and doesn't ever seem to hand in the finished project. This learner needs to know when they are finished and feel satisfied with his/her work.

As teachers we want to teach our students how to feel excited about getting started, determined to continue, tenacious when they get stuck, and ecstatic when they finish. There is no reason why, when they are at school, children can't go inside and remember being excited, and remember being frustrated, and get their frustration to lead to impatience, and this to lead to excitement. As teachers, we know in advance that learners are going to feel frustrated at some point and are highly likely to face a problem or task that feels too hard – it's happened to the best of us. When we chain the states and link them together, the feeling of 'it's too hard' leaks into feeling really frustrated, and the frustration leaks into impatience, and the impatience leaks into curiosity, then you really start trying to answer the problem. This process is going to build a tenacious child.

In this case the sequence is: **Frustration, Hesitation, Impatience, Curiosity, Desire** All too often when a child gets frustrated at school, the teacher will tell the child off and the result is the learning just stops. In our day you were sent to the corner or to the Headteacher. Even now 'time outs' are in common use. The effect of this is to connect frustration with stopping learning, rather than the teacher leading the frustration into curiosity or desire. Even the most caring parent can inadvertently create the belief in a child that when you get frustrated you stop. Recently, Kate observed a mother who intervened as soon as her child became 'stuck' or frustrated. When Mum was taught to say, *'oh dear, you seem to be a bit stuck there, it's time to think of another solution'*, the boy found another way and was consequently delighted with himself.

Children and teachers can learn to do this routinely and for fun until the point it becomes a game. Here is a game to try with your learners. Say to your learners, *'okay, think of the most frustrating thing we've done here today and how we hesitated to get going, but then feel impatient to get on with it and curious as to what we can learn next, so we really want to do it well and finish it!'* This literally loops the learners through the states so they don't stop in the wrong place, hit frustration and give up. Rather, they use their frustration as a motivation to continue and get to the end.

Humour, gentle teasing and chiding are an important skill for a teacher. By chiding children out of bad states they lead themselves from bad states into good states, and you build people who are self-propelled learners. **One of the most important things that a teacher does is to give the message to children - don't stop until you get to a happy place.** A bad place just means that you are doing it the wrong way and you have to take a step back and find the easy way.

A STEP-BY-STEP GUIDE TO LEARNING STRATEGIES

Learning doesn't stop at 3 o'clock in the afternoon and education doesn't just happen when you're doing homework. Everything you teach children, from cleaning their room, to washing the car, to doing chores, has a right state in which to begin, a way to know when you're doing it correctly, a way to know when you are not doing it correctly, and a way to know when you are finished. All strategies have a beginning, a middle and an end. It's just the same with learning strategies.

A strategy is a sequence of activities within our sensory representational systems that have become a single unit of behaviour. On a very simple level, imagine the process of answering a phone, or on a more complex level, of driving a car. When you first learn to drive a car, each activity has to be thought through individually, but as you practise over and over, driving becomes a single unit of activity.

A useful model for understanding strategy elicitation and installation is the TOTE model[2] **Test Operate Test Exit (TOTE)**

The TOTE model is the internal process we go through to successfully complete a strategy, whether this is getting out of bed in the morning, deciding what to eat for lunch, or learning something new. Here is a simple example of TOTE in action:

TEST – Have we done it yet? Test the present state (the workbook is blank) against the desired state (the workbook is completed). If the two don't match it's a no to the question!

OPERATE - Run the strategy with tenacity and determination, keep going and the more we get right, the better we feel, the harder the challenge the more determined we become to succeed. Using a variety of representations and submodalities the answer is worked out.

TEST - Have we done it? (The workbook is completed) Yes! Knowing that we have done just the right amount to complete the process, not going for closure too soon, leaving the question half completed and not persisting beyond what is necessary.

EXIT - We are done – feel great!

Good strategies are short and sweet! They have no additional or unnecessary steps and they have no unnecessary loops. Good learning strategies are driven by good feelings. Some people have really good strategies for motivating themselves to do things. Some people may have effective strategies but rely on pain rather than gain to achieve the result they want. For example, a famous horror story writer motivates himself to write scary books by scaring himself, which may not be the best way!

MOTIVATION AND PROPULSION
We wonder if you have ever heard teachers complain that their students *'just aren't motivated'*? Motivation is not a permanent state that you experience outside of any context. A friend went on a seminar with a famous self-improvement speaker. After the event our friend said he felt *'so motivated'*! We asked him *'motivated to do what?'* His answer was to do more courses with this speaker! Motivation is related to a particular context and everyone feels motivated to do something at some time, even if it is to stay in bed! Motivation is where you see that your homework is not done, and seeing it makes you feel like you **want** to do it, rather than you **have** to do it.

In addition to knowing the most effective steps and sequence of steps in a strategy, the rationale, desire and drive also need to be in place. Why you are doing it, what you have to do, how you do it, and where else it can take you. You also need to know when you are done! Any good strategy is not just about the steps to learn something - it includes the propulsion system to create the motivation to learn and find out even more, and has a sense of achievement when you have finished.

How do you motivate yourself? Do you motivate yourself **towards** feeling the gain or **away** from feeling the pain? Let's take a look at an everyday requirement to do something – getting out of bed! How do you motivate yourself to get out of bed in the morning? Are you up with the lark or do you roll over and leave it to the last possible minute before you get up? This example also illustrates the differences in effective and elegant strategies and ones that are clumsy and inefficient. It's also an opportunity for us to introduce you to the way we formally notate strategies.

Caroline is up with the lark. She knows she is awake when she hears the sounds in the room minutes before the alarm clock goes off. She imagines what she is going to do that day, sees herself enjoying herself, has a good feeling, throws back the covers and is up.
The strategy Caroline has, when the content is removed, goes like this:

Test: Am out of bed?	No	
Operate the strategy:		
She hears a sound	Ae	(Auditory external)
She sees a movie	Vi	(Visual internal)
She feels good	Ki	(Kinaesthetic internal)
She gets up	Ke	(Kinaesthetic external)
Test: Am I out of bed?	Yes	
Exit		

Duncan, on the other hand, wakes up when the alarm goes off, feels bad, groans, and turns the alarm to snooze. He says to himself, *'oh no, just 5 more minutes'*, and snuggles under the covers feeling how nice it is to be in bed. The alarm goes off again. He hits snooze again and imagines that if he skips breakfast he can have 5 more minutes. He snuggles back down in bed and feels how good it is to be dozing still. The alarm goes off again. He feels he needs to go to the bathroom, but puts it off and says to himself, *'just 5 more minutes'*. Then he imagines himself arriving late for work and what his boss will say to him. He has a feeling of panic combined with wanting to go to the toilet and he drags himself out of bed. The strategy Duncan has with the content removed goes like this:

Test Am I out of bed?	No	
Operate the strategy:		
He hears a sound	Ae	(Auditory external)
He feels bad	Ki	(Kinaesthetic internal)
He does something	Ke	(kinaesthetic external)
He says something to himself	Ai	(Auditory internal)

He feels good (still in bed)	Ki	(Kinaesthetic internal)
Test: Am I out of bed yet?	No!	

He loops this strategy round and round, adding bad feelings at each loop until the bad feelings he is using to motivate himself eventually get him out of bed.

Caroline's model goes: Test Operate Test Exit, which is short and sweet. Duncan's model goes: Test Operate Test Operate Test Operate (repeating over and over) Exit (eventually!)

If Duncan wants to enjoy getting out of bed in the morning he can change his strategy in a number of ways. Firstly he could 'try on' Caroline's strategy and see if it works for him. Or he can take some of the loops out of his strategy to make it shorter and more elegant and change some of the pictures, feelings and sounds to make it genuinely more pleasant to get up in the morning. Changing the sub-modalities of the sounds and images will often be sufficient to change the feelings associated with the activity. Or he could create an entirely new strategy that he likes much more and puts him in a great state for the day.

One of the choices that you make as a teacher in deciding how best to help someone is to choose which intervention to make. Recently, a black belt martial artist who was progressing very well in his studies wanted help with passing his examinations, which were demonstration-based. He said it took him too long to decide what move to make. He even used the term *'clunky'* to describe his strategy for choosing and making the move. His strategy was as follows:

He heard his master call out the move in Japanese	Ae
He would say the Japanese word to himself	Ai
He would translate the word in his head to English	Ai
He would look at the sequence of moves in his mind	Vi
He would rehearse the movement in his mind with his body	Ki
He would make the move	Ke
He was usually not sure he had it right	Ki

The strategy worked and was organised, but it wasn't elegant because it had more steps than he needed and he was unsure and not feeling good while running the strategy. The solution was to take out some steps and rehearse the new strategy a few times so he became confident in it.

There was no need for him to translate the word and say it in English. The Japanese word was already strongly associated with the movement, so his new strategy was to hear the instruction, rehearse the movement in his mind to check it was the correct one, and make the move with his body. It was clear that the new strategy worked because his whole body changed as he practised and he beamed widely as he finished, so it obviously felt good. So in this instance we modified a strategy to make it more efficient and elegant. His strategy wasn't broken, but as he said it was *'clunky'*, so streamlining was the answer.

Just as some teachers may use poor tonality to give instructions, many people put drudgery in the tone of voice inside their head when they think about studying or doing homework, see themselves being bored for a long time and feel bad about it. As children are great modellers, it's likely that they have your voice in their head as their teacher, so make sure it's a helpful and enthusiastic voice. Recently, a little boy was very sad because Mrs Troy wasn't his teacher anymore and he really liked her and said that she helped him. It was suggested to him that he could still ask for her help and she would probably tell him a great answer because he knew her so well. Mrs Troy's voice was in his head and so he could still utilise that resource to help himself.

Teaching students to have good strategies involves paying attention not only to the efficient way they learn something, but also to the good feelings about the activity. Being motivated by a negative feeling is generally not a good learning strategy. Instead, build propulsion through feeling good so that your body and your mind benefit from great neuro-chemistry.

Most children who enjoy reading have learned to enjoy books even before they can read. Cuddling up on a sofa with parents, grandparents, and carers makes book time a special time with good feelings associated with reading, which seems a great place to start. Contrast this with a child whose anxious/ambitious parents flash word cards to their 18-month-old, desperate to engage reading. As the child internalises the parents' anxiety, what is the feeling being attached to reading?

The 21st Century has seen a new phenomenon, the 'hyper-parent' - stressed to the hilt lest their child doesn't become a high achiever, while instilling in children that learning is hard work and that if they don't outstrip everyone else in their class they will be miserable for the rest of their lives! Since learning is state-related, these children may achieve great things, but they will not have good feelings associated with their achievements. If we are fearful and anxious every time we remember our times tables, is it any wonder that we prefer to forget them? A better option is to be like Una's father and install a love of reading with comfort and pleasure at the same time as using a simple strategy to teach reading.

ASSESSMENT FOR LEARNING NOT OF LEARNING!
One problem with the way the school system operates is that the **doubt** is with the child and the **certainty** is with the teachers. This means that the only way a child knows they are doing well is by an **external reference**. The teacher is the one who tells you when you have finished and whether you are right, rather than you solving the Maths problem and turning the page to see if the answer you got is the right answer. This teaches children to feel good by pleasing the teacher by the shortest route, rather than feeling good by self-initiated problem solving. This is the wrong kind of strategy installation.

At this point we can almost hear the cries of the teachers! *'Well the students won't do the work – they will just cheat and look at the answers!'* If the strategy the teacher installs isn't an effective one and the answer is on the next page, yes, you will just look at the answer without doing the problem. This is because the fun isn't in getting the right answer; the fun is in getting over the pain! The problem is not that the student is looking for the prize through minimum effort; it's what they have been trained to do. The problem is they are trying to please the teacher rather than themselves.

Richard installed a strategy to learn maths extremely quickly with John Sebastian La Valle, son of John La Valle – Richard's co-trainer and co-author with Richard of Persuasion Engineering®. The name of the game was get the right answer so you can please yourself! This is how the conversation went:

"I kept saying to him 'I don't give a hoot if you get the right answer. But if you do this you get the right answer'. John said, 'wow I got the right answer', so I said 'I bet you can't do 5 of them'. John said 'will you check them?' I said, 'no, here's the right answers'. I wrote them on 5 separate pieces of paper so he wouldn't have to look at all 5. I said, 'OK, here's the first one. When you're done, flip over the piece of paper and look at the answer. If it's the right answer you get to feel really cool and move on to the next one. If not, you have to go back and do it until that's the answer you get'. John said, 'what if I can't get it?' I said, 'well then you just keep going until you do and if you really can't do it then I'll show you how to do it, but why should I show you if you already know how? Maybe it might take you three tries'. Then he got one right, and the next, and did 6 months' homework in 4 days. Just like that."

Teaching a child to multiply 3 times 8 and get the answer 24 is all well and good, but there is an infinite number of numbers. Do we want to teach every single combination or do we want to teach the students to want to have the right answer? We need to design the learning to the strategy so that when the student sees those numbers s/he wants to find out what the answer is so they can feel good. As the students learn the answers they want to build the chart in their heads so that the answer pops out of their chart as fast as possible. The faster it pops out, the better they feel.

Why bother figuring out how to spell words? Because it feels good to do the right thing! If a child gets 10 words right, the next time the child will use the same process to learn new words. It makes your job as a teacher much easier. Build in the desire to get the right answer for themselves, not to please the teacher, so the child knows to focus on what they are doing that is right. If they grade their own tests, so nobody except s/he knows whether s/he is right or not, and the teacher gives exactly same test again, the child builds more and more right answers, and if s/he desires the answer s/he will go for it.

This way we could reduce the grading structure to simply an 'A' or an incomplete!

SUMMARY

During this chapter you have explored the key elements of effective learning strategies including chaining states, the representational systems, the TOTE model, and propulsion.

A key message to consider is how we equip our students to please themselves rather than gain satisfaction only from external and target-driven criteria. Armed with this information, we hope that the following chapters on specific strategies will build the desire for great learning for yourself and for your students.

REFERENCES

1. Alvin Toffler (1970) Future Shock, USA: Bantam Books,
2. Bandler, Grinder, et al 1980 Neuro-Linguistic Programming Vol.

ACTIVITIES

Activity 1

DON'T STOP UNTIL YOU ARE IN A HAPPY PLACE GAME
Spend 10 minutes with a group who could do with a bit more motivation.

Place 4 large signs on the floor in a row with a sequence of states such as:

INTEREST- FRUSTRATION – IMPATIENCE – DESIRE
Have the group move to each sign and discuss with the students each state in turn, asking questions that elicit that state for them, such as:
'What interests outside school do you have?'
'What's great about it?'

Move on to the next sign asking about frustrating experiences and have them share them until they all feel frustrated.
Move on to impatience and repeat the process.
Finally move on to Desire. Talk about what floats their boat, what do they dream of doing or having. Now go back to the beginning and move the group swiftly from one sign to the next so they just touch

into each of the feelings before moving onto the next one. Make it a race to link one to the next and the next. And of course end with the really good feelings so they are in a happy place. Remind them of this activity and their experience next time they need a little motivating.

Activity 2

ELICIT A STRATEGY IN PREPARATION FOR THE NEXT CHAPTER
Find a person willing to help you elicit their strategy for a process we have discussed. It could be for deciding to read a particular book, or getting out of bed.

Find out as much as you can about what they do inside to do this. Here are some questions to help you get going;

What happens as you are doing this?
What do you do as you are preparing to do this?
What steps do you go through to do this quickly?
What do you do first?
What do you do next?
How do you know when you have done it?

If you think you have missed something, back up and ask:
What did you do just before that?

How do you know when you have done it? Try the strategy on for yourself. If it works through to the end – you have all the pieces

HOW TO TRY ON A STRATEGY
Decide on something that you could do to have a better strategy to make the activity more exciting or enjoyable. Find someone who does this really well and elicit their strategy. Close your eyes and take some time to imagine going through each of the steps for yourself. Do this thoroughly and completely. Does this work better for you? If not, you don't have to keep it. If it does, then decide you like it and keep it for yourself.

PART 2

STRATEGIES FOR LEARNING

CHAPTER 3

How to teach anyone to spell

Scan this to see the videos

'Nanny Ogg knew how to start spelling 'banana',

but didn't know how you stopped.'[1]

Terry Pratchett

In this chapter

- Learn the secrets of how to spell well
- Discover the steps to teaching spelling from scratch
- Identify the steps to improve poor spelling
- Make spelling great for the whole class

We taught Louise to spell in 15 minutes during a tea break on a Neuro-Hypnotic Repatterning® (NHR) course. Afterwards she was furious! She said, *'I have been feeling stupid for 30 years – why didn't anyone teach me how to do this before!'* We explained that perhaps no one else she had met knew the precise steps to teach her to do this. The next day she arrived with coloured pens and large pieces of paper, set about finding every person in the group who had trouble spelling and proceeded to teach them her new-found strategy. She became an evangelist for spelling well, determined that no one else would feel like she had for all those years.

If you have been a poor speller in the past, apply the process we are about to teach you to yourself first, because a basic premise of NLP is 'you go first'! This spelling strategy is short, sweet and easy to learn, so it is also a good place to start developing your skills for all learning strategies.

Many people refer to the 'NLP spelling strategy'. This is a little odd since there isn't actually one spelling strategy and it doesn't belong to NLP. There is, however, one way that most really good spellers spell and NLP gives us the tools to discover the steps to the strategy (elicit the strategy) and teach others how to do it (install the strategy). Since it is so effective, it makes sense to teach people this way - so let's sit for a spell!

What makes a good speller is that they are consistent and remember very well what a word **looks** like. Ask a good speller how to spell a word, and invariably they look up to their left and see the word in their personal spelling database as a big, clear and still picture; when they see this they get a good feeling down the midline of their body – a positive yes!

Ask a person who is 'OK' at spelling to spell a word and the process is more cumbersome. They may look up to their left, but they have to check it by sounding the letters out or sometimes breaking the word into phonemes (small units of sound) and then get some sense of it being right – maybe!

Ask a poor speller to spell a word and they will do a whole range of other things. For example, they may look up to their left and discover the word isn't there, then they may say to themselves, *'oh no, I don't know how to spell this'*. Then they will look down and feel bad, and then try to work it out phonetically (foniks dosent werk for spelling in Inglish!) and finally they will get a feeling that lets them know they are still not sure.

A good speller who encounters a new word pays attention to the new word, makes a big still image of the word in their mind, and once they have the picture in their mind, feels certain they have the image which makes them feel good. So what we see is that a person who has a strategy for recalling information will also have a strategy for learning something new in the first place. Notice how quick the process is. Most effective strategies are as short as possible and have no unnecessary pieces or loops.

It is not that some people are naturally good at spelling and some are naturally bad spellers; they have simply worked out a way of spelling that may or may not work well. Invariably, those who have worked out a way of spelling that does not work well have done so because they haven't been taught a good strategy in the first place. It is our responsibility as teachers to put this right, hopefully before our learners create limiting beliefs such as *'I can't spell'*. When teachers teach spelling in the way they believe it works (this may just be the way they do it for themselves) or without sufficient detail in **how** to spell, the children have no option but to randomly work out a strategy for spelling. So it's inevitable that some of them get it right and others don't.

The qualities of the representations are important to an effective strategy. If you are making small, faint images it's unlikely you will remember these images clearly. To be confident in doing something you want to make a big, clear image of yourself doing it. One lady said during a class, *'I just can't see myself doing that somehow'*. It would be easy to assume that this person was speaking metaphorically and there could have been a long conversation about why this was, her past experience of learning, her confidence etc. Instead, she was asked to *'just move the picture closer so it becomes bigger'*. She said, *'oh, that's better, now I can see myself doing this'*.

Now think about how spelling is often taught in schools. The child copies the words down from the whiteboard into one of those narrow, half-size exercise books used especially for spellings. When children are small and learning their first words, they have not graduated to using a pen so the words are written in pencil so the writing is faint and grey. Is it any wonder that they have difficulty remembering small faint letters in a little book?

TEACHING SPELLING FROM SCRATCH

Spelling strategies are the easiest strategies to install in people who can't spell and it's a great convincer for a student when they discover they can overcome a previously strongly held limiting belief. You can easily test this out for yourself with a student who wants to spell well. The first distinction to make is whether you are teaching someone to spell a word *for the first time* or whether you are *improving or correcting* poor spelling. This is an important distinction because the strategy used is slightly different, depending on the situation.

TEACHING HOW TO SPELL A WORD FOR THE FIRST TIME

To teach the spelling strategy from scratch, select a word that the learner has no idea how to spell. It's not necessary to choose a simple word first; it's more important that it's a word they want to spell and they are motivated to learn to do it. With children, the word could be to do with a hobby or craze. With adults we often ask, *'what word always trips you up?'* or *'what word do you avoid using because you are not sure of it?'* One lady wanted to spell *'administered'* because she was a nurse and always had to write 'given' in patients' medical notes because she couldn't yet spell 'administered'. The length of the word is unimportant because the learner is about to make a complete image of it.

Now take some coloured pens - the NLP Education Team use scented pens (see later) - and ask the student to choose a colour for each letter. Write each letter in nice big lower case letters on a large piece of paper, eg., flipchart paper. Words are generally written in lower case, so this is the lettering to use for teaching how to spell. Have the paper straight ahead of the learner, not flat on the table, and when you are talking to the learner use the correct name of the letter, not the sound. This way you prevent the learner returning to an unhelpful part of their strategy - namely, trying to spell a word phonetically.

Say to them, *'now close your eyes and make a big picture of the word. When you have a clear picture open your eyes and check that the two words match'*. Repeat this process 2 or 3 times if it helps the student. This is almost always sufficient. The brain makes the image easily and quickly when directed with precision. When the internal and external images match, celebrate their success so the person feels really good – not just nice, but fantastic! (Remember, we are creating a great state to glue to the learning!).

Now ask them to close their eyes again, look at the picture and tell you in sequence what is the first letter, second letter etc. until you get to the end of the word. If the person can't recall the letter, ask them what colour it is, and then ask them what shape is the colour. This gives them access to the letter through a different channel or representational system. If you use scented pens, you can also ask what the colour smells like to help them further. Increase the celebration and excitement with each letter so the person has a good feeling every time the words match. Continue until they have named all the letters in sequence. (NB - the use of colour and scent does not make this multi-sensory learning, it just provides another route to the image, which is what you want the learner to access).

It's not just a matter of making sure the person can say each letter. They must also be absolutely convinced that they can now spell this word. So here is **the convincer**:
Ask the learner to start at the end of the word and spell the word from the last letter to the first. It's just as easy to do it in reverse as it is forward because they have made a big, clear and still image. Usually, the person will feel good now all by themselves as they realise that they now have a way of learning any word they choose, backwards or forwards. Make sure you celebrate their success to reinforce the good feeling they get when they do it correctly, so that they want that feeling again and again. This builds motivation.

IMPROVING POOR SPELLING
Here is the modification for poor or erratic spellers. Ask the learner to spell a word and observe their strategy as they do this. Ask some helpful questions such as *'which bit of the word are you unsure about?'* It's often the middle of the word that is confusing or vague, or it can be an unusual or irregular part of the word. When you ask the learner to look at the word in their mind, the person will often report that they can see some of the word but part of it is blurry, or they can't see it or it dances about. Select this part of the word and write the whole

word out in the same way as before, but this time use black for the part of the word they know and highlight the part of the word they had trouble with in their favourite colour (there is no need to write each letter in a different colour). Then go through the same process as previously outlined to make the image big, clear and still. Remember to celebrate their success and explain that because they can now spell this one word they found tricky, they have the strategy to do the same with any other word they like – forever!

There are lots of tricks to help someone spell, however the most important thing is to pay attention to what they are actually doing and saying, so that you can find the one key piece to change that will make the whole strategy work. So, for example, if someone says they can't make a picture, back up to show them how to do this first. If the picture dances about, help them to hold it still. Ask them *'what colour is your front door?'* or *'what does your favourite shirt look like?'*. Ask them to imagine sitting in a cinema and make a picture of a red rose that fills the movie screen. Do whatever is necessary to help the learner. Paying attention and being creative are essential attributes to using NLP for learning. NLP is a model based on elegance; that is, scientific exactness and precision. In NLP this means that we make the smallest intervention in a very precise way to create the biggest change.

TEACHING SPELLING TO THE WHOLE CLASS
The strategy outlined here can easily be adapted to whole class teaching and can have a profound effect on your students' spelling scores. The Durham Project[2] involved a group of teachers with no prior experience of NLP. The teachers were taught as much useful classroom-focused NLP as possible in a day and a half. The results in one particular school were astonishing.

The teacher, Andrea, and her Learning Support Assistant, Kelly, decided to see if they could improve the spelling of the whole group. They realised that they were already doing a number of useful things, so they just made some small changes to the way they taught spelling to improve the internal strategies the children were using. Small changes are not insignificant changes – they can be the ones that are the difference that makes the big difference. The children already looked at the words and wrote them out, then checked they were correct. But there wasn't a specific instruction as to how to check the words so Andrea and Kelly introduced colour to make the spelling pattern they were concentrating on stand out. This use of colour helps the children make better pictures of the word.

Andrea then changed her language. For example, she asked the children to **see** the word rather than **remember** it. The words were written on the right hand side of the board and the children were moved so they sat looking directly at the board and moved their eyes to their left to see the words. Armed with scented felt tip pens, the children wrote out the words on BIG sheets of lining paper. This, in addition to introducing colours, made the task more fun.

A number of the children were not improving as fast as the others, so Kelly made some lovely textured letters to help them recreate the words. Using the textured letters doesn't mean the children were learning spelling kinaesthetically, just as using scented pens doesn't mean learning through the olfactory sense. These simply provide **another route to learning the words visually**. The aim of a strategy is to be as simple as possible, with no additional parts or loops to the sequence. Kelly created the textures to introduce an extra encoding only for those students who needed it. The primary focus was to ensure that the children made really good pictures of the words and the addition of colour and texture aided this process for a few children, but it wasn't necessary for the majority.

Now look at the spelling scores. Week 1 was the baseline assessment before the changes were introduced:

RESULTS OF THE PROJECT

WEEK 1 — **18% FULL SCORE**   **46% 5 OR OVER CORRECT**

WEEK 2 — **66% FULL SCORE**   **81% 5 OR OVER CORRECT**

WEEK 3 — **71% FULL SCORE**   **92% 5 OR OVER CORRECT**

The step change in the results is nothing less than spectacular. Less than 20% of the children got a full score in the baseline week, whereas more than 70% got all the spellings right just 2 weeks later. This is why NLP learning strategies are a little piece of magic! The full report of this project is included in Part 5 of this book.

A great strategy for learning spelling goes like this:
Hear the word spoken	Ai (Auditory internal)
See the word externally	Ke (Kinaesthetic external)
Make a big still image on the inside	Vi (Visual internal)
Feel a positive 'Yes' feeling	Ki (Kinaesthetic internal)

Once the strategy is installed correctly and the person is a great speller, she/he will hear the word and automatically see a big, clear and still image on the inside, with a positive feeling attached to it.

This is about as short a strategy as a person can have and illustrates the elegance of effective learning strategies.

Of course a child doesn't need to know about notation, but it is important to keep the learning fun. Here is just one variation especially loved by little boys. It's best to use a very conspiratorial voice for this!

HOW TO BE A GREAT SPY!
'This is a secret and only you have the code. Spies have lots of special equipment and secret hiding places. Do you know you have a secret camera that is so small no one else can see it? So here is how to use your special camera to spell every word you see and remember it easily - just like a spy! Look at the word; now take a picture of the word with your secret camera, blink, and click the shutter. Blow up the picture so it is really big and check that your picture is the same as the one on the paper. It is? Good, now look up in your mind and store the picture in your secret filing cabinet. When you hear the word in the test, sneak up inside your mind, open your secret filing cabinet and look at the word. Then copy it down on your sheet. Don't let anyone know though because it's top secret and you are training to be a great spy!'

When you listen carefully to the language learners use, they will often tell you directly how they are processing information, especially when you take what they say literally.

For example, imagine a student comes to you saying, *'I am struggling with this assignment. I just can't get going with it and I'm stuck. I don't know what I am doing'.* How would you reply? Remembering the representational systems we mentioned earlier in this chapter, what clues do you have about the sensory channel this student is using to express her problem? Words like *'struggle', 'get going', 'doing'* indicate strong kinaesthetic representations. In order to gain rapport with the learner and **speak the same language** you need to use the same sensory-based language in response, such as, *'okay Anne, it feels like we need to get to grips with this so let's roll our sleeves up, get stuck in and unpack the problem'*.

However, if in response, a teacher uses a strong visual preference to solving this particular problem and replies, *'okay Anne, clearly you just can't see the wood for the trees. Let's take a good look it and see if we can shine some light on the problem, we just need to focus in on the big picture'.* Anne is expressing her (problem) experience using language that is primarily kinaesthetic, revealing that, at this time, she is using the kinaesthetic modalities to access her representation of the problem. By matching her language the teacher has a good chance of helping her, whereas by using his default (visual) language, he runs a great risk of alienating her and she may well retort, *'oh you just don't get it',* and she would be right! If you listen to the way she is representing the problem, you can respond using language which will make her feel like you can really help her. It's a case of speaking the same language – literally!

Similarly, improving your ability to notice a learner's eye accessing cues and other nonverbal cues (your sensory acuity), so that you notice 'how' people learn, gives you a huge amount of information without anyone saying a word. This can be especially rewarding when dealing with older children and teenagers, who are not known for their love of communicating with adults. Where a person looks, how and when they breathe, and their body posture are all clues to tracking the learning strategy they are using. It helps you to work out which parts work and which don't.

Take Adam for example, he hasn't done his homework and when asked why he hasn't done it, he reveals his strategy for not doing his homework. *"Well, I was going to do it and then I imagined playing football instead and I said to myself, 'what would I rather do? The football is much more exciting than sitting studying'. So I checked the time and decided I could do it later. But when it came to it I was too tired."* Adam's strategy for not doing his homework begins with him making a picture of himself doing something else. He gives himself a choice by asking a question in his mind and then compares the two different feelings – doing his homework and playing football – makes another picture of time and expands time so that he will have enough time to do both. Finally, he has another feeling (being too tired) and doesn't do it. Does this sound familiar?

It's also worth bearing in mind that many people have favourite or habitual ways of expressing themselves and assume that because they are communicating effectively everyone will understand precisely what they mean. This may not be the case! People respond to language at an unconscious level, literally. You may believe you are illustrating a point metaphorically, but the other person may be responding to it in a very different way. Remember the lady who couldn't see herself doing something?

Understanding how someone learns requires you to track the sequence that they go through using the representation systems. Listen and look for the combination of visual, auditory and kinaesthetic representations in the sequence. The sequence may work really well - or it may not. When you learn to track the sequence you will begin to know where and what to improve and just where to make the change so the strategy works really well and makes the person feel great at the same time.

SUMMARY

In this chapter you have learned how to teach the strategy for spelling, both with individuals and with a whole class. You have developed your sensory acuity further and begun to listen carefully to the language people use to discover their strategies for learning. So now you can begin to install exquisite learning strategies in all your students.

REFERENCES

1. Terry Pratchett, 1991 Witches Abroad, Victor Gollancz
2. Kate Benson and John Carey 2006 The Durham Project, META Ltd1

ACTIVITIES

Activity 1

NOTICE EYE ACCESSING CUES IN AN EXCELLENT SPELLER
Find someone who is an expert speller. Ask them to spell a word and watch very carefully their eye accessing cues. Pay really close attention, because this will happen very quickly. You may want to repeat this a few times so you become skilled at noticing what they do.

Activity 2

INSTALL AN EXCELLENT SPELLING STRATEGY IN A POOR SPELLER
Now find someone who is not confident with spelling and repeat Activity 1, noticing what they do with their eyes and body. This will be easier because the process will go on longer!

Ask if the poor speller would like to sit for a spell and improve their life by teaching them to spell using the strategy in this chapter. Keep it simple and remember, your enthusiasm is infectious!

Extension activity

What are the key terms your students need to know in your subject? Make some big, bright and colourful cards or posters and put them on the walls high up. Refer to them from time to time with the instruction to 'see' the correct word on the poster on the outside and the inside of their minds. Leave the cards/posters there for a week or two and then take them down and ask the students to write down the words. Notice how they look at the posters in their imagination.

CHAPTER 4

How to teach anyone to read – the mechanics and beyond

Scan this to see the videos

'One must be an inventor to read well. There is then creative reading as well as creative writing.'[1]

Ralph Waldo Emerson

In this chapter

- Discover how to create pleasure in reading
- Identify the strategies to master the mechanics of reading
- Explore the difference between learning to read and reading to learn
- Learn the strategies for reading for meaning and reading quickly

Consider for a moment the shocking facts that in the UK 1 in 4 people are functionally illiterate and 42 million adults in the USA can't read. Immersing yourself in the pages of Tolstoy and Shakespeare is not the issue here. Simply being able to understand a bus timetable or official letter is essential to day-to-day life and freedom of choice. Reading is a route to freedom and a basic human right rather than an academic choice. It is not just a question of accessing the rest of the curriculum, although this is important too. Regardless of what subject or age group you teach, we hope that every teacher equips themselves with the skills to teach reading and improve their learners' strategies for reading. Reading is a foundational pillar of all learning. It is not therefore about learning to read, it is about reading to learn. Once we begin to move on from teaching the mechanics of reading towards recognising the capability of reading as a skill that facilitates learning, we open up a whole new vista of possibilities for learning almost anything.

Let's start by making three distinctions:

1. There are the mechanics of reading - recognition of the letter pattern and the associated sound of words, and applying rules as to how the words are used (these are Mastery skills, see chapter 14).

2. There are the reading strategies for specific needs such as 'reading for meaning', 'reading for full sensory immersion' or 'reading speedily to extract information' (these are Developmental skills, also see chapter 14).

3. Underpinning both these activities is discovering the joy and pleasure associated with reading.

The assessment of whether someone can read or not is often treated as a yes or no question. Why do we talk about a person's ability to read in such digital terms as 'can do' or 'can't do'? To look at a sequence of letters and know how to pronounce the word is only one level of learning to read. Knowing what the word means and being able to manipulate the meaning in your mind is another step. Creating images, feelings and a virtual reality is yet another. Grasping the mechanics of reading is just a step and not the goal. What we really want is to be able to utilise the best reading strategy according to the context and required outcome.

LEARNING TO ENJOY READING
The problem with words on a page is that they are two-dimensional and, initially, less interesting to look at than the multi-sensory three-dimensional world we inhabit. A baby looking at, touching and feeling a cat and hearing it making interesting sounds is quite excited to learn that the thing is called cat. When s/he looks at the three flat letters C A T and is told that says cat, it's not such a rich experience. So it's

an advantage to quickly work out the mechanics of letters and words so that the child can move swiftly on to enter a world of sensory-rich imagination.

Strategies that encourage people to generate rich pictures out of 'flat' words encourage learners to read swiftly and efficiently, and this can start well before a child formally learns to read. Children who read really well have usually had books read to them. They have sat on the lap of a parent, grandparent or caring adult, staring at the page, listening to the story and making vivid pictures in their mind's eye. So when they look at the words they don't bother to see each and every word, they make pictures of the story. The story is also not in their own voice.

When you hear a story, it enables you build other voices in your head. For many of us remembering back to school, the best part about reading was the teacher reading to the class whilst we had the book, so that we weren't burdened with the process and could immerse ourselves in the experience, just as Una did (Chapter 2) when she sat on her father's knee when he read to her.

Once a child has discovered the joys of the written word, their desire to enjoy the process for themselves is awakened and the mechanics of reading are just the next step to more pleasure.

LEARNING TO READ
Words are connected to an experience, so that when your mother says *'get off the floor'* you know you are not on the ceiling! After a while, the word 'floor' means floor. We say to young children as they climb all over the furniture, *'it's a chair, it's for putting your bottom on'* and after a while 'chair' means chair – for sitting on. We don't say the word 'stop' to stop the car - when we see the stop sign your foot just goes down on the brake pedal. We apply a meaning that is associated with the experience. The experience of stop isn't the same as reading the word 'stop', but it is the physical experience of ceasing to move that keeps us safe when we see the word.

We believe that making a bundle of letters more important than the meaning of the words is a major mistake. Learning about the meaning of words can and should be fun. For example, we teach children to run over and put the right word on an object, so nouns then become 'things'. Children learn the meaning of the verb 'to run' through doing the action. Children wear stickers with 'run'/'walk'/'hop' printed on them so they do the action as they move towards a labelled chair or window, connecting the verb with a noun to start to build sentences that have meaning and make sense. Pronouns, adjectives and adverbs can be added, so the children then *jump quickly to the shiny window*. When children are taught in this way, the rules of grammar become intuitive; grammar becomes an unconscious process that 'feels' rather than 'looks' right or wrong. This is an important distinction to make. Yet we teach children to read by sitting still, rather than in a large interactive room.

Remember the value of connecting good feelings with learning (Chapter 2)? When learning is a game connected with good feelings then everyone wants the experience.

This is not just limited to children. A scientist who reads about an experiment in an academic paper instantly makes sense of laboratory conditions and equipment and pays little attention to the words. Most people who have high comprehension of written material think this way. The scientist probably couldn't recall the precise words s/he had read, yet they could describe the experiment in detail. So it's like being there. When Richard does this he makes life-size mental pictures with everything full scale, showing different points of view, and can gain more understanding than even the author by taking different positions and perspectives.

Now it is time to raise the on-going debate over the choice of reading scheme and methodology. There is a huge amount of discussion, some of it quite adversarial, over the 'right' reading method.[2] It is not our intention to enter into or add to the controversy; we utilise NLP to focus on the processes involved in reading to determine the right strategy. There are three main reading methods advocated and we can utilise aspects of each of the methods once we free ourselves from the rhetoric of the debate. The three main categories are:

1. Phonics – synthetic or blended or analytic, focusing on the sound of letters and letter sequences.[3]

2. Whole language – focusing on the meaning of the words.(4)

3. Look and say – focusing on the shape and recognition of a word.

60% of children will learn to read with any given reading method. Either the method will suit the way they like to learn at that time or they are able to adapt and translate the methodology and make it work for them. The other 40% may struggle. Change the methodology and the statistics will be the same, but the individual children involved will be different, because the new scheme will suit different children. So the solution is to understand what goes on in the brain when learning to read and have a number of different methodologies available to suit each child.

When a child doesn't read, it may be more a question of the flexibility of the teacher and the methodology, not the child's abilities. Change the method and the child will read very quickly. Our experience of teaching reading is that when a new approach is introduced a child will immediately get results after 1 hour and, provided the method is continued, the child will catch up in a matter of weeks.

Before a child can make use of phonics in English s/he needs to be able to sight recognise between 50 and 100 patterns that make up words. This means looking at the **word** and knowing what it says and how it sounds. If children can't do this they are likely to become bad spellers, because English is full of weird anomalies and a child needs to have a rudimentary understanding of these to make sense with phonics. For example, take 'through' 'threw' 'true' and 'trough'. Try working these out without any knowledge of the structure of the English language!

One young boy who engaged his mother in a conversation about 'abory-jines' had worked out how to pronounce the word aborigines by using phonics, and a Lancashire girl wrote 'slayd' in her story to describe her favourite activity in the park (the slide) based on how she pronounced the word in her accent. These children were being creative too quickly! Phonics is very inefficient in English, although it works better in some languages such as Spanish, and in others it is irrelevant. Try learning Japanese phonically!

Synthetic phonics is now prescribed in English schools and is working well in some of them.(5) However, we observe that these schools often have enthusiastic teachers who actively engage the children in the process of learning. The children are enjoying themselves and having a complete experience where all the senses overlap (synaesthesia), so of course they learn well. This begs the question - is it the process of being engaged or the model of synthetic phonics that is accelerating the learning process in some schools?

Take a lively and enthusiastic group of teachers, committed to teaching children to read with one system or another, and most of the children will learn easily. Take the same system and give it to a reluctant and unenthusiastic group of teachers and the children won't be engaged, won't learn easily, and may well struggle.

Strategies which encourage learners to make pictures of words, rather than sounds of words, encourage learners to read swiftly and efficiently. The most efficient readers are sight-readers. These readers don't say the words or make the sounds, either on the inside or the outside of their head. So why do we assess reading ability through speaking out loud? It's another case of doubt and certainty! The early reader will often read aloud in a doubt-filled voice, which makes it more likely that they will feel doubt when they read. The teacher may know that the child can read a particular word, but the unintended consequence is to slow the reader and the reading down.

Once a reader begins to develop a degree of competence it is preferable to ask him/her to read some pages and tell you what they are about. This begins to encourage children to read for meaning and understanding. Testing whether they can read certain words can be achieved through writing. Testing if they understand what they have read can be achieved by asking them to tell the story or act it out in their own words.

A common misconception is that a person uses the same strategies for reading as they do for spelling. The following example also illustrates what happens when there is insufficient focus on the **meaning** of words. A father told Kate that he had become concerned about his young daughter's reading ability. Dad, with a little NLP experience, had attempted to coach his daughter to make a picture of each word listed in a recent homework, in the same way as described in chapter 3 for the spelling strategy. However, the task was not a spelling one; it was a comprehension task to match the most appropriate word within each sentence listed. The child struggled and everyone became frustrated – how could the father's NLP spelling strategy fail? The answer is that the spelling strategy works for spelling and was not the correct strategy for this challenge. What was needed here was a *strategy to assign meaning* to each word, not to recall or spell a word. She would then know which words went where based on their meaning. For example:

Take your shoes off and _____ in the grass

It rained so the _____ in the park ended

Choose the correct word:
yield, blossom, romp, ambush

Here are some useful steps to teaching reading. First, teach a child to enjoy the reading process so that they want to do it for themselves and have great feelings about stories.

The strategy for building a love of reading looks like this:

Contentment and anticipating the story	Ki – Kinaesthetic internal
Child listens to the story	Ae - Auditory external
Child imagines pictures, movies	Vi – Visual internal
Child experiences a range of feelings (scary, happy, intriguing etc.) and finally excited, enjoyable and wanting more!	Ki – Kinaesthetic internal

Next create associations between objects, their meaning and the image of the word to build sufficient language structure and encourage sight-reading through games and fun activities.

See Activity 1 at the end of this chapter.

Use some phonics to enable a child to work out any unfamiliar words and encourage private reading with discussion to ensure progress. Encourage comprehension and understanding through discussion.

If you encounter a child or adult who isn't accessing reading easily, the trick is to use strategy elicitation to discover what isn't working. Take Emily, for example. When she was eight, her reading development was way behind her peers. Watching and listening to her read, it quickly became obvious that she just didn't get the phonics system she was being taught at school. Saying the sound of the letters one after the other didn't get her to the word: 'c......a......t c...a...t c..a..t – *DOG*', was one such response. She was basing her thinking on the picture (it looked like a dog) and what she already knew. However, her sensory acuity was fantastic; she never missed a trick and would notice immediately if something was moved in the room. She also loved to be active, especially singing, dancing and acting. So the new game was to put the names of objects on things around the house, then collect the labels, mix them up, and label the objects again. Next she moved on to labels for activities (verbs) and it took just 3 weeks for her reading to catch up with her peers. A few weeks later she was given a play to narrate and this year, aged 9, she is top of her class for reading.

READING TO LEARN
Mr Beadle was very frustrated with his group of 14-year-old History students. He would ask them, *'did you all read chapter 4 of the textbook?'* Yes would be the answer. *'So what were the key messages?'* Response – silence! They can read the words as instructed, but may not have been taught how to extract the information from the text.

Once a child has mastered the mechanics of the reading process, more strategies are needed to be able to read for meaning or pleasure, or skim and scan to extract information. We don't think our education system pays enough attention to developing these skills, Even though processes like SQ3R. Survey Question Read Recite Review[6], are useful, there is no mechanism to teach the reader **how** to survey or question or review. Fortunately, NLP offers more.

A STRATEGY TO EXTRACT INFORMATION AND MEANING

When it comes to reading for meaning, the most important thing is for the reader to have a good question in their head as they look at the words. A question like 'what is this about?' is a good start. Ask students to say this to themselves as they take 30 seconds to look over 2 or 3 pages, then answer the question. This creates an overview of the subject – the big picture!

The next step is to have them ask themselves, *'what are three main points on these pages about this topic?'*, scan through the pages again and answer the question.

The third question is *'find three things about each of these three key points'* and there you have it - within 2 minutes they can tell you 13 pieces of information about those pages.

You can try this for yourself. Pick a new chapter of this book. Before you look at the first page ask yourself *'what's this about?'* and make a mental note of the answer. Secondly ask yourself *'what are 3 key points in the text?'* and make a mental note of your three answers. Thirdly ask yourself to *'find 3 additional points about each of the 3 key questions'*; and make a mental note of three pieces of information you have arranged under the first three headings. Now close your eyes and **pay attention** to how you know the answers to these questions. This will give you a better understanding of your personal strategy for learning key points.

A STRATEGY FOR SPEED READING

During a Teaching Excellence seminar in Amsterdam, Kate was asked for help from Maria, who said she read very slowly and wanted to be able to read much faster than she did at the moment. What was interesting is that Maria was an extremely effective and efficient speller, but she read really slowly. She used a strong visual strategy for spelling but a slow auditory strategy for reading, saying each word to herself. She was taught the strategy outlined above and it helped a bit, but she was still struggling with the instruction *'scan your eyes down the page'*. Her eyes kept stopping on words whilst she said them to herself, until Kate said, *'not those eyes – use your spelling eyes!'* Maria said, *'OH, RIGHT! I was using the wrong eyes – now I can scan the page easily!'* In her excitement at discovering a new strategy she went home and spent the whole evening reading everything she could find.

To speed up **reading for meaning** you need to stop saying the words inside your head and it's important to teach the student this as a skill. When asking themselves the first question, have them just scan their eyes down the centre of the page. Ask them to do this quite steadily at first, just looking with the focus on the middle of the page. Their peripheral vision will take in the rest of the words well enough to know what the page is about. They can then repeat this process with the other questions and demonstrate easily to themselves how quickly they can take in information. This is the essence of speed-reading techniques. But don't tell anyone – you're supposed to go on expensive courses to learn to do this!

The lady in Amsterdam already had the right strategy in place and just needed the key to access it. It's worth noting that there may well be a place for her original strategy, such as reading poetry out loud. Every strategy can be useful in the right context.

During the course of researching this book, we made a study of how good readers extract information from a book and observed some key patterns. Firstly, lots of people have a kinaesthetic process to begin with. They will turn the book in their hands to get the feel of it. Then they will look at the front and back covers. Some people go straight to the end and look at the last page. One lady said she wanted to read the last page to decide if it had a good enough ending or not. That was how she decided it was worth reading the rest of the book. The next thing people did was skim over a few pages. When asked what they were doing, they said they were looking to see how well written it was. Some people find bad style irritating while others are drawn to a style they like, so the visual input led to a kinaesthetic response in this instance. At this point, most of the good readers were deciding whether to read the book or not. Once these criteria were fulfilled, they went on to read using variations of the strategies outlined above.

Remember that NLP is the study of subjective experience – and if you want to help someone do something, a good place to start is by studying what they can already do well. It's a matter of being able to back up from the particular difficulty and ask the questions about what is going on or what is not going on subjectively, and what needs to happen before the person can perform a particular task or skill. By studying the subjective experience of people who are already skilled in a particular task, we gain the resources to teach others to do the same.

SUMMARY

Now you have the fundamental strategies for teaching anyone to learn and enjoy reading. You have explored the strategies that progress students from the mechanics of reading to effective, efficient and pleasurable reading. These skills give you the opportunity to free others from limitation and have access to their fundamental human rights to information, decision-making and choice through the written word.

REFERENCES

1. Ralph Waldo Emerson 1837 The American Scholar: An Oration delivered before the Phi Beta Kappa Society, at Cambridge, MA
2. Kim JS. 2008 Research and the Reading Wars. In: Hess FM When Research Matters: How Scholarship Influences Education Policy. Harvard Education Pres, Cambridge, MA 3. Regie Routman, 1991, Invitations, Heinemann Educational Books
4. 2014, What's Whole in Whole Language in the 21st Century? Carn Press New York
5. Reading the next Steps, 2015, Department of Education
6. Francis Pleasant Robinson (1978). Effective Study (6th Ed.). New York: Harper & Row

ACTIVITIES

Activity 1

Make a set of cards with nouns, verbs, adjectives and adverbs printed on them. Play the 'find the word game' with a child or a group of children. First, put the cards printed with the nouns on objects around the room (or house) with the child/ren. Then collect the cards up and make a game of putting them back on the right objects. Immediately correct any places where the cards are not right yet, and keep going until they are all right. Then move on to the verbs. Give the child/ren the verb cards and have them move in this way to the objects. Add the adjectives and adverbs to the sequence to start building sentences.

Here is an example:
Window
Put the right word on the window
Hop
Do this to the window
Quickly
Hop to the window like this
Shiny
Hop quickly to the shiny window
Adapt this process to create more games.

Activity 2

Find a person who is a really effective reader and is willing to help you elicit their strategy for reading.
Find out as much as you can about what they do on the inside.

Here are some questions to help you get going;

- *What happens as you are doing this?*
- *What do you do as you are preparing to do this?*
- *What steps do you go through to do this quickly?*
- *What do you do first?*

- *What do you do next?*
- *How do you know when you have done it?*

If you think you have missed something – back up and ask,
- *What did you do just before that?*

Extension activity

Make some question cards as a new resource for your class to improve their comprehension of a subject as they read and review a text. Make the questions as sensory-rich as you can:

- *What would it feel like to have been in the jungle at that time?*
- *Build an image of the volcano in your mind. How hot would it feel? How would it sound? What are the smells associated with volcanoes?*

CHAPTER 5

Memory Strategies

SCAN THIS TO SEE THE VIDEOS

'The true art of memory is the art of attention.' [1]

Samuel Johnson

In this chapter

- How to build a great memory
- Remembering names
- Remembering lists and facts
- Making remembering fun and rewarding

'I can't remember! I have a memory like a sieve! I forget things all the time!' These are cries we hear over and over again. From children sitting with furrowed brows staring at facts, to adults panicking over failing memory, it's a problem for many people. This chapter teaches you memory and recall strategies that are easy to learn and use. It takes just a few minutes, once you know what the key steps are and how to drive your own brain, to develop a great memory for yourself and your students.

Like it or not, there are times when we have to remember information. Even in the age of technology, instant images and Wikipedia, some information needs to be memorised. It's a pleasurable experience for many people to remember information such as poetry or dialogue from a play or film, so if remembering information can be fun some of the time, why not make it fun all the time?

Good memory techniques use all the senses. The more senses that are engaged, the more powerful the recall will be.[2] A good memory technique has two key components. Firstly, remembering the item, and then, more importantly, recalling the item. Think of this as encoding and decoding the information.

By connecting the senses together we create synaesthesia. Synaesthesia occurs when one experience or representation immediately fires another experience in a different representation.[3] So, for example, smelling baking bread may immediately bring to mind an image of your grandmother in her kitchen. The olfactory sense fires a visual representation.

The ability to remember information is also the foundation of creativity. The process of memorising depends on how creative you can be in presenting and representing the information to yourself. The first question to ask is, *'how do I represent this information to myself in a way that is useful?'*

Having a great memory is about choosing the most helpful way to encode the information and store it so it can easily be decoded. For example, to learn the capital cities of different countries, the best place to put them in your mind is on a map. Then you can animate the map in your mind, so as you focus on each country it expands to make it really big and you make the capital city pop out of the country. Repeat this with each country and capital city. The more you teach children to do this in their imagination, the more it becomes automatic and the question is not *'can you look at the picture of Japan and make it big in your head?'*; but *'how big can you make it?'* *'How big can you make the letters of the capital city?'* If the word *'Mississippi'* is written in white on white you won't be able to see it. But it's easy to see it when you make the letters in a strong contrast and exaggerate them.

Concentrating on encoding means that people can decode easily. The result is they can recall the information in a number of different ways and contexts. Reciting poetry from memory is easy when it is written out on a huge screen inside your mind so you can read it from a distance. Children remember nursery rhymes perfectly because a nursery rhyme has a melody and a rhythm which is pleasing. Add the melody to the big screen and connect it to a body movement. So if you can't quite recall a line of the poem, look at the screen, listen to the rhythm or just put your body in the same position and the line pops up so that each representational system triggers all the other systems.

LEARNING NAMES
Many teachers worry that they can't learn students' names. It is particularly important that teachers, more than most people, have a good strategy for learning names, so let's use this common problem to show how a good memory strategy works.

Caroline is a teacher who used to believe she was incapable of learning her students' names. During a Teaching Excellence seminar she learned this strategy and now she uses it to learn 200 students' names in the first week of the new term. She turns it into a competition with all the students in the school hall. The students test her by mixing themselves up in the room. She names them all and she wins every time. The students love her more than ever now.

When people complain about remembering bad things, they typically make very large pictures of the situation. They may even say they have *'blown it out of all proportion'*. To get rid of the bad feeling, we do the reverse and make the picture very small until the feeling goes away. Every strategy is useful in a different context, so the way we *'blow something out of all proportion'* is a key to a good memory strategy.

To begin, we want to ask questions about encoding. People have different encoding strategies for different contexts, and this is a good thing because you do not want to use the same strategy for buying lunch as you do for picking a husband or a wife. One is just a shortterm decision - the other one lasts a lifetime! So the questions you ask about how someone encodes something should be similar in nature to the issue you are dealing with. So ask about objects that they already know about. How many chairs do you have in your house? How many pairs of socks do you own, etc.? This tells you what works well for them. Once you discover how someone encodes remembering something else, you have some clues to use in encoding names.

The next step is to ask how they **don't** remember names, so you discover what isn't working. One teacher said, *'it doesn't take me very long not to remember'*. Well if we used that strategy we would forget very easily too! This of course is a very useful strategy for remembering to forget things that are unhelpful, like bad memories, so store this one away for those times. Remember, all strategies have a context in which they are useful!

Next, build confidence in the certainty that the person is able to do this and care enough to make it worthwhile. Failing to remember someone's name is often about not really paying attention and not really caring about remembering who the person is and what they are called. This is why students really like the teachers who remember their names. A name is the call sign for who you are.

The next step is to consciously begin to use a strategy that works:

Look at the person	Ve Visual external
Make a picture of the person and morph some characteristic of their face so that the image becomes a caricature of the person	Vi Visual Internal
Do this until it is funny and absurd and you get a good, strong kinaesthetic response	Ki Kinaesthetic internal

At this point you are beginning to make the image memorable because it is different. It is important to know that people like sameness, but learn through difference.

Ask, *'what is your name?'*	Ae Auditory external

Say their name on the inside	Ai Auditory internal
Write it phonetically under or over the image you have made of their face	Vi Visual internal
Say to yourself on the inside *'his name is....'*	Ai Auditory internal
Ask the person *'is your name ...... ?* Listen to the 'YES' reply	Ae Auditory external
This verifies the certainty feeling. There is no point in feeling certain if the name is incorrect	Ki Kinaesthetic internal

You are creating a strategy that uses the main representation systems. Repeat the steps a few times so the person becomes quicker and quicker at remembering names. It's then a good idea to take the strategy from a conscious process to an unconscious process, so that the learning happens in the right state of consciousness and becomes automatic. So now ask the person to *'close your eyes and go back through in your mind and replay what you did'*. Good encoding requires verification, so lay the foundation to remembering. Ask the person to *'find a good memory and spin the feelings so the experience intensifies. Notice where the good feeling is and which way it moves'*. As they do this, tell them, *'make the feeling spin more in the good direction so it feels wonderful'*. Whilst they do this, go through the steps again. In this way we create unconscious motivation and attach it to the strategy. Say to the person, *'speed it up in your mind so that you can do it faster and faster so that it becomes a little addictive as the conviction that you do this well builds'*. The more we run through a process making it faster and faster, and each time we get to the end, we feel even better and this builds our motivation to do even more.

Lastly, to make it worth doing, make the learning generative. So it's not just names of people that you can remember; you can remember dates, places, names of countries, the periodic table or anything else that is worth remembering.

Installing good strategies creates efficiency in your mind so you build the target and aim for it. As you get better at something, notice the improvement and make the feeling of improvement something that feels so good you want it even more.

REMEMBERING LISTS

Mnemonics are often used to help learners remember a chain of information and associate one thing with the next thing, but it is really a matter of transforming the list in some way so the information stands out in your mind. If you are asked *'when was the Battle of Hastings?'* it should have something attached to it, so 'the Battle of Hastings' triggers a really loud **1066**. When you teach it this way, learners will encode the information in a similar way on the inside. So rather than have them say the answers, why not have them shout or sing the answers as a group? It's important that you look at the date, say the name differently, and then blow up the size of the date, so saying the name makes the date pop up. This means that the link works both ways - encode so you can decode and memory functions well.

We know of some teachers who get a little upset when students use their phone camera to capture information from a flipchart or whiteboard. This seems to stem from the belief that the process of writing things down helps students to remember the information. This is not necessarily the case. Firstly, the image that they capture on camera may be clearer and easier to remember than in their own writing. The problem with a digital image is that you won't have it with you at all times, but then you won't have your list with you at all times either. What you do have with you at all times is your body, so here is another way to use the representational systems and synaesthesia for remembering lists:

MEMORY PEGS

This is just one of many powerful and effective memory strategies and a fun activity to do with any group. Everyone can utilise this strategy easily and quickly, and once you know the steps and the key components, it is easy to adapt and create your own unique strategy. When taught to one person in front of a group, there is often a major change in belief among the other people in the group. Test the strategy a few days later with one learner and the whole group will remember all the items and be keen to shout them out!

As the strategy is content-free, it can be used for any subject. It raises a learner's confidence in their own ability because it is not just a learning strategy - it is also a strategy that convinces them they can remember a whole list. As with all great NLP, the learning is generative and the improvement in ability also creates a powerful belief. The learner moves from a belief that they have a bad memory to one of *'wow, I really have a great memory!'*

Although we are showing you how to teach others the strategy, teach it to yourself first and make the changes you want to make in your own ability and beliefs. Remember - you go first!

THE MEMORY PEGS STRATEGY
Connecting the new learning to prior learning and experiences builds more synaptic links in the brain.(4) Human brains recognise and like patterns. Memory Pegs use something that is instantly recognisable and always with us – our own body - and connect the learning to it. Different parts of the body already have strong associations, so it's ready-made for a memory strategy.

Our best and most vivid memories are often funny or absurd. Memory Pegs utilises this by ensuring that the process is funny and the whole activity is ridiculous in a nice way.

As with all strategies, it's important to be thorough and ensure all the steps are completed with a certain amount of checks and repetition included, so the learner knows very quickly that they are progressing. Success breeds success!

Like all good strategies, this is as short it can be and has no unnecessary loops. Some people think that if they add extra steps it will get better, but actually it becomes less efficient. As you know by now NLP is based on a model of elegance, which means we take the smallest number of steps to create the most powerful change.

This technique utilises a process called 'anchoring'. Anchoring is the process of associating an internal response with some external trigger. We establish anchors so we can re-access the state we were experiencing at the time the anchor was established, and we remember the learning associated with the state simultaneously. A trigger or anchor fired in one sense or representational system will re-create an experience in that sense and in other senses too.

HOW TO LEARN THE MEMORY PEGS STRATEGY

Ask your group to suggest a random list of 11 items. Write the list up so it is visible to the whole group. The first time you do this, make it as silly and funny as possible so everyone is engaged and enjoying learning. This way, remembering becomes fun

1. Test the person's (or group's) ability to remember the list. Challenge the person/group to remember the list in 1 minute. Most will remember around 4 items; the most anyone without a memory strategy will remember is 7 items. If someone remembers them all – elicit their strategy because it's a good one! Choose the person with the lowest score to volunteer.
2. Now 'place' each item on the body of the volunteer as shown in the diagram below:

Starting at the top, touch the crown of the head (check that the person is OK with this first) and ask them to visualise a sandwich on top of their head. Use humour and ask questions such as *'what type of sandwich is it?'* Have fun discussing stinky cheese sandwiches or imagining tomato sauce running down your forehead, so that the person is laughing or having another strong response. Remember to utilise all senses when installing the items (words, objects) onto each memory peg so on sense is linked to all the other senses

3. Now move on to the next 'place' the nose. Repeat the process, having the volunteer imagine a bunch of keys dangling from their nose. Have them think about how heavy they are and the sound they make.
4. Once you have got to the ears, check back on the head. Continue to work through the sequence in the order on the list. Make the images big and bold and the sensations powerful. When you get to the hands, check back on the mouth and ears. Then start to check randomly and out of sequence. This is so the sequence builds, firstly in a linear way and then holistically, so the person doesn't have to run through the whole list to find the one they want.

This is very useful for recall later. 6. Test, feed back and immediately correct any mistakes until the person has them all instantly available as recall. This shouldn't take more than 3 minutes Here is one list to start with.

Change it in any way you like so long as it is fun and entertaining:

	BODY-PEG	ITEM	ASSOCIATION
1	Top of the head	Sandwich	What sauces are running down from the sandwich?
2	Up your nose	Bunch of keys	Which one would you use to start a car?
3	In your mouth	Watering can	Your mouth is the rose of the watering can – water the garden
4	Hanging from your ears	Bananas	Sing Yes, we have no Bananas!
5	Right shoulder	Owl	Instead of a parrot - you have an owl perched on your shoulder!
6	Left Shoulder	The Sun	How would the sunshine feel on your cheek?
7	Right hand palm	Glass of water	Don't spill it!
8	Left hand palm	Door handle	Which way does it turn
9	Waist band	An elephant	Leave this one to your imagination!

	BODY-PEG	**ITEM**	**ASSOCIATION**
10	Between your knees	Computer	Is it a laptop or desktop?
11	Under your feet	Tree	Stand firm on the branch

HOW TO DEVELOP MEMORY PEGS FURTHER
- Begin with each peg which then becomes its own body of 10 pegs; you can start to build a memory palace!
- Now try this with a theme based on facts or information you really want your group to learn well. Try it out with your shopping list and practise at the supermarket. How about French vocabulary or the planetary system?

By the time you have reached this point you have probably already installed the Memory Pegs in your brain. Speed improves the technique, so act fast and enjoy!

Although there is a vast amount of information stored on computers, machines are infinitesimal compared to your brain. One of the best medical diagnosticians Richard knew could rattle off 5 symptoms and every disorder that fitted would pop into his mind. Then he would go and check them. You could load that into a computer and it would find the disorders connected to the symptoms, but the human brain does it better. This is because the human brain can sort and select for relevancy. When this doctor was in front of a person, he picked up on signals such as smells, breath patterns and skin temperature unconsciously, as well as his knowledge of symptoms.

Think of those people who learned to programme computers 40 years ago. Compilers learned to translate one computer language into another computer language. They don't even have compilers anymore. If the compilers only learned that one thing, they would all be out of a job now. But their ability to know how that was done meant that they could think about other problems and find solutions. In years to come, all the knowledge taught now may no longer be relevant, but the process of remembering, encoding, decoding and pleasing yourself when you get something right will enable everyone to learn new things.

SUMMARY

In this chapter you have learned the key components of a good memory, including how to encode (remember) information so that you can decode (recall) it in a range of ways and contexts. You have explored two strategies for remembering which you can apply and adapt to any subject area for yourself or your students.

REFERENCES

1. Samuel Johnson: Idler #74 (September 15, 1759)
2. Willis J. MD, 2006,Research-Based Strategies to Ignite Student Learning: Insights from a Neurologist and Classroom Teacher, ASCD
3. Diamond M. Hopson J., 1998, Maic Trees of the Mind, New York, Dutton
4. Nash J.M., 1997 (February 3) Fertile Minds, Time 48-56

ACTIVITIES

Activity 1

IT'S ALL IN THE NAME

Do you have a good strategy for learning names? If not, work through the steps for learning names methodically and thoroughly with a group of 10 people. If you have a great strategy, elicit your own strategy and compare it with the one in this chapter. Which steps are the same and which differ? Remember Caroline, the Teaching Excellence student who learned the names of 200 new students within the first week and had a competition with the students at the end of the week to prove she can do it? The students loved it and felt very special because she remembered their names every time. Can you challenge yourself to do the same?

Activity 2

TEACH A GROUP MEMORY PEGS

Test them first and then record the results after teaching the strategy. Compare their recall on the next test with their previous test. Here is the list to remind you. You can of course vary the body positions to suit your group of learners.

	BODY -PEG	ITEM
1	Top of the head	
2	Up your nose	
3	In your mouth	
4	Hanging from your ears	
5	Right shoulder	
6	Left Shoulder	
7	Right hand palm	
8	Left hand palm	
9	Waist band	
10	Between your knees	
11	Under your feet	

Extension activity

Do you know someone who has a terrific memory for something special? Elicit their strategy for remembering and try it on for yourself.

CHAPTER 6

How to teach anyone to calculate: Strategies for Mathematics

Scan this to see the videos

'In mathematics you don't understand things.

You just get used to them.' [1]

John von Neumann

In this chapter

- Developing your 'Mathematical Mind'
- Counting and Skip Counting
- Attractive Addition
- Sublime Subtraction

One day, we were discussing a strategy a little boy used to prepare for his SATs test in Mathematics. The school Kate had visited was one of the few schools in the UK where all the staff are trained in NLP. The little boy explained to his teacher how he went into his very own maths room in his mind and all the answers to the maths questions were on the walls of this room.

His teacher said to the whole class, *'let's all have a maths room so maths is easy'* and set about teaching each child how to have a room in their minds too. Richard began to laugh as he explained that when he had elicited the strategy of a genius mathematician some years before, he had discovered that the mathematician had a maths room where all the equations were calculating automatically on the walls. Both this child and the mathematical genius had mathematical minds!

The poor literacy level in the USA and the UK (Chapter 4) are nothing in comparison to the percentage of people who have difficulty with numeracy and mathematics. Up to 40% of people in the UK are functionally innumerate, nearly one in three adults in the USA have only low level numeracy skills, and in some ways, being no good at maths has almost become a badge of honour [2]. Often, the primary emotion associated with mathematics is fear. This is the opposite of the feelings we want to associate with numbers – the feelings of comfort and certainty.

Many people think of maths as complex and difficult. Sadly, the unpleasant feelings that adults have about maths directly affect children. When mothers express to their daughters that they are no good at maths, their daughters' grades go down[3]. We want to reduce the process to the simplest and easiest way of doing maths, so that everyone feels great about making it simple.

When a group of students complained to their teacher that they couldn't do maths, the teacher responded by saying *'that's OK, neither can I, so I'm going to show you the tricks to get around it'*. He was telling the truth, because the solutions to mathematical problems are processes and procedures which resolve problems or puzzles in the simplest way possible; they are the tricks of the trade!

Learning maths in a sequence and making sure all the pieces are in place will ensure people are confident and enjoy maths. Missing a few steps along the way often leads to the confusion that makes people move away from maths rather than towards the fun of solving puzzles and problems. So to be great at maths and to enjoy learning it's helpful to begin at the beginning and make sure each stage of learning connects to the next stage, and that the steps at each point are explicit in that they clearly show the learner what to do on the outside **and** what to do on the inside of their mind.

We want to do even more than this though. We want to create a **Mathematical Mind**. When you learn to have a mathematical mind, it is full of numbers that are pleasing and comfortable to have in your head. The numbers move by themselves, automatically finding simple and easy solutions and the quickest way to find answers to all kinds of problems. A mind that enjoys the magic of maths is filled with numbers and patterns, so that a problem reduces logically to the simplest and easiest level, so maths becomes natural and comfortable.

It may be that you want to teach a small child to begin learning maths, or you want to help an adult to improve and enjoy Mathematics. Either way, the key stages to building a mathematical mind are Counting, Addition, and Subtraction. Later you may want to teach fractions and percentages, or ratio and proportion, or statistics. However, each of these disciplines requires the fundamentals of counting, addition and subtraction, so let's start with these. Here are some approaches to Mathematics that are based on how the brain works, so you can start to adapt and create your own strategies based on sound neurological principles and NLP.

When we learn to ride a bicycle or a scooter we don't just learn to ride. We learn to balance, steer, and push with our feet on the pedals. The activity becomes ingrained or encoded. So much so that, even after years of not riding a bike, it comes straight back to you at that magical moment when you sit on the saddle; the foundations are laid in just the right way and with just the right state attached to the learning. We want to encode Mathematics in the same way.

As with other strategies such as reading and spelling, you know that if you are to remember something visually in your mind, it is best if it is big and bold. It is the same with numbers. When children start at school, numbers are made bright, bold and big. As they progress through school, more and more numbers appear on the page, they get smaller and smaller and are usually reduced to black and white.

Fortunately, the inside of your mind is not limited in this way. We want the look and feel of numbers to be interesting and engaging. Have a go at this exercise for yourself to discover how you can change the submodalities of numbers so they are pleasing to you. Once you have this experience for yourself, it will be easy to create comfort and fun around numbers for your learners.

Think of a number you are **certain** about. Look at it in your mind and **know** it is right. See it in a certain place, a certain size or colour. The bigger it is in your mind, the easier it is to be sure of, so make it at least 20 centimetres tall. Make it just the right size so it feels comfortable. Now move on to another number and do the same thing. Is it a different colour? Is it in a different place? How big is this number? There are only nine numbers plus a zero - so there are not that many to remember and not that many to make every one of them special, developing a great feeling of certainty and comfort with each number.

Whether you are starting to teach little people or helping adults with numeracy, this is a good place to start, because if you are going to fill your head with numbers, it's a good idea that you enjoy having them inside your mind!

COUNTING
We have a vast heritage of counting songs and the internet offers endless animated versions of these songs. Songs that count up and count down help to encode the sequence with feelings of fun and laughter, laying the foundations of a mathematical mind filled with number certainty, pleasure and comfort. Do you remember singing *'1, 2, 3, 4, 5 once I caught a fish alive'*, or *'10 green bottles hanging on the wall'*, and *'there were 10 in a bed and the little one said 'roll over, roll over'*? Were you singing along as you read those phrases? Combining the internal visual representation of the numbers with the auditory sound of the numbers and the good feelings associated with the activity are the foundations of enjoyable numeracy and **magical maths**.

The unconscious mind repeats this learning over and over and very quickly encodes the learning. So whatever the age of your learners ensure that you count up and down, not just to 10, but on and on to higher and higher numbers, running the sequence over and over. Unlike the monotony of rote learning, this is best done as fast as possible, so make it a race. The brain learns quickly and the patterns form effectively when it happens all at once. Think of the metaphor of the little books with one picture on each page, which you flip with your thumb to make a little movie. You are encoding numbers in the same way!

SKIP COUNTING
Once a person can add any combination of numbers together and race through them up and down, all the combinations they need become encoded and automated. Counting leads to addition. When someone can add up numbers they can easily learn to subtract, and are ready to learn to multiply and divide.

The next step to learning to add numbers is to count and add at the same time - sometimes called **Skip Counting**. The more fun the counting game is, the better it feels. Einstein and other great mathematicians paid more attention to how the numbers made them feel than focusing on just the visual images.

Start with sequences that are easy for the learner. Often, small children will find counting in 2s easiest, but older learners and adults will often find 5s and 10s easier. Ask your learners which sequences are easiest for them and remind them of the feelings of certainty and comfort about the numbers they have in their mind before you begin. Beginning with the easiest sequence enhances these feelings, so you can build the belief that all the other sequences are easy too.

Now the game to play here is to see how quickly you can count in sequence. Have a competition to see who can get to 100 or to another specified number first. Your learners may not know all the numbers to start with, so have them write out the sequence in a long list to start with, so they are not burdened with trying to remember the numbers and they have all the information to keep up with the game. Very quickly, the learners will stop using the list as the number sequence becomes easy to remember.

Some people may think this is an odd thing to do, as you are giving the answers to the learner. But remember - we want the learner to have certainty, and this certainty feeling is connected to what will quickly and easily be memorised – the sequence of numbers.

As an example, start with counting-up and down in 2s: 2, 4, 6, 8, 10, 12, 14, 16, 18, 20 ... all the way to 100 and then count back down again.

Or in 10s:
10, 20, 30, 40, 50, 60, 70, 80, 90, 100 and then count back down again.

Now move to 3s: 3, 6, 9, 12, 15, 18, 21, 24, 27, 30 all the way to 102 and back again.

Repeat this with each set of numbers so you have the complete set of sequences up to and including 10s, which will be so easy for your learners now.

Each time the learner succeeds, ensure that you reinforce how easy this is and how fast they are getting. Remind them that the bigger the number they are counting with, the fewer numbers are in the sequence and the less there is to remember; the bigger the numbers, the easier it gets! Whether you use this strategy for yourself or with your learners, the more you repeat this process, the more your unconscious will identify the patterns emerging in your mind.

The wonder of the human brain is its plasticity. Children find this so easy and so much fun. Adults are surrounded by numbers and sequences - phone numbers that just pop into your mind, email addresses, money and change. Just those 10 digits that match your fingers and toes create exquisite patterns in your learner's mind.

Once you have had fun running each sequence in order, continue to play this game by mixing up the number sequences. For example, do 4s followed by 7s followed by 3s and 5s and 8s etc. It's not about being able to understand mathematics, but about being able to take the steps to build a more organised and more numbered mind.

These games encode the number sequences so quickly that you will see rapid improvements when you begin to teach addition and subtraction, multiplication and division. These are great games for the car or on school trips and can involve, *'let's get to 100 before the next petrol station'*, or *'can we do the 6s before we get home?'*

MOVING TO ADDITION
Once your learners are confident and comfortable with skip counting, you can move on to a range of skills to make addition fun and easy. You can experiment with these:

DOUBLE-UP
Once your learners can count and skip count, they already have some addition skills. Now they can easily move on to how to double up numbers:
Double two: 2+2 is 4
Double six: 6+6 is 12
When they have all the double numbers encoded the next step is easy!

DOUBLE PLUS 1
This strategy uses the information they already know and builds on it. Take 5+6 - the learner already knows 5+5 = 10, so add 1 more and the answer is 11.
Continue with each of the doubles and add one more.

COUNTING-UP
The first step is to add two numbers together. Look at the two numbers in the sum and choose the biggest one. So in the sum 4 + 3; the biggest number is 4.
Start with the number 4 and count up the same number of times as the smallest number – in this case 3 times.
4 (count up 3 times): 5 - 6 - 7
Now the learner knows 4 + 3 =7 and 3 + 4 = 7
Move on to bigger numbers such as 8 + 5.
8 is the biggest number, so count up from 8, five times
8 (count up 5 times) 9-10-11-12-13
Now the learner knows 8+5 = 13 and 5+8 = 13
Continue practising with other sums, counting up from the big number

by the small number so that all the sequences become familiar. Very soon the learner will automatically remember the sequences and see the patterns in the numbers.

GETTING TO 10
Remind the student of all the nice pictures and feelings they have about the numbers, then begin to use the counting-up strategy to work out all the numbers that make 10. Begin with the biggest ones: 9 +1=10, 8+2 =10, 7+3=10, 6+4=10, 7+3=10, 6+4=10, and look - now 5+5=10 and so does 4+6! So, once they see the pattern they realise they already know the rest! Once your students know 'getting to 10', all the other additions become easy with this next game.

BUILDING A NUMBER COUNTER
Now it's time to learn to manipulate much bigger numbers whilst realising that there are really only 10 digits to deal with in any number, however big it gets. The problem with larger numbers is that learners try to hold too many numbers in their mind. What we want them to learn to do is just hold the last and biggest number in their mind, so it is clear and easy to remember.

The strategy for doing this is to build a number counter in the learner's mind that is big, bold and clear. So now take a number such as 24 and see it in your mind as big and colourful and clear so it looks something like this:

24

Now add 2 to each of the numbers starting with the number on the right. 4 + 2 = 6 make a click sound, and see the counter move from 4 to the number 6.
Now take the number next to it on the left: 2 + 2 = 4, make the click sound and move counter from 2 to 4.
Now this is the only number to have in your mind. A really big colourful number:

46
A useful representation to
have here is a digital meter, or digital calendar, where the numbers

automatically go back to zero after 9. As they roll around, add a 'click' sound to the movement, you know it has moved on.

So now the only number we have in our mind is 46. Add 2 to each number and hear the click each time the number rolls around: 6 + 2 (click) the counter moves to 8. 4 + 2 (click) the counter moves to 6. Now the new number is 68 and this is the only number in your mind, big, bold and clear:

68

Move on, adding 3 to the number and then 4 to the number until the machine inside your head is working by itself.
Move on to adding a number to a 3-digit counter such as 423, so the meter gets bigger and bigger.
Keep going until the meter has as many numbers as you want it to have. Keep playing the game, (remember the 'click' each time) until the counter is encoded in your student's mind and they are ready to move on to the real addition strategy.
Remember, we are building a head full of numbers to be manipulated and played with for fun!
Now there comes a point where the numbers added together are 10 or more. So now it's time to talk about real addition.

REAL ADDITION
Once the digital meter is working all by itself, the next step is to adjust the numbers every time the number goes around the clock past zero. So start with the big number 99 and add 11 to it:

99

The 9 moves up to 0 and the next 9 goes to 0 plus 1 and a new column appears with 1 in it, so the new number is 110 and this is the only number in your mind:

110

Move on to even more interesting numbers! Have 626 as big and bold at the top an`d underneath have the number 333, still clear but a little smaller. Like this:

626

333

Now add the top right number (6) and the bottom right number (3) and turn the number on the meter to 9. Next do the same (remember the click) with the top middle number (2) and the bottom middle number (3) and turn the top number to 5. Now do the same with the left hand numbers 6 plus 3 and turn the top number to 9. Now you have a new big number at the top:

959

Carry on adding 333 to this number. This time, when the number goes past 0 click the big number up one -so 3 plus 9 is 2, and the 5 clicks to 6. 3 plus 6 is 9. So the left hand numbers are 3 plus 9 so this number clicks to 2 and a new number appears in a new column 1292 and this is the only number in your mind:

1292

It doesn't matter how big the numbers get, it's just as simple as adding one column and moving to the next using just the numbers 1 to 9 plus 0.

When learning maths, children are instructed to 'show your working out'. With this process there is nothing to show on the outside - it's all happening on the inside. Showing how the answer has been achieved is often for the teacher's benefit so that they can be sure the child has gone through the process of carrying numbers and number placement. This is not the purpose here. We are building machines inside our learners so that the basics of mathematics happen automatically. With these strategies installed inside young minds, multiplication, division, algebra, and geometry become easier processes and maths is fun!

SUBTRACTION

Once we have the machine in our heads to add numbers, the same machine can subtract numbers. So all the same games can be played in reverse to build a subtraction machine. Start with the counting game, but this time the counting counts back from 100. Move on to the take away game, which is the same as the addition game, but this time with the question *'who can get to zero first?'*

Doubling up becomes halving, getting to 10 becomes getting to 0, and the addition game becomes the subtraction game. Starting with two numbers and take off 2 at a time, move on to 3 or 4 first and then make the big number at the top drop down one rather than adding a number on.

Maths is about finding the simple solutions and the easy way to do things. Adding 4+4+4+4 may seem quite a bit of work, but if your mind sees that it is the same as 2 lots of 8 and double 8 is 16, it's easy. It doesn't matter how big the number is, it is always made up of smaller numbers.

Humans are neurologically wired for the decimal system. We have 10 fingers and 10 toes. Discomfort with numbers is often because we haven't found the right voice and the right place to have the good feeling; when we find the most comfortable place you can find the solutions and strategies for your students to have inside their minds.

SUMMARY

In this chapter you have discovered strategies that work on the inside to build mathematical machines. You have learned that maths isn't just a process of manipulating numbers on a piece of paper, but creating a mind full of numbers and strategies that make manipulating numbers and solving problems easy. You have built the basis of a mathematical mind with counting, addition and subtraction - and next we explore how the fun multiplies.

REFERENCES

1 Reply, according to Dr. Felix T. Smith to a physicist friend who had said "I'm afraid I don't understand the method of characteristics," as quoted in The Dancing Wu Li

Masters: (1979) by Gary Zukav, Bantam Books,

2. Skilled for life? Key Findings from the Survey of Adult Skills Ref http://skills.oecd.org/documents/SkillsOutlook_2013_KeyFindings.pdf

3. Gunderson E, Ramirez G, Levine S. C, Bellock S.L, 2011The Role of Parents and Teachers in the Development of Gender-Related Math, Published online

ACTIVITIES

The digital meter in your head

Install the digital meter to learn addition and subtraction. Practise adding bigger and bigger numbers to each other as above.

THE BIG COUNTER
Using a smart board, create a BIG counter on the screen and play the counting games with the whole class

ELICIT EXCELLENT STRATEGIES
Elicit strategies from 2 different people for subtracting large numbers. Find out what they do inside their minds to make it easy. Try them on and see which one works best for you.

THE METER METHOD
Teach someone who is convinced they are no good at maths to add numbers using the meter method outlined in this chapter. Simplify your language so concepts are really easy to connect to the learner's previous experience and create states of certainty and comfort in the learner.

Extension activity
How could you utilise this method for teaching decimals and negative numbers?

CHAPTER 7

Mathematical Magic

Scan this to see the videos

'Doing mathematics should always mean finding patterns and crafting beautiful and meaningful explanations.' [1]

Paul Lockart

In this chapter

- Mastering Multiplication
- Fast and effective Division
- Geometry made easy
- Engineering successful strategies

Mathematics is often taught as a conceptual subject with no real application to the world; only those students who enjoy the logical process love maths, while others can see no real purpose to learning multiplication and division. However, maths is part and parcel of everyday life. The chef knows how to multiply and divide ingredients, the traveller needs to estimate arrival times and calculate money exchange rates and distances, and artists and photographers need to calculate angles, depth and perspective. It's a great stress saver; can you imagine the headache of trying to solve a problem without the short cuts and easy tricks that Mathematics teaches us?

When many of us think about learning multiplication tables we are transported back into the classroom, sitting at a small table and monotonously repeating our tables over and over. Then, at the end of the week or on Monday morning there was the 'test', which was often frightening. This traditional method attempts to install times tables auditorily, and creates unpleasant feelings of dread and fear of failure. There is rarely a visual element to the strategy. However, people who manage to learn their tables easily somehow work out that making a picture of the numbers is a good way to remember them. It's unlikely that anyone showed them how to do this; the phrase 'learn your tables' does not specify to the student what to do inside his/her mind to find the easiest way to remember.

MULTIPLICATION
Adding and subtracting are processes that are carried out consciously in the mind. Multiplication is just a fast way to remember repeated additions of the same number – a quick way to add a series of the same number to each other. Multiplication happens unconsciously because we memorise the sequences rather than add each number to the next and the next. So ask a person who has learned a multiplication table really well, *'what is 5 times 5?'* and the answer just pops into their head. This memorising process is the one that we as teachers need to teach by specifying precisely what the learner needs to do on the inside of their mind to achieve this. There is a huge difference between the instruction to *'learn these tables'*, and an instruction to *'picture these tables and make the numbers jump out and grow really big!'* Just notice for yourself the difference in the quality and detail of your mental processes when you say these two instructions to yourself. Once the process has been correctly installed, multiplying becomes unconscious and natural.

TEACHING EXCELLENCE

The good news is that when a learner has learned to count up in sequence (see Skip Counting in Chapter 6) they already have the basis of the multiplication tables and have encoded the numbers so that multiplication and division are easy and already familiar.

The trick is to enable learners to visualise the times tables as a big chart. The instructions to your students are to see the big square, which has the (by now) familiar sequences of numbers completing the grid, as one complete image.

The human brain likes patterns and learns them easily, so before you begin with the mechanics of multiplication introduce the big picture first. This also means that the student knows where they are going, so they begin to learn to track forwards and to track backwards on the grid.

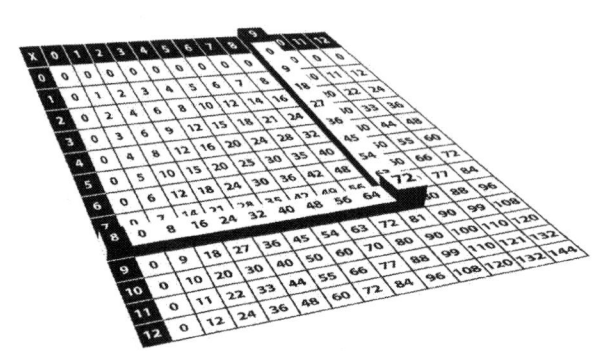

Start by exploring the grid and looking for familiar sequences and patterns. Look at the unit tables and across the top row:

X	0	1	2	3	4	5	6	7	8	9	10	11	12
0	0	0	0	0	0	0	0	0	0	0	0	0	0

Now the learner can see that when there is nothing to times a number by there is nothing to do!

PART 2 - STRATEGIES FOR LEARNING

Now look at the next row:

X	0	1	2	3	4	5	6	7	8	9	10	11	12
0	0	0	0	0	0	0	0	0	0	0	0	0	0
1	0	1	2	3	4	5	6	7	8	9	10	11	12

Well fancy that – it's just counting! Now look at the next row:

X	0	1	2	3	4	5	6	7	8	9	10	11	12
0	0	0	0	0	0	0	0	0	0	0	0	0	0
1	0	1	2	3	4	5	6	7	8	9	10	11	12
2	0	2	4	6	8	10	12	14	16	18	20	22	24

How familiar are these numbers now? Because in the last chapter we played at racing our way up to 100 in 2s, we can go way beyond this chart. Each row has the same sequence of numbers that you learned when skip counting to 100, and each column has the same set of numbers too. Also notice that the pattern is symmetrical along the diagonal, so you only need to remember half the numbers because the answer is the same for, say, 8x9 as it is for 9x8.

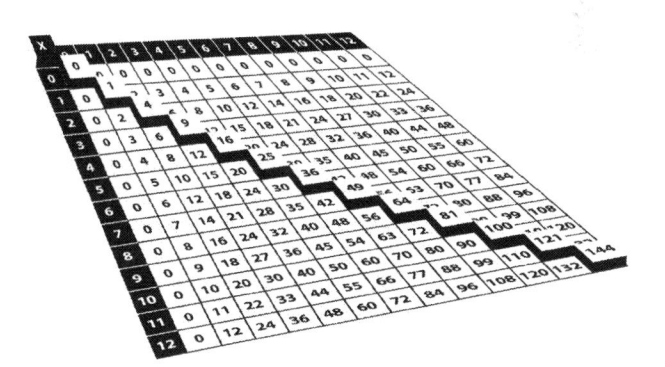

So now the task is not to multiply the numbers - the task is to track to the number that is in the left hand column horizontally, and track to the number from the top row vertically until the two numbers meet in the square and make the number jump out in your imagination. This trains the mind to pop the right number up automatically.

The image above stops at the 12 times table, but of course your mind is not limited in size, so the chart inside a learner's head can be as big as they want it to be and the numbers can be coloured in any way that makes the learner happy and comfortable.

Each time you ask *'what is four times four?'*, track along the line from 4 on the left side to meet the number 4 coming down from the top line and see the number 16 pop up in the correct square.

Ask *'what is four times five?'*, track along the line from 4 on the left side to meet the number 5 coming down from the top line and see the number 20 pop out.

Then move to the 10s and make the table bigger and bigger, with large numbers that are easy to see. When you do this enough times the correct numbers pop up by themselves, because the numbers are in the squares. It is just a question of paying attention to the two starting points and playing the tracking game lots of times, just for fun!

The brain is capable of memorising an infinite amount of information. An idiot savant may be able to memorise all the numbers in a phone book and tell you the name of the person each belongs to. For a few such individuals, the information is all there, all of the time. However, this isn't useful - you don't want the chart to stay there all the time, you just want the chart to determine the number, so the more you look at your chart, the more the number pops up by itself, so that it becomes unconscious. As soon as somebody says *'what is 12 times 12?'* rather than having to compute it through some long process, the brain will flash up 144. Once you have all the 10s it's easy to get the 100s, then you can do the 1,000s, which happens just as easily. This is because it is the mechanism of learning how to make it happen automatically that makes the fast mathematician.

PART 2 - STRATEGIES FOR LEARNING

Some multiplications will be easier simply because they are more familiar. Others may seem harder in the beginning, but when we start to look for what we already know even unfamiliar numbers become easy. For example 3 x 18 might seem quite hard until you notice that you already know that 3 x 20 is 60. The bit of the number that is too big is just the number 2 (the difference between 18 and 20) which just has to be multiplied 3 times to find out how by how much 60 is too big a number. Go back to your table and you easily know that 2 x 3 is 6. Subtract 6 from 60 and you have 54. So 3 x 18 = 54. Easy! Looking for the patterns in what you already know and finding the tricks makes maths fun.

When numbers get bigger in multiplication, remember you are still only dealing with 9 digits plus 0, just like with addition. Getting to the answer for 17 x 17 might seem like a lot of work, but if your brain thinks in simple terms and breaks the problem into simple steps it becomes easy - like this:

The 10 times table is easy, so just add a zero to find 10 x 17 = 170
Using the 10 times table in the same way, 10 x 7 =70
Add these two numbers together to get 240.

That just leaves the 7x7 bit to find. 7x7 is on your chart and pops out at 49.

Add this to the number you already have and even a large multiplication like 17 x 17 = 289 is easily discovered.

The message for our learners is that they want to look for the easy way to get to the answer. Debbie had a complete fear of the 9 times table until she was shown a pattern that she hadn't been aware of before. The pattern was that all the multiples of 9 add up to 9 when the two digits are added together, so it was a really easy way to be certain the number was correct.

The pattern is 18, 27, 36, 45, 54, 63, 72, 81, 90. So to find 2 x 9, drop down one number from the multiplier - 2 down to 1 and make this number up to 9, which is 8, so 2 x 9 is 18.

For 7 x 9 drop the multiple 7 down one to 6 and find the number that makes this number up to 9, which is 3, so 7 x 9 is 63.

As soon as Debbie saw the pattern and practised a few multiplications she had the pattern installed and felt really good about herself.

The traditional and somewhat tedious way of multiplying already presupposes that the 10 times table works by itself. So if you multiply 12 x 12 traditionally, you multiply 2 x 2 and then 1 x 2 and add a 0.

But you still have to be able to multiply 2 x 2, so there is no reason why you can't multiply 12 x 12. It's easier to increase the numbers on the grid so they pop up by themselves.

If for some reason a learner doesn't know the answer they can go back and dissemble the multiplication, but they will still know some part of the sum which will help them. They already know 10 x 10 equals 100, so all they have to worry about is how to get 144 with the bit that's left over! They also know that 2 x 10 is 20 and 2 x 12 is 24. So you can do it the long way or you can just do it with the chart in your mind!

DIVISION
Here is a secret to share with your learners - long division doesn't really exist! The process of division is simply multiplication and subtraction with a bit of guess-work thrown in. The bigger the numbers you are dividing, the more often these steps are repeated and long division just repeats the sequence more than once.

Now that you have the strategies for multiplication you have the basic strategies for division, which also happens to use the same multiplication chart. Imagine you are dividing 108 by 9. You are really asking yourself the question, how many times will 9 fit into 108. Your brain tracks across the multiplication chart to 108. The two numbers that correspond to the intersection with the square 108 are 9 and 12. So 9 fits into 108 12 times. 108 ÷ 9 = 12. As the chart has the same numbers for multiplication and for division, it's easy.

Now the chart in your head doesn't have to stop at 12 so now divide 119 by 7. Remember, you are asking yourself how many times will 7 fit into 119. Your brain tracks across the multiplication chart to 119. The two numbers that correspond to the intersection with the square with 119 in it are 7 and 17. Just as easy when you have a big chart in your head.

With the process of long division, the trick is to find the biggest number on your multiplication chart that is below the number you want to divide. So you know that all your brain has to do is scan the chart. Imagine you are dividing 124 by 7. (124 ÷ 7). Your brain finds the biggest number that's below 124. The question is how many 7s are there in that number so you can tell what is left over? It's really another multiplication task. So you simply track across the line of multiples of 7 until the number is bigger than 124 and then go back one square and the number pops out. So there it is again, 119. 7 divides into 119, 17 times. (119 ÷ 7 = 17). Subtract 119 from 124. (124 – 119 = 5) which gives you the number left over, known as the remainder. 119 ÷ 7 = 17 r5. The more you train the brain to do this, the more automatically it finds the biggest number and then of course what's left over is simple subtraction.

It's important not to underestimate the power of these simple methods and how quick and effective they can be. One day, sitting in the back of the car, 8-year-old Maisy announced, *'I'm rubbish at maths'*. After 20 minutes of playing number races, she was doing long division easily and enjoying the process.

To divide 377 by 6, we asked her to take the first two numbers in the sum and asked, 'how many times can you get 6 into 37?'
'I know it fits into 30, 5 times' she said.
'Can you squeeze another one into the 7 that is left?'
'Oh yes one more – that's 6 times', she said with delight on her face.
So that leaves us with 1, which is in the 10s, and so is 10 and the next number to it is 7. Add these together and we have 17 more to fit 6 into.
'How many times can you squeeze 6 into 17?' we asked.
She said, *'3 times 6 would be 18, but it is too big so it has to be 12, which is 2 times 6'*

Yes, so add the 2 to the 60 and the answer is 62 with 5 left over'
A very big sum for a little girl who used to think she was rubbish at maths!

Teaching these processes to your students is now very much easier. At one time all we had as visual aids were posters and grids in books. Now we have computer programmes and phone apps which can create and animate the multiplication charts on the screen. Although some teachers lament the use of mobile phones in maths classes, we don't agree. When learners can see the process of numbers popping out of a grid on a screen with their real eyes, it's much easier to create the representation on the inside of their mind with their inner vision.

A computer programme or animation can pop up the number and blow it up so it fills the screen, so that when we ask what is 5 times 7, the number 35 pops up, fills the screen and then shrinks back down again. This way the brain gets used to taking the numbers, going to the intersection of the grid where the two points meet and the picture is BIG. If the question is 5 times 9, it goes to the 9s and to the 5s and then tracks to the intersection of the two points and the number 45 gets BIG. If the question is 45 divided by 9 it goes to number 9 and tracks down to 45 and then across to 5. The brain is always looking for the point of intersection. This way it's not about taking five lots of nine and adding them all together very laboriously; it's about geometry, because if you learn maths this way, you are already set up to do geometry.

GEOMETRY

Shapes and form surround our world. Just look out of your window and notice the line of the rooftops, or walk down a city centre street and notice the angles of entrance lobbies. How much geometry can be seen in buildings such as The Shard or The Gherkin in London? The natural world is also full of beautiful geometric shapes - a snowflake, a nautilus shell, a sunflower. Geometry is in our DNA. Just close your eyes and imagine some of these fabulous shapes in our world.

PART 2 - STRATEGIES FOR LEARNING

The ability to see and rotate a visual image as if it's a movie allows learners to extend their visualisation skills to geometry. Once you have the images of the geometric shapes, equations have a context and make sense.

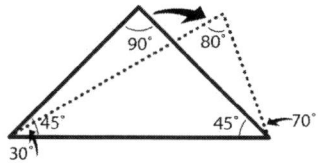

Geometry obviously has to have pictures because it's about shapes. So when you draw a triangle and add the angles in the triangle, you can start teaching the children to rotate, stretch and shorten the angles and watch the numbers change, so that it happens by itself. Again, years ago you couldn't do this so easily because we didn't have computers to create the images, whereas now teachers have built websites to do just this. This way, when you pick two angles, whatever the third one is automatically adjusts. Instead of having to add all the angles up and subtract from 180, the numbers can be there by themselves.

It's not a question of whether you can name a trapezium (trapezoid), it's a question of seeing the pictures of shapes and writing the angles in the corners and the lengths of the sides. As the lengths of the sides extend or shrink in the same proportion, it's still a trapezium. As one line gets bigger, the other one does too. And if the line on one side gets bigger, the other one has to get even bigger too! You can watch the numbers go up and down so that the numbers shrink and expand together.

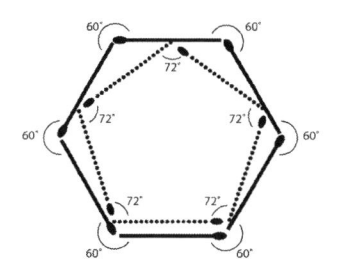

This process works for understanding shapes and changing shapes from one to another. Take a picture of a hexagon and write hexagon on it, adding the lengths of the lines and the size of the angles. Take a line out and have the picture change shape and as the shape changes to a pentagon so the name changes too. Then you put the angles in the pentagon.

Two builders were building a house extension and were asked if they would use Pythagoras to ensure the building was square to the original wall. *'No'*, they said, *'we are using a 3 - 4 - 5 triangle!'* They were using geometry the easy way. Learners often believe that Pythagoras's theorem is a long complex equation that has to be computed, when the truth is that it's a way of solving a puzzle. If we know the length of two sides of a right-angled triangle, we can find out how long the third side is. It is quite complicated to figure out the area of a triangle, but quite easy to find out the area of a square, so you put two triangles together, work out the area of the square and just chop it in half! When learners can see the process of the squares forming on the edges of the triangles and merging together, the brain knows what it is aiming for with the calculation. So the learner knows where they are going and why.

As soon as you think of a circle as a whole bunch of πs (Pi) then it's just a whole bunch of triangles. So all you need to do is work out one triangle and multiply it to figure out how many triangles are in the circle. Suddenly it's easy. You can use the $πr^2$ formula, but really all you do is figure out the area of one triangle and multiply the triangles. So if you look at the circle and know how many triangles are in it you know that the reason you are taking the radius and computing it is just because of the curve on the circumference. This way learners understand that a formula is just a shortcut, and as long as you follow the formula it gives you more information about the object.

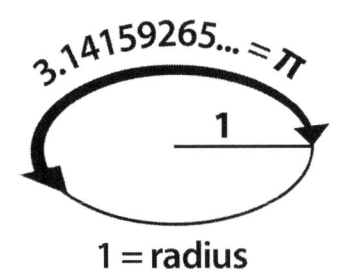

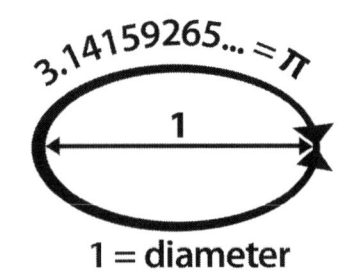

$3.14159265... = π$ $3.14159265... = π$

1 = radius   1 = diameter

Of course, plane geometry is about flat shapes. When you take the object and make it 3-dimensional it becomes a number of shapes added to the sides of the original shape. So a square becomes a cube by adding more squares to it. When you want to think about the surface of an object as opposed to the bulk or mass of the object, you want learners to look at the object and rotate it in their minds. Learning to observe objects in motion enables a learner to begin to make the connections between objects in space. If you are shown a still picture of a triangle and then shown another still picture of a triangle, it's hard to make the connection to a pyramid. But when you are shown how to morph a triangle into a pyramid, it's easy to realise that the surface of a true pyramid is just 4 of the original triangles. This way it's all connected and every machine you build in your mind is a machine that works.

ENGINEERING SUCCESSFUL STRATEGIES
We can build the machine that visualises moving shapes in the minds of learners. To do so we need to make the steps very explicit, and teachers don't always know how to do this. Sometimes we need to reverse engineer the problem to find out what the learner needs to be able to do, that they are not doing currently.

Paul was a really bright 11-year-old boy with good literacy and numeracy skills. He had a problem with non-verbal reasoning questions. His teacher's strategy was to give him more past papers to practise, which actually meant he just got very good at not being able to do non-verbal reasoning questions.

The questions showed simple geometric objects on a page and asked the learner to identify which object was the same as another drawn from a different angle, or how many pyramids would fit into a box. Paul didn't like drawing and actually said he wasn't any good at it. Often, children who say they are no good at drawing are judging themselves by comparing what something looks like with what they have on the page. If it's not accurate enough by their reckoning, they will decide they are no good at drawing!

Now think about it. What does he need to be able to do to work out these problems? Firstly, he needs to look at a 2-dimensional drawing of some lines on a page and turn the lines into 3-dimensional objects in his mind. Then he needs to do the same thing with each of the other drawings so they become solid objects.

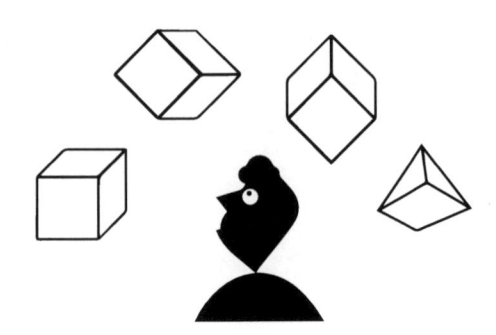

Look at the drawing of the cubes above. Represented in this way it is simply 9 lines on a page, which isn't a cube! Paul also said he had a horrible feeling in his tummy when he thought about tackling the problems. This wasn't surprising, as every time he tried to do the questions he got them wrong and didn't know what else to do.

So to make sure that the horrid feeling changed at the outset, all the activities we gave to Paul were designed to be fun. Some good suggestions were given about how the teacher may have just forgotten to teach some pieces and when Paul knew what they were, he could surprise her!

The first activity was to exercise his 'imagination muscle'. He spent a fun evening painting his thoughts and feelings whilst listening to Vivaldi's Four Seasons violin concerti and imagining the seasons. He said it was fun and not like homework.

The next task was to take digital photographs of cubes, pyramids and balls. Using lots of coloured pens, he drew lines around the edges of the shapes and traced them onto plain paper. This activity reversed the process so that he could see a 3-dimensional shape and conceptualise it as a 2-dimensional line drawing, making the link between how a cube looks in real life and what it looks like when we represent it on paper. You see, he hadn't got that bit; previously, when he was asked which of the drawings on the page was the cube, his answer was *'none of them, they are just squares with extra lines!'*

Now the representations he had in his mind of the shapes looked more like this:

Next he did some drawings directly from shapes to see how many ways he could represent each shape. What did it look like from the bottom, the top, the side? And finally what does it look like when it's behind my back? Once he could go from a 3-dimensional object to a 2-dimensional representation of the object, he could do this in reverse and go from a 2D representation to a 3D object. He could rotate the shapes in his mind and put them back on the paper as a 2D representation, compare it to the ones on the paper and tick the right box!

ALGEBRA

Some mathematicians are said to be 'intuitive mathematicians' - they know the answer and work backwards to check the answer is correct. Others do it by working out step by step. This is inductive and deductive reasoning. But when we say intuit, this simply means that the number just jumps off the chart. Then they go back and do it the slow way to verify the answer.

This is good because you should always have two ways of doing everything to know you have arrived at the right place. That's why you solve an equation one way and then go back the other way to make sure you are right.

So that X equals B+C and then you can solve Y, you should be able to solve back and forth in both directions. If you can multiply a number, you can divide it and go back the other way. In Mathematics, everything has those checks and balances within it.

When teaching algebra the checks and balances can be felt kinaesthetically. Watch a great mathematician working on a really long equation on a blackboard and one thing you will notice is that s/he stands back every now and again and looks at the board and feels whether it is balanced or not.

To begin teaching algebra, it's good to present the process as a detective story where you are solving the mystery. You are trying to find out who the main character is. Most algebra teaching stops with the quantity, but the nature of the quality you are trying to discover isn't introduced until higher maths. But to find out that Y is the main character because 2 Xs equal Y means that Y is the more significant character.

Maths, by definition, is a human endeavour. It's not about the real world, it's about how the human mind formulates. As is often the case when strategies are elicited from mathematicians, those we have studied didn't know consciously how they were doing it, but we discovered that they did maths in the way we have explained it. The fact that they don't see the chart in their mind anymore doesn't mean it's not there. They say, *'the number just pops into my head'*, and the same thing is true with triangles in geometry and many other learnings.

The mathematician who gets to the answer and then goes back to do it the way s/he was taught in school to check it's right is really doing reverse mathematics. It's reverse engineering again; if you intuit the answer and don't double check the answer that popped up, you might be getting the wrong square. So it's useful to constantly check you have the right answer. Just as if you write a word in your head, you should look at the word on paper to make sure you have the right letters. It's the same process; just with maths it's a little more linear than it is with spelling.

When you go to school you still have to go home. If you are going somewhere and only looking at where you are going, you don't know how to get back to where you were! A friend of ours was visiting Copenhagen and went out to dinner. He got in a taxi at the end of the evening, the driver asked where he was going and he said *'back to the hotel'*. Which hotel? Oops, he'd forgotten to take notice of the name!

When you park your car at the airport you look at the car and notice where it is so you can find it again. You have to do this with numbers. So if 5 x 5 is 25 then 25 divided by 5 will be 5. The motivation to learn to do this is that down the road, life will be easier. So through the process of proving your work, and the process of learning to multiply, you learn to divide. This is a better way of doing maths. Jump to the answer and then work back. You track your way back until you get to the answer and if you can't then you track your way forward until you get to the answer.

Have you noticed how the answers to the maths tests are in the teacher's book? Because whoever wrote the teacher's book knew that was the best way to do it. The trick is not to GET to the answer. We are taught that the whole rationale is to get the right answer but it's really to get the right **process**, so people will always be able to add subtract and multiply.

Teachers can create the desire for the children to go *BOOM! I got the answer*, check if it's the right answer, and if it's not, go back to the process. Instead of having to wait a day to find out if you did it correctly, the student should know which process was wrong and which was right immediately. One of the problems with our current methodology is that the teacher has the certainty (the right answers) and the student has doubt until the teacher gives them certainty! When we reverse this process, the student has the certainty of when they are right or not and the teacher has the doubt, so they constantly check that the students are learning in the right way. Fortunately, with the advent of learning platforms more and more learners are able to know the answers straight away, correct what they are doing and move on, so the motivation is to get better and better and faster and faster.

As part of the New Wave Project[2] to teach adults maths in the workplace with the technology of NLP, we ensured that the answers were not just at the end of the book, but at the end of each section. Interestingly, even some of the learners questioned this, saying 'well we will just cheat and look at the answers!' Of course they didn't do this. What they did was get more and more enthusiastic about working the answers out and seeing immediately whether they were right. When they were correct, they felt great. If they were not, they went back to find out why and work it out again. Answers at the back of the book are great motivators for learning when it feels good to solve a puzzle and know you are right.

As we mentioned, most great mathematicians are not just working visually; they are working kinaesthetically too, in that they are trying to get to the good feeling. You get that good feeling by bending the numbers. The more you build in the strategy that makes a child hungry for the right answer rather than dreading the wrong answer, the more successful the child will be. Knowing that this one is right, this one is right, this one is not right yet so go back a few steps, installs the strategy that works rather than installing the dread of what doesn't work. Whether it is maths or any other subject, the more you get it right, the better the good feeling. Education is about Design Human Engineering® for kids. We are teaching children to do things that are conceptual, not natural. The target is to have the mechanism or strategy of learning connected to the learning itself and connected to other learnings. So instead of looking for mistakes they are looking for how the dots fit together. So they become better than inductive or deductive thinkers; they become learning machines. In future generations, knowledge is going to change so fast that what you learn won't be useful by the time you get out of school. What will be useful will be the rudimentary skills of learning. So what you learn may change, but how you do it will not.

SUMMARY

In this chapter you have learned to use maths charts in your head to find easy and simple ways to multiply and divide numbers. You have discovered ways to teach geometry and algebra using visual representations. You can now begin to identify steps that are missing in a learner's strategy, to correct and improve mathematical ability and to have more than one way of finding a solution. By applying these processes you also build propulsion and motivation into your learners so the more they learn the better they feel and the more they want to learn.

REFERENCES

1. Paul Lockhart, 2009, A Mathematician's Lament: How School Cheats Us Out of Our Most Fascinating and Imaginative Art Form, New York, Bellevue Literary press
2. The New Wave Project 2011, Meta Education Team, Funded by Cornwall Learning Partnership

ACTIVITIES

Activity 1

Create a multiplication chart in your head and see how big you can make it! Most people have a chart that goes up to 12 x 12; how high can you get yours to go? Practise using a relaxed and alert state to focus your attention

Activity 2

Design an activity to build a multiplication chart in a group of learners. How big, bright, colourful and memorable can you make it?

Extension activity

Search the web for really great examples of moving geometry – there are lots out there. Watch the numbers morph and install the same machine in your mind so you build bigger and better learning machines. To get you started have a look at www.mathsisfun.cov

CHAPTER 8
How to nurture Creativity and Talent

SCAN THIS TO SEE THE VIDEO

'Creativity is as important now in education as literacy and we should treat it with the same status.' [1]

Sir Ken Robinson

In this chapter

- Strategies for Music
- Strategies for Art
- Strategies for Creative Writing

Throughout the ages, humankind has sought to find expression through artistic endeavour. Think for a moment of Neolithic cave paintings, the drumbeats and music of indigenous peoples around the world, the poems of the Greeks and the story ballads of the Dark Ages. It seems that creativity is hard-wired in people. Yet in Education today, creativity is given a low priority against the 'hard skills' of literacy and numeracy.

Just imagine how interesting it would be if you and your students could study the greatest artistic geniuses of all time and identify their creative processes for painting, composing and playing music, or writing great literature. Well, this is now possible using NLP strategies, so read on to discover how you can learn the creativity of past masters and future geniuses.

Sadly, many people have a belief that they are just not creative. They believe they can't sing, paint or make music. This is such a shame because everyone is capable of creativity. Children who are encouraged to enjoy creativity have a great resource, both for their academic and future working life and for their own pleasure and enjoyment. he ability to think creatively has many more applications than just the arts. It enables people to take a different perspective and look for solutions in many different ways. So here and now is a good time to change.

The first step to creativity is to create in every learner the strong belief that they are a creative person. Many people have to overcome the unhelpful suggestions given to them by other people, often unintentionally. A teacher may have given a child an instrument to play and they couldn't make a sound out of it, or someone may have told them they can't sing. People often think about painting and automatically feel bad and say to themselves, *'I am not artistic'*, just because of a silly suggestion long ago. So, seeing yourself in your mind's eye being creative, playing music, designing or writing is the first step. Beliefs guide our behaviour, but the nice thing is that they are not true and we can change them, so our new beliefs guide different behaviour.

Next, teach learners to feel excited when they think about being creative. Sometimes, the very foundation of creativity is starting with a really strong and different feeling instead of starting with a really bad feeling. Most of the time when people begin a new project with really horrible feelings they just don't create good work. Even people who claim they have to have pain to be creative actually feel the pain, then get excited about it and output it as creativity. Vincent Van Gogh was one such artist although, unlike him, you could just skip the pain of cutting off your ear because it's a lot better to just feel good in the first place. Otherwise you will run out of ears very quickly!

Although NLP may have started by curing phobias and resolving people's problems, the co-founders soon became interested in the many talented people in the world, asking the question, *'how do they do that?'* Fortunately, NLP allows us to ask very precise questions about states of consciousness, and all creative states seem to involve an altered state of consciousness and focused concentration. Altered states are the rule that creates talent - not the exception. We want to create states of concentration, enthusiasm, tenacity and ferocity, so that the learner keeps going and the more they do, the better they feel and the more they enjoy being creative. The more sophisticated or challenging it becomes the more excited the learners become. When we have the right beliefs and the right states created, just a small piece of a strategy will mean that people will be able to be creative.

ART

Take a walk along the River Thames and you may see street artists at work. One day, one of them was drawing the buildings on the other side of the river, producing an amazingly accurate picture, as Richard passed by, and he asked the artist how he did it. The artist said there was a big hand in the sky with a wire attached to his own hand, and as the hand in the sky moved, so did his hand on the paper. *'You have to keep the wire tight!'* he said.

This one piece of strategy is enough to give a child a really clear instruction as to how to recreate an image in front of them. By doing this, the learner begins to really open their eyes and see more detail, more colours, more shade and light, so that their representations become more and more detailed.

Being creative in art is different in some ways from the person who sits by the river and makes the painting exactly like the river, although some of the same skills can be useful. Creativity in art is the degree to which someone looks at something and responds to it with their feelings, taking part of what is actually there and adding elements using their own imagination and internal world. Some people look at Van Gogh's work and are convinced that he actually saw the world the way his pictures looked. We doubt that. His pictures are creations of how he could distort reality.

PART 2 - STRATEGIES FOR LEARNING

THE PICASSO STRATEGY

Think for a moment - compared to the number of things you can see, how many things can you imagine? Let's imagine being in Picasso's mind. To begin, start to draw something you can see, like a circle, a triangle or a square. To do this, first have a connection between the images in your head and your hand. See a hand in your mind drawing around a circle. Connect a wire from the hand on the inside to the hand on the outside so when the hand on the inside moves, the wire moves and the hand on the outside moves too. This way you make sure what you see in your mind matches what you put on the canvas.

The next step is to take something like a circle and see what you would have to do to it to make it a different shape. So take the circle and pop it up so it has a pointy edge, and pop it out so it has another pointy edge somewhere else, and pop it out again in the other direction too. What would happen if you popped it in a few more directions? You now have a shape that no one has ever seen before. So now you have created a 'something'. If you took a square and put it inside the circle and started bringing some of the lines in and pushing some of the lines out, you would have a more sophisticated shape that no one has ever seen before.

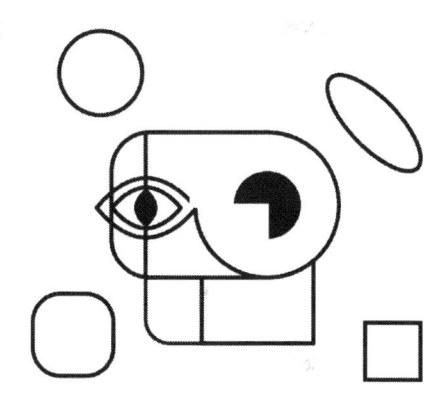

Now take this never-seen-before shape and put it inside the square and manipulate the shapes from the inside and the outside of the square and even between the new lines you have just created. Then take your finger inside your mind and swirl it in a spiral and draw that. Now you can take something that no one has ever seen and draw it on the outside. Then take something from the outside world, perhaps a fish, a bird or somebody's face, and start doing the same thing. You can take just one idea or image from the real world, mix it with your own responses and emotions and morph it using your own imagination into a piece of art that no one has ever seen before. Then your name is Picasso!

Another skill in a great artistic strategy is to create first on the inside of your mind. We all produce some material that we aren't happy with, but great artists produce very little poor work. This is because they create on the inside before they create on the outside

THE CHAGALL STRATEGY
The artist Marc Chagall would paint things in the back of his mind and as he did so, he would think, *'this area is going to be reddish, this area is going to be greenish and this bluish'.* So when you step back far enough from one of his paintings, to where you can't see the objects, you can see there are colour centres. Even though there are colours inside the colours, when you stand 20 yards away, the pictures have colour areas which are like tonal centres in music. So instead of just seeing one thing at one distance from you, you can create something that is one thing from one distance and another from a different distance, angle or perspective. This way you change your perspective and look at things from different angles and different points of view, making them bigger and smaller inside your mind.

Maybe you can look at something and in your mind make a picture of it and start to pixelate it, so you could make it very different to the original view. It may be that Monet was losing his sight, because if you visit his garden at Giverny which features in so many of his paintings and squint whilst looking at it, you will find it looks just like one of his paintings! Whether he was blind or whether he squinted isn't important, because if you want to paint the way Monet did, you can squint too so that the world looks that way, or you can make a picture of what you are seeing, distort it inside your mind and then use this image as the representation of what you paint.

These are some of the distinctions between drawing something you are looking at and creating a representation in your mind so that you draw something that has never existed before, by taking your feelings and letting them swirl out onto the paper. The truth is, there are different strategies for different types of creativity. Learning to read and interpret a piece of music that someone else wrote is entirely different to writing a piece of music and is different again to playing by ear. A key point is that **the more distinctions we can make in the creative process the more we can unleash people's creativity**.

MUSIC

There are people who can read any piece of music but can't play unless they are looking at a music score. One of Richard's friends had a perfect musical ear. When someone tapped a glass, he could tell you what key the sound was in, because when he heard the note made by the glass he would see the key go down on the keyboard in his mind. Yet he couldn't improvise music or play jazz.

It's possible to teach perfect pitch. One mother did this deliberately with her son. He sat on one side of the room away from her, and she would ask him what note she was playing on the piano. If he didn't get it right, he would go to the piano and watch the key go down physically and see the key go down on the imaginary keyboard in his mind. He reached the point where he always knew which note was which. It was a good teaching method. His mother was a piano teacher and oddly enough she didn't do this with her piano students, only with her son, because it was just a game they played together.

However, what this mother didn't give her son was the ability to take this beautiful, crystal ear and hear something inside his head that nobody had ever played before. Creativity doesn't start on the outside, it starts on the inside. Most of the great solo artists hear the melody and their fingers play it automatically. But the notes come on the inside first and their fingers go down simultaneously - almost as an afterthought. They hear a good melody and they play a good melody.

People often say, *'oh I just can't hold a tune in my head'.* Well, the truth is, there isn't anything solid to hold on to! The first step in playing music is to hear the tune in your head. Listen really closely to it and start to hum along with it. If it doesn't match, listen again and match it again so that what is on the inside of your mind matches what is on the outside.

All music has a certain melody and feel to it. Some people start with the words and then make a melody for them, and some people make a melody and find words for it. There is no limitation to the possibilities. There does seem to be a restriction with each individual in that they have to do it one way, because that is the only way they know – so far.

Learning to play classical music is totally different to learning to play jazz, and writing classical music is totally different to writing jazz. They are completely different tasks and there's no reason why a learner can't learn to do both. Consider the genius Leonard Bernstein; his music draws on every genre and type of music. What made him such a genius is that he cognitively understood each type of music. He would think, *'this is part of opera, this is how opera works, it has these motives and I am going to pull them out of here and I am going to put them in a musical'*. He would add a little of this and a little of that. By understanding how to function in each of the different structures he was able to put together something that was greater than the sum of its parts. Teaching children how to do this, not just with music but with art and all creative activities, means it's going to start leaking out in many different areas of their lives. Their ideas will not simply be about how to get the music or the art right, but how to make it even more than it was before.

POETRY AND CREATIVE WRITING
Poetry is an area of creativity where asking great questions can kick-start the creative process. Many people, children and adults alike, claim that they can't do creative writing, so begin by asking your learners about what could never be the case. Ask, *'what is the strangest thing about looking in the sky?'* They may say *'well, the clouds'*, so ask *'what is the weirdest cloud that you have ever seen?'* They may say, *'I saw a cloud like a hippopotamus'*. Say, *'what sound does the wind make? It howls. The hippopotamus in the sky howls'*. Connecting unrelated ideas together creates great poetry. Children are so animated they can write great poetry, draw a picture of their poem and create beauty in many different ways.

Creative writing is a perfect example of where people are not taught enough about creating language. People often say, *'I have writer's block'*. Ask, *'where are you blocked?'* and they may respond that it is in the first sentence. So write what comes first, such as *'I am blocked'* and ask the question *'while?'* Because as soon as you add linkage words, whatever comes next is connected to what went before.

Creative writing is about linking ideas that have not been put together before. Rather than worrying *'am I doing this right?'* you will always keep going if there is a link that prompts your brain as to what comes next. This differs from the norm in writing, where a great deal is taught about stopping. Is it a complete sentence? Oddly enough that's a question! Am I dangling a participle? If you worry about that you will never get to a participle! We love the child who said *'my teacher said I was dangling a Popsicle'*. So if you don't have good grammar you will dangle a Popsicle!

Here is an illustration of how to kick-start the creative writing process with children and adults alike created by our Teaching Excellence student Tanya. Tanya begins the lesson by introducing the class to her beach hut and her hobbies, one of which is writing in her beach hut. She invites the group to join her on a magical journey to inspire their imaginations for writing. The journey is to the seaside (see Chapter 12 for how to create guided journeys). Guided journeys using artfully vague language exercise the imagination 'muscles', enabling learners to create a rich internal world to draw upon in the next part of the lesson.

In the second part of the lesson Tanya models the writing process by engaging the group in a conversation about thinking aloud, describing what it was and how it moved, so that in the third part of the lesson the group begin to create and innovate their own poetry lines and verses to end with the phrase, *"Down at the beach"*. The learners then combine ideas together, evaluate how their poem is progressing and rehearse reading their poems. In the plenary session, the learners perform their poems and celebrate their success.

Here are some examples of the poems created using this process.

Children's outcomes - example:
"Brown crabs crawling,
Shark tails splashing,
Fast fish flying,
Down at the beach"

Adults' outcomes - example:
"The seagulls high will fly
As tourists their souvenirs will buy,

Down the throat will go beer
As I look at my peer/ pier! Down at the beach"

For Tanya's full lesson plan and mind map of the lesson see the activity section at the end of this chapter.

BEYOND THE ARTS
One interior decorator had every piece of furniture he used built by cabinet makers. When he wanted antique furniture, he would have it built, leave it outside his house for a year and tell people that it took him a year to find it – so that put up the price! What was interesting is that he would walk into an empty room and start trying objects out in the room in his imagination. He would start with objects he had seen, and if the object wasn't perfect he would start morphing it into the perfect object for that place. If the best object he could conceive of was a bookcase that looked a particular way, he would start changing it into something even better in terms of how it would fit his vision of the finished room, and when he looked at the finished room it would feel right. He would begin with the feel of what he wanted and change the objects until they matched the desired state. The key here is to oscillate between your images or the sounds that you make on the inside, the feelings you are aiming for and the output channels – the music, the art or the interior design.

The creative process extends beyond traditional 'arts' to areas such as design, architecture, landscape gardening and many more. The only limits are a person's imagination and beliefs. An architect has to be able to see an empty piece of land and hallucinate a building in its totality. A gardener has to look at a bare patch of land and see a garden there.

To do this, your internal world has to supply variation. In other words, if you are going to be an interior decorator you have to have a reservoir of possibilities. This reservoir of possibilities can include things that you have seen before, things you know you could find, and things you could create or invent. The architect, systems theorist, author, designer and inventor Richard Buckminster Fuller was an exemplary example of creativity across multiple fields including architecture, design, geometry, engineering, science, cartography and education. Although best known for his geodesic domes, Buckminster held 28 patents, authored 28 books and received 47 honorary degrees for his creative work.[2] Much of the time it's a case of starting with an idea of what you want and then following it to see if you can make it better on the outside, and the more you like it the more you do it and the less you like it the less you do it. So teach people to use their feelings as a guide to what they are creating.

If we teach children how to vary from one system or method, we are teaching them to think. We have to teach people 20 ways to remember, 20 ways to create, 20 ways to paint. Every time we have a different variation on these things we add the possibilities. If you have ever visited the Van Gogh Museum in Amsterdam you can see the way Van Gogh learned to paint in many different styles, including his 'Old Dutch Masters' period, his 'Parisian' period, and finally he found his own distinctive creative style.

First you can learn one way and then try another and another, blend all three in sequence and all three backwards. Creativity doesn't come from having one mechanism working, it comes from having a variety. Creativity is about finding various combinations, so learners can do things that have never been done before. This way they discover which ones please them and which ones don't.

Of course if you have to paint everything on the outside first to decide if you like it, it's a lot slower than if you can do it on the inside first. That's why people we consider to be real geniuses don't seem to have a lot of poor output. Most of their output seems to be really good because they run through it first on the inside, find the best selections and then do it on the outside. This makes for efficient productivity.

The difference between human beings and inanimate objects is our ability to **respond**. The way that we as individuals work with clients is different from everybody else, and so it should be. The more variety of strategies and approaches we have to choose from, the more we can use them to alter the way things are for people, and this is very true for teachers. Teachers want to have lots of strategies available so that if somebody has trouble with one, they can offer another or take a step back and provide the precursor to the strategy.

Learning and teaching creativity is also about asking good questions. Rather than asking, *'what is wrong with this?'*, ask *'what would happen if I added this?'* If there is a picture inside your head, ask *'well I've got a tree in mind, what would happen if I took the weirdest colour I could find and made the leaves that colour?'* Or *'what would happen if I had a normal face on one side and I distorted the other as much as I possibly could?'* Anything that exists in normal reality can be altered in another reality, so teaching the *'what would happen if'* question to your students develops creativity and imagination.

In schools, learners are sometimes admonished for not drawing what is on the outside. If a child draws an apple that is purple he may be told that he hasn't got it right. On this basis, Picasso, Monet and Van Gogh would have all failed Art at school and only the people from the Renaissance who painted perfect three-dimensional images would have been considered artists. The truth is, creativity is having a sense of experimentation. Sit down and experiment to make colours; first you can match colours that exist, but then you want to make colours that are like the ones only you can imagine. If you start imagining and changing all the different tones, you can take a colour on the outside and think, *'I like this blue, maybe we can make it into a tree'*

SUMMARY

During this chapter we have outlined the basis for creativity in a number of different arts and forms. Within each strategy there are some consistent factors. First and foremost is the belief that the student is a creative person. Secondly, that the right states are created, not only to begin but to continue so that the more they create the better they feel. Thirdly, that a few helpful techniques will get people off to a great start and that is all they need to become creative. Next, ask the *'what would happen if'* question and create on the inside as well as the outside of your mind and stretch your imagination muscles. And finally, remember that the more distinctions we can make in the creative process, the more we can unleash people's creativity.

REFERENCES

1. Sir Ken Robinson, 2010, Changing Education Paradigms, RSA Animate, www.thersa.org
2. The Buckminster Fuller Institute, https://bfi.org/about-fuller

ACTIVITIES

Activity 1

FOR YOURSELF :
Decide on an area of creativity that you do not believe you are good at or have never tried. Sit quietly and imagine in every representation system yourself creating in this form. Notice the good feelings and spin them so they intensify. Add in some excitement and some tenacity. Then go out and have a go. Find a really creative person and ask some interesting questions, such as *'how do you do that?'* / *'How do you know when to start?'* / *'How do you know when it's done?'* Keep going until you have found one key part of the technique to add to your repertoire.

Activity 2

Design a list of questions to stimulate creativity with your students and build a lesson around creativity, whatever your subject.

Activity 3

FOR YOUR STUDENTS :
Write out an introduction to a session that convinces your students that they are creative. Use a journey where they relax and imagine themselves creating something wonderful and enjoying the pleasure of the process. Then teach your class and notice what is different (see Chapter 12 for more guidance on how to do this).

Extension activity

Build your introduction into a full lesson.

Here is the Poetry lesson plan and an example of a mind map to guide you:

LESSON
Focus: Year 1 class [Original] - Adapted for NLP Master Practitioner Students
Subject: English [Poetry Writing]

SUCESS CRITERIA FOR PROGRESS :
- **Satisfactory** - Use words from the word bank
- **Good** - Choose own nouns/adjectives
- **Outstanding** - Choose adjectives/verbs that are different, ambitious or sound effective, e.g. Verb continuous

NTRODUCTION/GREETING:
- Rapport: My name...My beach hut...My hobbies... [writing at my beach hut] Create beach scape while talking...sea, sand, shells, etc.
- Hook: Invitation to come with me on a magical journey to inspire our imaginations for writing

LESSON FORMAT :

1. **Episode** 1: Generate vocabulary & creative states [Process: Guided meditation to 'sea' music using artfully vague language to enable the learners to choose their subject and language]

2. **Episode** 2: Model writing process [Talk for writing: Describe what it was...Say how it moved...]

3. **Episode** 3: Learners to innovate their own poetry lines/verses ending..."Down at the beach"

4. **Episode** 4: Combine ideas, evaluate and rehearse.

5. **Plenary** - Perform and celebrate!

PART 2 - STRATEGIES FOR LEARNING

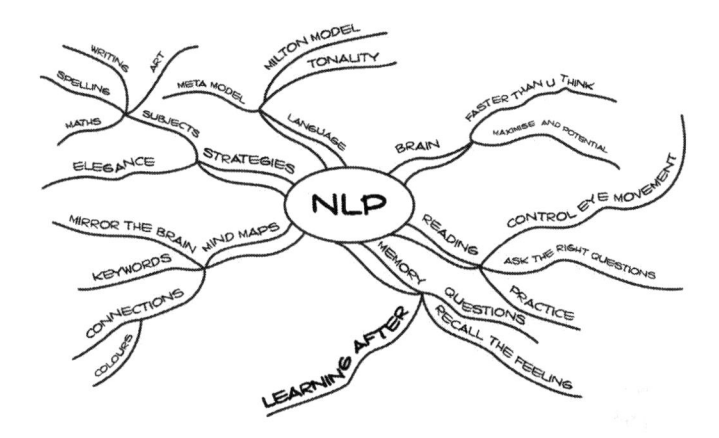

NLP

- STRATEGIES
  - SUBJECTS
    - WRITING
    - ART
    - SPELLING
    - MATHS
  - ELEGANCE
  - META MODEL
  - MILTON MODEL
  - TONALITY
  - LANGUAGE
- BRAIN
  - FASTER THAN U THINK
  - MAXIMISE AND POTENTIAL
- READING
  - CONTROL EYE MOVEMENT
  - ASK THE RIGHT QUESTIONS
- QUESTIONS
  - PRACTICE
- MEMORY
  - RECALL THE FEELING
- LEARNING AFTER
- MIND MAPS
  - MIRROR THE BRAIN
  - KEYWORDS
  - CONNECTIONS
  - COLOURS

PART 3

HIGHLY EFFECTIVE CLASSROOM TEACHING

CHAPTER 9

What makes a Highly Effective Teacher?

Scan this to see the video

'The last of human freedoms - the ability to choose one's attitude in a given set of circumstances, to choose one's own way.' (1)

Victor E Frankl

In this chapter

- Discover the core beliefs that Highly Effective Teachers hold true
- Translate these beliefs into effective behaviours in the classroom
- Develop the 7 Habits of Highly Effective Teachers

We don't believe our students get up in the morning wanting to screw up our day. It might feel like that sometimes, but it's not a helpful belief to have and it's not true. However, one teacher on a seminar we ran protested, *'you haven't met my Wednesday afternoon group. I KNOW they get up and plan how to screw up my day!'* It wasn't at all surprising to discover that this class succeeded in screwing up this teacher's day every Wednesday, for this is what he expected them to do, and they obliged.

As a teacher, you may be familiar with the Pygmalion or Rosenthal Effect.[2] Robert Rosenthal and Lenore Jacobson informed teachers that, following progress tests a number of students were showing great promise and were expected to 'spurt' in their development over the following terms. In fact, these children were a random selection and showed no such particular promise over other students. The 'prophecy' was self-fulfilling; the study showed that if teachers were led to expect enhanced performance from certain children, then those children did indeed show that enhancement. It became clear that the children were not responding to the expectations of the teachers directly, but were responding positively to the behaviours and attitudes of their teachers, who in turn **believed** that these children were of higher intelligence.

Teachers are powerful influencers, and when we carefully choose our beliefs or assumptions about our students, to a great extent those assumptions will manifest in our students. The premise is simple - **what the thinker thinks the prover proves**.[3]

When your mind holds a belief, it biases and filters all incoming data to substantiate and support that belief, and we can use this to powerful effect in the classroom.

Highly Effective Teachers choose useful beliefs that support learners as individuals and learning as a process. In teaching, as in all other areas of life, our beliefs drive our behaviours, so any decision to act or behave in a certain way is based on the beliefs we hold at that moment in time.

Most of us probably only spend time thinking about what we believe in relation to the very weighty questions, such as our religion or values. Beliefs are by their very nature not 'true'. If they were true they would be facts, not beliefs. Some of our beliefs are extensive, like breathing is a good thing! Other beliefs evolve and change as we grow and learn, such as a belief in the tooth fairy. Just as our beliefs change and develop over our lives, you can adopt helpful and supportive beliefs in relation to your students.

The beliefs of Highly Effective Teachers correspond to many of the basic assumptions or presuppositions of NLP, which in turn form the basis of NLP interventions. Deciding in advance to 'pre-frame' or presuppose success in ourselves and in others ensures that we think ourselves and our students into successful outcomes. The assumptions of NLP provide operating principles that are conducive to motivated, resilient and tenacious teachers and learners.

Some of the presupposed beliefs of Highly Effective Teachers include:

- My students are doing the best they can at this moment in time
- My students are making the best choices with the resources they have
- Given better options, the students will make better choices
- There is a positive intention behind their behaviour – they may just not have the right strategy to achieve what they want
- Failure is a result. All results are outcomes, whether or not they are what was intended

Some people may think that beliefs don't change–*'I can't help it, I've always been like this!'* However, even pervasive beliefs can and do change and we are all able to choose our attitude at a given time when we start to think on purpose.

Of course you are not responsible for a student's experiences prior to your meeting them, and one of your first jobs may be to help them to change some of their less helpful past learnings. They may have beliefs about being stupid, being unable to learn, or that learning serves no purpose for them. Fortunately, you can be proactive in changing your students' minds. Consider the following behaviours used by Highly Effective Teachers:

1. HIGHLY EFFECTIVE TEACHERS ARE SYSTEMATIC IN THEIR BEHAVIOURS

The reason for carefully choosing the beliefs that support and sustain learning is that our behaviours will follow directly and be driven by our beliefs. Whatever a highly effective teacher does, s/he does it in a systematic and consistent way. They base their decisions to act on the operating principles they have adopted and they engage in certain behaviours as a habit. NLP is a systematic field; it is not based on intuition, charisma or other innate qualities. The skills of NLP can easily be learned and transmitted to others.

2. HIGHLY EFFECTIVE TEACHERS ARE PROACTIVE AND OUTCOME-FOCUSED

In some languages such as Welsh, Serbian and Maori, the word for 'teaching' is the same as the word for 'learning'. In English, we could have 'tearning', which is probably better than 'learching'! Even in some English dialects, the word 'learn' is used rather than 'teach', for example, *'she learned me to ride my bike'*. This shift in focus reframes the concept of teaching. When we begin to take responsibility for our students' learning processes, we move the focus from the teaching to the learning. The key approach here is to keep your eye on the prize (the outcome you want for your students) and be proactive in finding creative ways to achieve the outcome with the student.

Have you ever heard, or even said, *'I taught them X last week/month/ year – they must know it!'*? And the students' response is a blank or confused stare? You know you taught this subject, but you don't know the students learned it. This common misunderstanding about learning suggests that the responsibility of the teacher has been discharged at the point of delivery. However, the reality is that if they haven't learned it, we haven't taught it! If you are not getting the response you want, then it's time to change the way you communicate. This requires the teacher to be a great learner and to look for new ways to understand what works - and what doesn't work - for a student. One NLP assumption - **the meaning of the communication is the response you get** - puts the learner at the centre of the learning and the teacher in the driving seat of being 'response-able'.

Simply put, if the way you are explaining or teaching isn't working – try something else!

3. HIGHLY EFFECTIVE TEACHERS SEE PROBLEMS AS CHALLENGES AND OPPORTUNITIES TO LEARN

Students are making the best choices they can with the resources they have right now. Making this assumption provides the opportunity to resolve challenges rather than simply accept that this is the way they are. For example, when we believe that everyone gets up in the morning wanting to do their best and a student does something we don't like or is inappropriate, we can then ask ourselves, *'what is the student trying to achieve with this behaviour that isn't working for them?'* This question provides a direction, so we can then ask how we can help them to find a better way to achieve what they want. **When people are given better options they make better choices**.

You will have heard teachers say, *'Oh, that student is just attention-seeking'* Well, guess what - they are! Attention-seeking behaviour means that the student wants attention. There is nothing wrong with that; everyone wants attention, especially when they are young. The problem is, the behaviours they use to get attention may not be appropriate in that context. We can show that young person how they can get the attention they want through more appropriate means. The behaviour that isn't getting a student what they want is not a 'bad behaviour'; it just doesn't fit within the context. We can help students to either find a more appropriate behaviour, or find a context where that original behaviour is acceptable. Some years ago there was a scheme on a rundown housing estate just outside Manchester, where tutors worked on the streets with boys who had been excluded from school. Most of these teenagers had police records and probation officers. Despite an inability to work independently, they were exceptionally good at working together as a group. This wasn't really surprising considering how they spent their spare time. This group could steal a car and strip it of everything that was of value in minutes, one big lad removing each wheel and propping the car up on bricks, the smallest boy inside the car removing the radio while someone else acted as lookout and the most athletic boy was the runner. Within 4 minutes, the car was stripped of everything of value, and within hours most of it had been sold.

Obviously, we are not condoning this activity. However, think for a moment of the behaviours and activity in a different context, focusing on the process, and it's clear these young men had Formula 1 racing pitstop skills. These young men had developed team-working skills, communication skills, dexterity, business skills, and physical prowess. It was not a question of re-training them in something useful; it was a case of moving their skills into a different context so their skills could be recognised and respected - hopefully keeping them out of jail in the future!

As we discussed in Part 2, behaviour relates not only to what someone does on the outside, but also how s/he behaves on the inside. The decisions they make, the way they represent situations to themselves, the sequence and steps they go through to engage in an experience are all internal behaviours. We have all seen kids completely engrossed in something on the TV in a room full of other distractions. They have learned how to turn the volume down on noise they don't want to pay attention to, and to turn it up on what they do want to pay attention to. This proves they can change the way they experience the world so that it works for them. If you have experience of teenagers, you may recognise this form of selective deafness. Similarly, many people will experience very difficult and painful situations, but no two people will respond in the same way or make the same decisions. Some people will continue to see a difficult experience in multi-colour surround sound, whilst others will push it to the back of their minds and turn down the sound and the brightness. Lots of children experience sad or unpleasant events in their lives, and we have a responsibility to intervene and protect them when necessary, but we can also do more. We can help them to process their experiences in ways that enable them to grow into healthy and happy adults, rather than staying stuck in the bad feelings as they grow up. NLP offers many techniques for fast intervention and transformation by changing the way a person experiences their past and creating new and resourceful states to move on into the future.

4. HIGHLY EFFECTIVE TEACHERS ARE PROCESS RATHER THAN CONTENT ORIENTATED

How is it that when the curriculum content of a particular subject is the same, the scheme of work is the same and even on occasion the lesson plan is determined, yet learners in one class learn with ease and pleasure and those in another class struggle and dislike the subject? The answer is that it has little to do with the content and much to do with the process. Most teachers focus on 80% content and 20% process. Highly Effective Teachers reverse this and focus 80% of their energies on process and only 20% on content. From planning a lesson to teaching it, the processes the students use to learn are at the forefront and form the focus of the lesson, rather than the content.

Pass rates and failure rates are regarded as measures of the success of both teachers and children. However, we need to distinguish between failure that is externally imposed, such as in a test, and formative assessment during the learning process where we learn what works and what doesn't work. In formative assessment, **there is no such thing as failure, only feedback**. This means that all outcomes are results and opportunities to learn more.

It's useful to reframe students' beliefs about failure as simply mistakes. A useful acronym for FAIL is First Attempt In Learning! All results and behaviours are achievements, whether they are desired outcomes for a given task or not. You may have heard the fable about the inventor Thomas Edison. After multiple unsuccessful attempts in his bid to create the first commercially viable light bulb, he was asked if he felt like a failure. He replied, *'why would I feel like a failure? I now know definitively over 9,000 ways that an electric lightbulb will not work'*. This story may or may not be true, but it's a great illustration of the assumption that there is no such thing as failure only feedback. If a student writes an essay on the French Revolution instead of the Russian Revolution, there are still things that they have learned and got right. They have used a pen or computer, created sentences, thought up ideas, researched and learned something about revolutions, etc. So make a point of ensuring students know what they have done that's good learning, and then let them know what they need to do next.

Assessments and tests can be devised which have success built into the process. Take, for example, the basic numeracy assessment test devised by a Maths teacher. Normal tests usually get harder and harder, so essentially the instruction is to keep going until you fail. As an alternative approach, this tutor put the questions onto cards and gave an instruction to sort the cards into three piles: One pile for the questions you know you can answer, one for the questions you know you can't answer yet, and one for the ones you are not sure you can answer. This gives the teacher an immediate and useful assessment and the student succeeds in the task of creating three piles – which was all they were asked to do. It's often just a matter of creating an assessment process without creating the feelings of failure.

Learners already know how to learn. One of the differences in our approach to learning is our total belief that people are natural-born *exquisite* learners. The question is not how do we teach people, but how can we discover what stops people learning, or what motivates them to continue. The 20th Century's view of education was that children were empty vessels waiting to be filled with knowledge from the teacher, yet when you think about that, it really didn't work, did it? When we act on the premise that **the resources a person needs to learn and change are already within them** we create learning opportunities.

Most of the really important things in life, like learning to walk, talk, use imagination, create exciting worlds and make friends, are learned without a classroom or a teacher. Many people even suggest that 'problems' with learning only actually begin once the child gets into the classroom!

Human beings are hard-wired for learning and for learning about learning, and it is our responsibility to remain mindful of these innate qualities so as to drive next generation thinking. Our job is to help students by giving them additional tools and strategies to learn and drive their own brains, so they develop independent learning and thinking.

Creating the link between existing skills and strategies for learning with the subject in hand is just one way a teacher can help. Take, for instance, the student who complains, *'why do we have to do more of this when we did it in class?'* Ask them what level they are at on an activity they enjoy, say their favourite PlayStation or Xbox game, and use the information, saying, *'Great, you're on level 7 of your new PlayStation game, did you just do level 6 once?' 'Of course not,'* they will tell you. *'I was on level 6 for a week before I got good enough to move to level 7.'* And this is your cue: *'Oh really, so practising something and feeling excited about it means you get really good at it – right?'* Remember, people are not broken so they don't need fixing - they are just uneducated as to how to apply strategies for learning, motivation and change.

5. HIGHLY EFFECTIVE TEACHERS ARE FLEXIBLE IN THEIR BEHAVIOUR
Each person's version of reality is not the same as the next person's. Imagine for a moment that you want to give directions to your house. You might describe in words how to get there, or you might draw a map. What would you focus on as important? Would you use road numbers, landmarks like shops, or street names to identify the key features of the journey? Having done this before, you will probably make a great job of it. What you won't have on your map or detailed in your directions is every blade of grass, every paving stone or the minute details of each house on the way. We all construct an approximation of the world in order to take some shortcuts and decide what is important to us and our understanding. We each have a different map of the territory and each person's interpretations of external data will be unique.

One of the key jobs of a teacher is the ability to understand how students map their world. Because the territory is so vast and detailed, we process the information in our unique way so that we can make sense of it, reduce it, sort it out and prioritise the input we receive. The illustration relating to the word 'dog' in Chapter 1 is one such example of how the map is not the territory.

Humans over-generalise, distort and delete information. This can be very useful - it is part of the learning process, like generalising the many shapes, styles and colours of seating objects as 'chairs'. However, if on one occasion you didn't learn your times tables and your teacher said you were stupid, and you decided you would never learn your tables again, this generalisation is really unhelpful. As a teacher, your job is not only to ensure that learning takes place, but also to ensure that your students make good decisions about what their learning means to them.

6. HIGHLY EFFECTIVE TEACHERS TAKE NOTICE, WATCH AND LISTEN

People **cannot not communicate**, which means that a great deal of information about a student's state and their learning can be discovered by paying close attention to the messages they give, both verbally and non-verbally. Non-verbal cues are particularly useful with teenagers who are not known for their high level of communication skills! During one-to-one progress reviews, students often say very little, and when they do speak, it may be just to ask, *'what do you want me to say?'* Teachers then create all sorts of prompts to cajole the student into talking. However, the student has literally given you the answer – they're not speaking to you because they haven't figured out what it is that YOU want them to say! They haven't learned yet that you are genuinely interested in what they say; they believe that there is a right answer and you are waiting for them to give it to you – like a test!

When we are unsure about the meaning a person is trying to convey, it is often helpful to simply listen to the words spoken and respond to them literally. So in the example above the response might be, *'I want you to say what your thoughts and opinions are and it doesn't matter if I agree with you or not.'*

Imagine for a moment a student who is silent after you have asked them a question. There are many assumptions that could be made about what this silence means. We may assume s/he is sullen, stubborn, or upset. The problem is, all these decisions are based on a guess about what is going on and we really just don't know. So what information is available to us? Well, you can observe the way s/he is sitting, where s/he is looking, their breathing rate, facial skin tone, the symmetry of their face and body. All of this is valuable communication and **Highly Effective Teachers accept and utilise all communication and behaviour presented to them.**

Some teachers are very adept at reading body language, often on an unconscious level, and by understanding even more about non-verbal communication, NLP adds new skills and resources to better enable teachers to make effective interventions.

We are sure you are aware that you have already learned a great deal about the senses, the representational systems and the submodalities of the representational systems in Chapter 1. The NLP assumption here is that **all distinctions people make about their environment and behaviour can usefully be represented through the five senses**.

As a reminder, people make pictures, hear sounds and have feelings inside themselves. The more skilled they are at utilising all their senses, the richer their learning will be, the more they will remember and recall and the more applications for the learning they will find. Similarly, the more the teacher uses all his/her senses and internal representations the more effective they will be in the classroom. When a teacher communicates using sensory-rich language s/he creates what is known as 'semantic density', which engages strongly with the internal representations the student is making and thus makes learning bigger, stronger and more memorable.

7. HIGHLY EFFECTIVE TEACHERS ENDEAVOUR TO LIKE THEIR STUDENTS

Consider the young men on the Manchester housing estate for a moment. Do you think of them as 'bad' individuals? Could you 'like' them? It's not often said openly that to teach well it's fundamental to find a way to at least like your students. Reflect on your own days at school; which teachers and therefore subjects did you respond to best? One of the messages they almost certainly gave you was that they liked and cared about you. However, they also probably cared about you enough to not tolerate behaviour that didn't serve you or the wider community. An NLP assumption holds that **the positive worth of the individual is held constant, while the value and appropriateness of their behaviour, whether this is internal or external, is questioned**. Love the sinner, hate the sin!

It's easy to think of the young men in Manchester as 'bad' people because they did bad things, but they are not. Once they were given better choices, they made better decisions. Words such as positive regard, unconditional respect and care actually mask something much more fundamental, which is that humans thrive on love and compassion. So as teachers can we care about our students enough to refuse to allow them to fail?

As teachers, we are very familiar with challenging inappropriate behaviour. Some of us are often taking control of behaviour before we can even begin to teach a class. However, in this context we also consider internal behaviour, that is, behaviour that someone is engaging in inside their heads, as well as how that is manifesting outside, in their external behaviour. It is not usually a teacher's intention to criticise a student as a person - rather, we aim to focus on the behaviour. Unfortunately, this is where you really need to pay attention to your language, because unless you do, a student may interpret what you say as being critical of them as a person.

The techniques of NLP change and develop over time. What remain constant are the attitude and beliefs of NLP. Using NLP effectively in the classroom requires tenacity, determination, and thoroughness. Never, ever give up on a student. We don't know when we will make a difference - we cannot not make a difference, the question is in which direction and what's the difference that makes the difference?

SUMMARY

During this chapter you have considered the key behaviours of Highly Effective Teachers and some of the assumptions of NLP that underpin the skills and processes which generate powerful learning experiences and effective teaching. Our beliefs drive our behaviour, so it is important to choose assumptions and attitudes that serve us and enable us to create positive and worthwhile learning for our students, and to intervene in a helpful and supportive way. The side effect might just be that you gain a happier and more relaxed disposition too! We know that many students arrive with unhelpful beliefs about being stupid, being unable to learn, or that learning serves no purpose for them. When you experience the impact of having adopted the assumptions outlined in this chapter, then your students will achieve beyond what you, or they, could previously conceive.

REFERENCES

1. Viktor E Frankl, 1959, Man's Search for Meaning, Beacon Press
2. Rosenthal, Robert; Jacobson, Lenore (1992), Pygmalion in the classroom (Expanded ed.). New York: Irvington.
3. Robert Anton Wilson, 1983, Prometheus Rising, New Falcon Publications

ACTIVITIES

Activity 1

Here is a list of some of the assumptions of NLP utilised by Highly

Effective Teachers we have discussed in this chapter:

- The meaning of the communication is the response you get
- There is a positive intention behind every behaviour and a context in which every behaviour has value
- The ability to change the process by which we experience the world is more valuable than changing the content of our reality
- The map is not the territory
- Given better options, students will make better choices
- There is no such thing as failure, only feedback. All results are outcomes whether or not they are what was intended
- The resources a person needs to learn and change are already within them
- Highly Effective Teachers accept and utilise all communication and behaviour presented to them
- All distinctions people make about their environment and behaviour can usefully be represented through the five senses
- The positive worth of the individual is held constant while the value and appropriateness of their behaviour, whether this is internal or external, is questioned

Take a little time to consider which of these assumptions you accept and hold as true in your teaching. Are there any that you would challenge or change in some way? Discuss the assumptions with your fellow teachers and compare their responses to your own.

Activity 2

You can now begin to think about how you can utilise these assumptions in your classroom so they become your default operating principles. Take a look at the following set of classroom beliefs created by Mark, NLP teacher practitioner for his Year 7 History class (age 11/12):

1. Everyone deserves respect - always

2. All lessons will be useful

3. Appropriate state + correct strategy = the outcome you want

4. The outcome becomes possible the moment I see, hear and feel it is mine

5. Getting into my best state is my responsibility - especially my learning state

6. I can answer any question if I know the right strategy

7. Awareness of my progress gives me the choice of changing my strategy

8. The person who knows the most strategies wins

9. Everybody has the ability to succeed

10. My language predicts my results

11. Feedback is the only friend I must use

Consider the teacher's work above and compare it to any current assumptions you may hold. Think about what you would include in a new and more resourceful list for you and your learners. Replace your rule list and design a short session with one of your classes where they create a new and useful list of helpful beliefs for learning. Notice their level of commitment to this list with their commitment to the class 'rules'.

Activity 3

Create an assessment tool for your subject that measures progress without the possibility of 'failure'.

PART 3 - HIGHLY EFFECTIVE CLASSROOM TEACHING

CHAPTER 10

The Mind of a Highly Effective Teacher - The Art of the State

SCAN THIS TO SEE THE VIDEOS

'To handle yourself, use your head;

to handle others, use your heart.' [1]

Eleanor Roosevelt

In this chapter

- Choose success ahead of time
- Be ready for any challenge
- Control the variables in the class
- Drive your own neurology
- Optimise your pleasure in teaching

Have you ever enthusiastically spent time and energy preparing lesson plans and resources, hand-outs, presentations, interactive resources, etc. then started your class and as the students arrived discovered they just weren't in the mood, were disruptive, or not joining in, despite your best efforts? When a class goes well, we bounce out of the room feeling great. If not, we may end the
lesson feeling drained of energy and despondent that all our efforts seem to have been wasted.

Teenagers in particular have an uncanny knack of pressing our 'crumple buttons'. Parents, other teachers and managers may also affect our mood, however unintentionally. The question is, if other people can impact or change your state, who is in charge of how you feel and what you think? Perhaps, until now, you haven't considered deciding which state would be most useful in a forthcoming class **ahead of time**. And even if you have thought this through, how successful were you in creating and maintaining your ideal state? Imagine that you can build a better strategy, one that takes care of itself, freeing you from feeling impacted by others around you, leaving you free to focus entirely on the best brain states of your learners.

Remember, in Chapter 3 we defined the NLP term 'State' as the total on-going mental, emotional and physical conditions a person experiences at a given moment in time. In short, this is what you remember, what you imagine is going to happen, and what you hear inside your head and feel in your body.

A major factor in using NLP for excellent teaching is the ability to take account of and manage as many as possible of the variables involved in the process of learning. We wonder why teachers are not taught to view the management of their own state as one such variable.

When you think about planning your state 'ahead of time', it may sound fanciful, yet people already do this. If a teacher wakes up on a rainy day and thinks about how awful their group was the previous day, then makes a picture of himself failing to teach well today, saying to himself, *'it's going to be worse than yesterday'*, it's not a good idea to imagine what feelings are created! Most people resonate with that scenario, and that's a good thing, because if you can do that, you can begin to consider what other states you can choose, practise and take with you into your class.

Take the example of a teacher who wakes up and changes her mind – literally – and does whatever is necessary in order to make feeling good a priority. She imagines the class going well, remembers the time when she taught brilliantly and everything was easy, makes the picture really bright, and says to herself, *'this is going to be such fun'*. Imagine the feelings she has created for herself now.

All that is required is a decision to take control, not of **what** you think, but **how** you think. You could make a gloomy picture brighter and more colourful, or the sound of the voice in your head softer. NLP enables people to be exceptionally good at these skills, giving you the opportunity to play with your own state, driving your own brain and neurology to deliberately decide to be in the best state possible for teaching.

Equally, we can all learn to maintain our state in the face of provocation and adversity. Imagine going into work full of the joys of spring and feeling wonderful, then you walk into the staff room and encounter a grumpy person. You say *'good morning!'* in your joyful tonality and he says, *'is it? Yeah, right!'* How do you feel? If this grumpy person manages to change the way you're feeling, the important question is - who is in control of your state?

If your students or other staff can change your state and have you feeling stressed and reactive, then they are in charge of your state. Basically, the person with the most stable and powerful state wins out - so make it yours!

Many people feel they are subject to the vagaries of external forces in determining their state of mind and mood. But the reality is that their state is often habituated and not something they actively and consciously pay attention to. Some people will say, *'I can't help it – it's the way I am'*, because they haven't yet experienced good state management. This isn't a very helpful belief and so it is time to change it.

Consider the situation Nigel found himself in. As a Hairdressing tutor in a large college, Nigel taught the same programme each week, to two different groups. Most of the variables were the same - group size, age and demographic, subject matter, scheme of work, lesson plan, activities, etc. However, one group he described as his 'Angels' and the other group as his 'Devils'. He said it didn't matter what he did - one group was responsive, happy and eager, and the other group was difficult, challenging and unresponsive.

Nigel chose to work on this problem as part of his NLP Practitioner training. On the fourth day of the training he had a revelation, suddenly announcing, *'I realise that when I think about or talk about my 'Angels' I smile and feel good, and when I do the same about my 'Devils' I frown and feel bad'*. He determined to use his new-found NLP skills to convince himself, as he was going in to teach his 'Devils', that they were really his 'Angels'. Nigel planned this carefully and practised beforehand. He imagined the group, happy and smiling, attentive and enthusiastic. He imagined hearing himself teaching and the group responding with enthusiasm. He paid attention to the good feeling this gave him and intensified the good feeling by spinning it so that it spread throughout his body. He entered the classroom in this state and kept the good feeling going, whatever was actually happening in the room. It took just 20 minutes for the 'Devils' to 'miraculously' transform themselves into another group of 'Angels'.

What changes first? You do!

Nigel chose his 'state' and his response in relation to this group. He also demonstrates the fundamental attitudes of NLP that include tenacity, determination and creativity to find the variable that makes the difference. It's reasonable to assume that there was some history in the situation between Nigel and his groups, which led to the point where Nigel developed the unpleasant feelings towards one group. However, in NLP we don't need the 'back story' or an understanding of the history behind a situation. The circumstances that lead to a situation don't contribute usefully to the process required to get out of it. Nigel simply determined to try everything he could to bring about change, and once he determined which variable would make the biggest difference, he kept going until he very quickly had two fantastic groups of students.

In summary, the goals Nigel achieved were:

- To engage comfortably with both groups, so as to teach efficiently and effectively
- To decide what was within his control and gather the necessary resources within him
- To rehearse the acquired skills until he was unconsciously competent and behaving automatically in the way he chose

- To believe it was possible and imagine the result by running the movie of his success in full Technicolor and quadraphonic sound
- To be clear that the goal would benefit everyone concerned

Of course no one can or would want to live in a constant, full-on exciting state of deep joy at all times. Sad and bad things do happen and it wouldn't be human to feel happy during such times. The important thing is not to dwell on the sad times and to take control of our state the rest of the time. We can be really specific about creating the perfect state at any moment. We may want to be in a state of relaxed alertness or comfortable contentment - any combination we choose - what's important is to learn how to do it, enjoy doing it and know how to create really great states in others. Later, we will consider how to create states in others, but for now how would you like to be in the best state possible?

Let's take a moment to consider what is happening in our brains and bodies when we are in a particular state. Most people understand that thinking takes place in the brain and that connections are made through the neural pathways. The chemicals that our bodies create, such as Serotonin, Oxytocin, Dopamine and Endorphin, act as neural transmitters, ensuring our brains work optimally and we feel good.[2]

What many people don't realise is that we have another system in our gut, which impacts on our thoughts and feelings. This is known as the enteric nervous system. Just like the neurons in our brain, the neurons in our bodies send and receive impulses, record experiences, and respond to emotions. The body's nerve cells are bathed and influenced by the same neurotransmitters. The gut can upset the brain just as the brain can upset the gut, and the gut can create feelings of wellbeing just as easily. It's easy to see why it is often referred to as 'the other brain'.[3]

In the early days of NLP, the neurochemical processes could not be verified because we didn't have the benefit of technology such as MRI scans to study these influences. Now we know more and can utilise this knowledge to create exquisite states that bathe your whole neurology in good feelings, especially through processes recently developed by

Richard known as Neuro-Hypnotic Repatterning® (NHR). Think about designing the perfect cocktail – take a dash of playfulness, a measure of calm, and a squeeze of excitement. There are numerous NLP techniques for creating great states; however here we introduce you to this NHR process, which we can explore with the help of Denise.

Denise is a lovely lady and a very enthusiastic teacher. She bubbled with confidence when working with children, but was moving into teaching other teachers and was extremely nervous. By using NHR she was helped to develop an exquisite state to support her in her new life. Asked what 3 feelings would be most useful for her in this new situation, she said she wanted to have a feeling of acceptance, a feeling of excitement, and a feeling of coolness. This last one was because when she got flustered she often had a hot flush which led her to feeling more flustered, and she would spiral into imagining what others were thinking instead of concentrating on what she was doing and noticing the responses she was getting.

Denise has now learned to take each feeling in turn, first finding a time when she felt completely accepted and loved, and building that feeling so it courses through her body, She notices which way the feeling moves in her body so she can spin the feeling faster in that direction to intensify the feeling. As she pays more and more attention to that good feeling it becomes really strong and powerful. She mixes this feeling with the next feeling of being excited to create a new and brilliantly good state. Denise then imagines standing on top of a mountain in a wonderful cool breeze with a river running below, amplifies that feeling and mixes it with the feelings of acceptance and excitement. She gives herself a word and a colour to re-access the feeling whenever she wants it.

Creating an entirely new state is different from re-accessing an existing state - Denise stood in her own pillar of power, and that evening she discovered for herself how powerful the technique is and was instantly convinced to study NLP to become a better teacher and also learn how to optimise other people's brain states for learning.

The anchoring process Denise used is explored in the next chapter.

Of course, the same principles that apply in the classroom apply to teachers outside the classroom. If as a teacher you don›t have any control over your state you can become stressed and either burn out or become numb to the process and cease to enjoy it. If you are stuck in a system where you have to do things rigidly by the rules of others, or you are under time pressure, you can prepare yourself for the challenges. Instead of running yourself down and becoming frustrated, you can accelerate yourself so you become more motivated, and make it so that having limited time becomes an asset rather than a liability.

Teachers often say, *'I have to teach 30 students, and that's too many'.* We believe that you can teach 1,000 people if you're in the right state. If you free up your time by giving kids the acquisition skills and installing in them the enthusiasm, there is no limit to what you can achieve. People can be enthusiastic about all sorts of things that may seem strange to others - stamp collecting, knitting, pottery or politics, for example. We don't know how politicians get excited about any of the things they have to vote for, but they do and enthusiasm isn't in limited supply in human beings. It only becomes depleted if you are not in the right state of consciousness.

Learning to go inside yourself and access great feelings, spin those feelings and attach them where you need to is a skill that teachers especially need. Above and beyond everything else, the school system puts teachers on an uphill climb. It's not having 30 kids that is the problem, it's having 30 kids and having nothing that makes you feel excited. When you have control over your own state, you can pay attention to what is really important, and that's being a great teacher

SUMMARY

In this chapter you have learned the fundamentals of creating great states for yourself, so you can begin to take control of your thoughts and feelings, think on purpose and lay the foundations for helping your students to be in the best states for learning. You have been introduced to the powerful technology of Neuro-Hypnotic Repatterning® (NHR) to enable you to easily and effortlessly create exquisite states in your teaching and in your life generally. Now it's time to spread the good feelings to your learners!

REFERENCES

1. Eleanor Roosevelt (1884-1962)
2, Carey, Joseph, ed.1993 Brain Facts, A Primer on the Brain and the Nervous System. Washington,
DC: Society for Neuroscience,
3. Emma Young, 2012, Gut instincts: The secrets of your second brain New Scientist issue 2895

ACTIVITIES

Activity 1

Some people don't realise how they can take charge of their states of consciousness. They believe that their moods, feelings and thoughts happen to them, not the other way around! We want you to realise that you are in charge of your brain. You do not have a 'monkey mind', as the Buddhists call it. You have the ability to choose your responses. So take a pen and paper and take a few moments to make some notes on two contrasting situations. First, think about the last time you had a challenging group or lesson: Now compare each question for each situation and notice the differences. Look for the 2 questions where the differences are the greatest and imagine going through the challenging lesson with the state from the great lesson. How different does it feel?

What were you seeing with your real eyes?	
What were you seeing in your imagination?	
What were you hearing on the outside?	
What were you hearing on the inside of your head?	
Name the feeling you had	
Where was the feeling in your body?	
Which way did the feeling move and where to?	

Activity 2

Now it's cocktail time, so take a few moments to relax and follow the process below:

1. Decide which 3 states would be really good for you to build into your neurology in preparation for teaching a class (or any other situation you choose).
2. Choose words that are powerful and stated in the positive. For example, rather than thinking about 'being not nervous or not interested', use positive words like 'being calm and curious'.

Our brains go where they are sent and can process positive instructions (e.g., being calm) much faster than having to negate the thing you don't want (e.g., being not nervous), so it makes sense to take the shortest route to the best result.

3. Remember a time when you felt this feeling absolutely and see what you saw, hear what you heard, and notice where the feeling is and in which direction it moves. Now begin to spin the feeling in a way that intensifies the feeling. Once you feel this, continue to spin the feeling faster and more fully as it radiates throughout your body.
4. Repeat with the second, and then the third feeling and have them mix together, just like Denise did, to create a new feeling cocktail.
5. Give this new mixture an anchor. This is a strong association, such as a name, symbol, colour or sensation. So this time squeeze your thumb and index figure together to create your own anchor. When you do this at the same time as feeling your new state, each time you repeat or fire off the anchor the wonderful new feeling comes straight back to you.
6. Have your mind's eye imagine yourself going through a lesson in this brilliant new state and notice the likely responses from those around you.
7. Take your mind off this for a while and make a cup of tea or catch up on emails.
8. Now test your anchor by squeezing your thumb and index finger together and feel really good just because you can!

Extension Activity

Next time you go into class, fire off your anchor by squeezing your finger and thumb together and see how you can take the wonderful feeling into class with you.

CHAPTER 11

Winning your class over

Scan this to see the videos

'Education is not the filling of a pail,

but the lighting of a fire'. (1)

William Butler Yeats

In this chapter

- Discover the secret of super-fast rapport
- Create powerful learning states with your students
- Control the variables in the classroom
- Learn how to anchor great learning states

Chain states together to lead students into resourceful learning states The other day, Anne, a highly experienced retired primary school teacher said, *'In over 35 years of teaching I never once asked my class, 'do you want to learn something today?'* There are many ways to gain commitment and engage learners in learning and asking this question isn't *onze of them! If one child didn't want to participate, I would spend all night thinking of different strategies to engage him/her in learning tomorrow.'*

What a great example of tenacity in teaching! We hope newly qualified teachers learn from Anne and her determination to engage her learners. Together with this kind of tenacity and the skills discussed in this chapter, every teacher can have an enthusiastic and happy class. In the last chapter you learned how to create great states for yourself. This is important because the key to getting your students into the best learning states is to go first and feel the way you want your students to feel. Creating powerful and resourceful learning states for your students requires you to pay attention to the minute details of your interactions with them. Often, teachers are looking for the Holy Grail that will solve all their problems in one fell swoop. They want someone to say to them, *'here, if you do THIS your class will do exactly what you want them to'*. However, it is the totality of the very small details that makes the difference. The small details are not insignificant, in fact they are absolutely crucial to engaging students and make a big difference!

SETTING UP THE GROUP
Put any number of individuals into a space together and they will form groups, as will your class when put in a room and left to their own devices. You may have noticed the way various alliances are formed and how sometimes someone can be excluded. Groups, as you know, generate their own identities and within that a set of accepted norms, behaviours and 'states'. Then, enter the teacher to try and take control of the group!

So let's switch the focus from control of the group to management of the process of group formation. Whether you're meeting a group for the first time or seeing them on a regular basis, ensuring the group has **you** at its centre, at the hub of the wheel, gives you command over the states and behaviours within the group. Rather than imposing control, you are determining the useful and resourceful feelings, thoughts and behaviours that support your students' learning. As John La Valle, President of the Society of NLP®, says, *'a class is not a democracy – it* *is a benign dictatorship!'* Your job is to lead the learning; therefore, the teacher is the leader of the group and should place him/herself at its centre.

To place yourself at the centre of the group, there are many key vari-ables beyond curriculum content and lesson plans, which you can be responsible for and manage. These include your state, your language, your non-verbal communication and to some extent the environment in which you teach your students. By paying attention to each of these variables, you not only establish rapport with your learners, you also manage the dynamic of the group. There is a great deal of discussion in NLP literature about rapport. Rapport is very simple and can be summed up as the presence of trust and co-operation in a relationship. It's about letting the other person know you understand something of their map of the world in the present moment. It is useful in teaching, because it enables us to pace our learners' starting position and lead them into better states, towards smarter decisions to maximise learning. Rapport is not, however, essential in all situations. Some people have said that in order to influence change in another person it is necessary first to have rapport. This is incorrect; if you need rapport there are ways to get it. It is useful to know how to build rapport and know how to break it. There are times to be in rapport and times not to be!

CREATING LINES OF LIGHT
One essential time to build a strong personal connection and rapport with each learner is within the first seconds of your encounter with a group. This ensures that you build the first connection with each learner before members of the group have time to establish their own connections with each other. This puts you in the centre of the group as the person with the strongest influence to determine the states the whole group will utilise for learning. Once group members begin to get to know each other, they will establish rapport (or not) with each other. However, the main reference point for the group will be you, so your ability to influence the state of the group begins at that very first moment. They become the spokes of the wheel around your hub.

How long do you think it takes to establish rapport? 5 minutes? 10 minutes? We've read many books that tell you this. However, the truth is that it can take just seconds, which is just as well when you have a group of 20 or 30 students.

To establish rapport with your students, simply open your senses and take notice of what is happening for them right at that moment. For example, if a student looks proud of their new haircut, compliment them on it. Maybe a student has arrived flustered and nervous about whether they are in the right place, so reassure them that they are OK and say, *'well done, you've got here!'* Of course, many teachers do this naturally, but few are aware of just how important it is. Often, teachers are distracted by concentrating on their own teaching needs, such as prepping materials or fixing their technology, and they miss a valuable opportunity.[2]

Consider the difference between putting your attention on yourself and your attention on others.

SUPER-FAST RAPPORT IS BUILT THROUGH ATTENTION ON OTHERS
Once you have rapport with each individual, you can begin to 'pace' the group. This means matching the state of another person or people verbally and non-verbally so that you can lead your student/s into the states that are really conducive to learning.

When groups of teachers are asked during training, *'how do you want your students to be in class?'* their responses invariably include words like *attentive, quiet, receptive, listening, compliant, interested, and well-behaved.* What would your list look like? Notice how passive some of these states are.

LEARNING IS AN ACTIVE PROCESS!
Regardless of whether engagement with learning is obvious through external behaviours or not, the truth is that we do not want our students to be passive at all. We want our students to be engaged in a learning process through states of fascination, inquiry, challenge, laughter, enthusiasm, curiosity and sometimes even noise! These are active states, and learning is an active process.

Active learning is sometimes very obvious to others but at other times may be less so. You are sitting reading this book and an observer focusing only on your external behaviour may assume that you are in a passive state. But pay attention to the internal behaviour, to what is going on inside you. Are you excited or curious right now? Are you referencing your past experiences or running forward to future times? Whatever your reaction and interaction with our words, you are probably not disengaged or unemotional.

Our priorities for learning are that people are physically comfortable (warm, fed and dry), safe, and able to giggle easily. People like repetition and sameness because they make them feel safe and comfortable, but people learn through difference. So the states you create should create sufficient comfort to enable the person to take the risk of learning something different. Then make the learning dramatic, so it stands out as something really unusual. You may have a different priority for the states that your students find most useful, and this is good - the key is to be systematic.

Consider which 'states' you want your students to be in at any one time during your lesson. If you could pick 3 from the following list, which 3 would you choose?

CALM | CURIOUS | EXCITED | FASCINATED | CREATIVE | FOCUSED | FRUSTRATED | TENACIOUS

How might you create those states in yourself first so that you can lead the group into the same states?

It would be very time-consuming if we had to create the states conducive for learning in our students every time we met them from scratch. It's much more useful to be able to build upon earlier exchanges and re-access states quickly and easily. It's fantastic when you realise that you've become so good at building learning states that you have created a super-fast trigger to change the state of your students instantly, without having to go through the process of setting up a new resourceful state for learning.

So how do you do this? Well, we mentioned anchors in the last chapter, so let's explore this some more. Anchoring is the process of associating an internal response with some external trigger. We establish anchors so that we can re-access a state as and when we need a particular resource, such as curiosity or determination. A trigger or anchor fired in one sense or representational system will re-create an experience in that sense and other senses too.

We can anchor states as they arise, or we can induce them so that we can easily get our students back to those states whenever it is helpful to do so. If your students are laughing and having fun, or fascinated with something, anchor it for later. If they are not, create the laughter or good feeling in them and then anchor it.

Some people mix up this process with the system Pavlov used with his dogs, but this is not the case. Humans have the capacity for one-time learning, so there is no necessity for constant repetition, as in Pavlov's model. Also, Pavlov was looking for external, physiological associations, while we are interested in re-accessing internal states.

HOW TO CREATE AND ANCHOR A GREAT LEARNING STATE

First, we decide what we want to happen and set about creating our learning state with a story, a joke or a visual aid. We then pay close atten-tion to the non-verbal responses from the person or group, so we know just the right moment to anchor the state. This is a calibra-tion process. The external trigger can be in any of the representational systems - visual, auditory, kinaesthetic - or any combination of any of these. Anchors can also be olfactory and gustatory. In class, the easiest anchors to use are auditory and visual, including a visual anchor associated with a particular place in the room, which is known as a spatial anchor.

Anchors are not an NLP invention, they exist naturally. The creators of NLP simply noticed how people do this and started to use anchoring systematically. Think about how easily a particular feeling or state is invoked when you smell baking bread or hear a piece of music that takes you back to a moment in time, a place and a particular feeling. You may instantly see images of the place and the person you were with. This is more than just a memory, because the strong feelings you re-access are real in the moment. How about your response when someone puts their finger to their lips? What about a particular tone of voice? A raised eyebrow? Have you ever heard someone call a child's name (which happened to be the same as yours) using the same tone of voice as your mother or father used with you? Did you notice how you experienced age regression and instantly felt like a little child again?

Do you encourage students to answer a question by raising your hand as a signal for them to respond in the same way, without offering a verbal cue? What other anchors are you already using - a facial expression perhaps, or indicating a particular spot in the room? Think again for a moment which specific states it would be good for your students to be in at different times in your class. Maybe you would like quiet curiosity, wanton go-for–it, fascination or a fun state? When you stand at the front of the room, what states do your students go into now? This is the state or combination of states that you have already anchored to you in that spot. Is it what you want, or can you change it for something even better?

This recently observed class illustrates opportunities to quickly and easily create good learning states and the opportunities for creating anchors to return to these states at another time. The class are teenagers, they are disengaged, and it's the last class of the day.
The teacher is at the front of the class and engaged in last-minute preparations, waiting for the students to arrive. The teenagers drift into class in twos and threes. Some wander around, others sit in their favourite places. Some are wearing baseball caps and hoodies, while others have MP3 players or mobile phones glued to their ears. Most are chatting. Jane is at the back of the class, in her usual place.

Eventually the class is seated and the teachers says, *'hello everyone, let's begin'*. She asks the students to remove their hoods and turn off their music and introduces the topic with the list of objectives for the lesson. This process has taken 5 minutes and the students, although reasonably compliant, remain disengaged from the learning and focused on their own agenda.

During a conversation with the teacher afterwards, some of the variables explained in this chapter were discussed. Simply but systematically the teacher made some key adjustments for the next lesson and the outcome was quite different.

This time, the teacher uses the few moments before the class arrives to put on a piece of music which she has chosen to signal the beginning of class. She creates a warm and welcoming state for herself and then, as she stands at the classroom door, she greets each student with a smile and makes a suggestion or comment to each one. *'Hi Dawn, lovely to see you on time today'. 'How are you doing, George?' 'Alex, put your hood down so I can see your cheeky face – wow, that's great!'* She smiles at Freddie, who is wearing earphones and mimes words to him until he takes off his ear plugs, when she continues out loud, saying, *'and that's the most important thing to remember!'* Smiling again, she greets other students - *'Hi Amy, how's that dog of yours?' 'Jane, I'd like your help today so sit near the front please. I just know you're going to do so well today'* (Jane messed about at the back last week).

The teacher returns to the front, turns the music off and says, *'OK, I've got such a treat in store for you today'*, and then waits with a look of anticipation on her face. The total time to reach this point is 3 minutes and she has total silence and a group feeling good and anticipating the class.

Our golden rule in teaching is **never do one thing for one reason**. That's simply a waste of energy! Every sentence can be an instruction for an activity **and** to elicit a state. Every activity can meet multiple objectives and small things make a big difference. So what has this teacher achieved in the first 3 minutes? Here goes:

The music: If you haven't until now used music, we guarantee it will create an automatic state change. It can create a surprise or convey a message through the mood, tempo or lyrics. When you regularly use music, the students will respond to each piece differently and you can plan to invoke the response you want by repeating particular pieces. This then becomes an anchor for the state you have elicited. Think about having consistent pieces at the beginning and end of the lesson, and varying this occasionally for surprise or a state change, such as calm relaxation and reflection. Switching off the music signals another state change, indicating time to listen to the teacher.

Greeting at the door: The purpose of this is to establish rapport with each student and establish your relationship with them as the primary one in the room. It also means that students feel good about themselves and you, and are likely to be more co-operative with you and the learning. It also signals that they are entering your space, where the primary relationship is with you. This is also an opportunity to manage some of the things that might otherwise get in the way of the learning. When suggestions and instructions are given positively they maintain the value of the individual. There is in each case a benefit to the student. This is not to say that using negative consequences is wrong – sometimes it is necessary. In NLP we call this 'away from' moti-vation because the motivation comes from thinking about what you don't want to happen. However, a focus on moving 'towards' something maintains rapport, especially if it is combined with a statement that demonstrates how you value and respect the person. It also sends the person's brain in the right direction! (We will explore this further later in the book).

The teaching space: The area at the front of the class is already a spatial anchor, and by standing at the front the teacher automatically triggers responses to the anchors associated with this space. Unfortunately, standing in this space also fires off the anchors created in this space by other teachers. Remember, this is your space, so use it to maximise the teaching and learning experience; make sure only great learning states are anchored to you here!

Bringing a class together is so much more than voicing instructions; it is not only **what** you say, but **how** you say it that makes a big impact. Consider your voice as a power tool; your state will be conveyed through your voice tone and your ability to influence your learners' states is also carried by your voice. A sound is heard not only with the ears - it is experienced as waves that bathe the neurology of the listener, so you can use your voice to elicit desired states such as curiosity and anticipation. You can make your words onomatopoeic, so that when you say 'curious' it sounds *'cuuurrriooous?'* We are sure you are aware that exciting words used with an exciting voice tone create excitement, just as calm words with a calm voice tone create calmness. If you don't create the desired state in your students straight away, continue with a story using a voice tone of curiosity or excitement. You can be even more elegant by having different gestures or facial expressions for these states.

Many teachers will spend a few minutes talking to their students about things that are of interest to them to create some rapport. Once this few minutes 'fun' is over, the teacher says *'OK, enough of that, time to get on with some work'*, often with a tone of resignation. This is a great waste of the opportunity to utilise the states that you have just helped to create in your students. It is much more powerful to link the state you have just created to the learning that is about to happen and this is really easy to do. Consider these examples:

'We saw our team win the match last night, so now let's see how we can all win the day with our Geography challenge.'

Or

'How about we solve our Biology mystery in the same way as Detective X did on TV last night.'

Creating a really great state in your learners so they are ready to learn is only the first step. Now, we want to chain states together so that we lead learners swiftly and easily from one state to another, sometimes through hesitation or frustration, to a better place. Peter, a head teacher on an NLP Practitioner training for teachers, demonstrated how to elicit and anchor states particularly well. As an experienced teacher, he realised the importance of creating curiosity, but hadn't realised the impact of being systematic. He regularly collected odd items in a special box for his group of 8-year-olds to guess what they were. So, something goes in the special box, he rattles the box and asks, *'can anyone guess what's in the box?'* The children are interested and begin to make guesses. The more outrageous the guesses are, the more intrigued the children become. Peter continues, saying, *'no, it's not Mr Brown's* nose', and, 'no it's not my dog', etc. After a minute or two he asks who would like to see what's in the box. All the hands go up. He picks Martha and says, *'have a look, but don't let anyone else see'*. She peeks in and makes an *'Ooooh'* sound. In this process, Peter's class members are led from interest, through curiosity, to enthusiasm to anticipation. The box at the front of the class becomes a visual anchor any time Peter needs to re-access the state of intrigue with the children.

Now the interesting thing about this example is that when Peter shared it with other teachers during his NLP Practitioner training, he got the same response from the adults. As soon as Peter used his *'what's in the box children?'* voice and looked really curious the other participants on the course instantly regressed to their 8-year-old states! They gave answers with the enthusiasm of children and were back to their optimum learning state of fun, curiosity, and abandonment.

Peter was completely congruent in this process. This term 'congruent' means that all your internal beliefs, strategies and behaviours are fully in agreement and aimed at a specific desired outcome (in this case, eliciting and anchoring states). And guess what? The box didn't exist, either. Peter just mimed the box – and he did this so congruently our imagination created the box. Thus, everything lines up and the result is elegant!

Sometimes, all a teacher needs to do to create great states in learners is to confidently and congruently exude and demonstrate the state powerfully, so that it becomes contagious. Even laughter or the odd sneer will be won over. However, it can be tricky, going from feeling disengaged to enthusiastic in one move, and sometimes the gap between where your students are and where you want them to be is too big a leap, so you may want to build baby steps to bridge the gap and lead them from their current state through to the desired one for optimum learning. We call this **chaining states**. A typical sequence would be:

BOREDOM→ HESITATION→CURIOSITY→FRUSTRATION→GO FOR IT!

So we pace and lead step by step through a variety of states until we get our students into a great learning state.

How do we do this? Well, if you have students who arrive in class bored and uninterested, first match the boredom and anchor it by talking to them in a bored voice and yawning as you do it. Stand in a slumped position to one side and create a visual and spatial anchor for this state. Next, create a state of hesitation, maybe by discussing something disgusting, such as eating mouldy pizza; something they would avoid so they 'hesitate'! Pull a horrible face and move to a different place in the classroom as you do this. Then, move on to curiosity by talking about something strange on a TV programme or using a prop such as a bag with *'do not look in here'* written on it. Anchor this state with a curious *'Ooooh'* sound as you point to the prop.

Now create a state of frustration and anchor it. Why? Because this is your propulsion mechanism! To do this, tell them that they are going to have fun working together – but not yet! Repeat this a few times – now – but not yet – now but not yet. The more you feel frustrated the more likely you are to just go for it when you finally get the opportunity. Finally, create a state of 'wanton go-for-it'.

To do this all you need to do is to talk about something that your students would really desire; that delicious sweet on the sweet trolley, the top-of-the-range iPad, winning X Factor.

You can anchor these states in many different ways. You can use a look, a gesture, a tone of voice. If you choose to, you can anchor these states in different parts of the room by standing in one specific spot as you create a state and you can easily move back and forth between the states. Many primary school teachers already use this process without realising that is what they are doing. Think about the 'curiosity table', the story mat, the naughty chair! All these are examples of spatial anchors where a particular state is established in one place and re-accessed when the children return to it.

Whenever you want to re-access a particular state in your students, simply go back and stand in exactly the same place, use exactly the same gesture or facial expression and voice tone, or mention the story you were telling when you set the anchor. You may notice that any one of these actions will re-access the state for your students.[3]

PART 3 - HIGHLY EFFECTIVE CLASSROOM TEACHING

Once you have a series of anchors and have created a sequence that leads from one state to another so that the students can move into the most resourceful states for learning, the trick is to chain the states together so that the sequence runs automatically. This means that rather than having to move from one to the other and fire off each anchor, the state, for example boredom, automatically leaks into the state of curiosity, or the state of confusion, say, swiftly leads to a state of understanding. Running the sequence over and over, faster and faster will create in the students the ability to move themselves from an unhappy place to a happy place where they are achieving and feeling good.

Now, armed with your use of language, voice tone, gestures and facial expressions, notice the point at which your students go into the exquisite learning state that you are eliciting and use the tools explained above to create an anchor for that state. If you have these anchors established spatially, simply move from one space to the next and the next, quickly.

The truth is that you are always communicating something, so choose what is best for your group, and remember to go there first! Remember, you cannot not communicate, and the opportunities to create wonderful, effective learning states are endless, so go ahead and do it on purpose and have fun succeeding!

SUMMARY

In this chapter you have learned how to recognise many of the variables that are useful in creating great learning states for your learners. You may not be aware of how easily you can now anchor these states in your classroom so you can enable your students to re-access the most resourceful states to continue learning. You can now chain states together in a classroom context so you can lead students from unhelpful states such as boredom to resourceful learning states such as curiosity and motivation quickly and easily.

REFERENCES

1. Attributed to William Butler Yeats (1865-1939)
2. In a study by Matrix (Theory into Practice Ltd) of the evaluation grades given to

trainers by participants, the key variable between a grade 1 (excellent) and a grade 2 (very good) evaluation was determined to be where the trainer's attention was on entry to the training room. Where the attention was on the participants the trainer gained a higher proportion of grade 1 grades. Where the attention was on the technology and training set up at the front of the room the trainer was given more grade 2 evaluations

3. For an example of kinaesthetic and auditory anchoring see the first 2 minutes of this video https://richardbandler.com/snake

---------- ACTIVITIES ----------

Activity 1

Take a few moments to relax and recall times when you learned really well and enjoyed learning. What were the states that were most condu-cive to your learning? Here's a list to help you. Circle the ones that work for you:

Excitement	Awareness	Interest	Receptivity
Sleepiness	Openness	Fascination	Curiosity
Flexibility	Dreaminess	Frustration	Calmness Determination
Creativity	Pragmatism	Laughter	Relaxation
Confidence	Fear	Joy	Enthusiasm

Add any others of your own that are not listed. Now spend a few moments thinking about how you can systematically generate these states in your students:

- Where can you stand?
- What words express the state best?
- What stories can you tell?
- What facial expressions can you use?
- What tonality expresses the state?
- What props can you use?

Activity 2

Pick one lesson you are teaching in the next few days and build in as many opportunities as you can to generate great states for learning.

Pay attention to the little things that make the biggest difference. Recall the differences in response from your students. What do you want to take forward into the next lesson?

Note them down here:

OPPORTUNITY	STATE	ACTIVITY

CHAPTER 12

Building an Effective Learning Environment

Scan this to see the videos

'And will you succeed? Yes indeed, yes indeed!

Ninety-eight and three-quarters per centh

guaranteed!' [1]

Dr Seuss

In this chapter

- The success focus attitude
- The keys to engagement and motivation in the classroom
- Building exciting learning outcomes
- Removing barriers to success

A 13-year-old girl was struggling with Physics at school. She hated the lessons, thought the teacher was 'boring', and wanted to drop the subject at the earliest opportunity. Her dad had different ideas. As a scientist, he wanted his daughter to enjoy science and keep studying it for at least a few more years. So what did he do? Get extra tuition? Tutor him herself? Change classes? No, he took her to the fairground! Do you want to know why?

Many teachers are taught that the very first thing they must do at the beginning of a lesson is to make it clear to the students what the aims and objectives of the session are. The received wisdom is that we must ensure students know the objectives so they can check their understanding. Some schools even insist on a pro forma to standardise introductions. Unfortunately, this practice ensures a minimum standard, but does not create excellent lesson introductions.

When we study the great teachers, we find that they rarely go straight to the point. Instead, they ignite engagement, where the students' faces look enthused rather than bemused, and where heads begin to nod slowly as activated minds begin to get the ideas being conveyed. Great teachers stack the odds in favour of their students being successful before they start, and often teach the learning through metaphors and anecdotes first, so the students unconsciously learn and understand before they become conscious of learning something new. This makes the learning easier, because it creates a sense of familiarity with the subject and a feeling that they already know what they are learning. After all, is it easier to do something for the first or the second time?

The young girl at the fairground learned about velocity, speed and centrifugal force by going on the fairground rides with her dad. The thrills of the rides created a wonderful state of excitement at the same time, so she became enthused with learning how the designers of these rides created thrills using physics. And it isn't necessary to actually go to the fairground, however much fun this might be, because students can understand the effect of these forces kinaesthetically|, through a story or metaphor and by remembering great times at fun fairs, before they consciously explore the science. Thus, you have the added benefit of creating excitement and thrills as they re-experience their last trip to the fair.

Even if there are constraints imposed by the school or Education authority on how to introduce a lesson, we have a secret weapon to ensure that we inform students of the content of the lesson whilst also ensuring that they are going to learn easily and enjoyably. The other good news is that it only takes small changes in what you do, it costs nothing and it doesn't require extra preparation to make this happen. All we do is use our greatest tool - our language - in elegant and effective ways to send our students' brains in the right direction. People are hard-wired for language and communication, and these are the tools of the trade for teachers - hence more than 40 years of developing the 'L' (Linguistic) in NLP (Neuro Linguistic Programming). As teachers, we not only want to communicate content, we want to use language elegantly and precisely. Language has power and it would be folly to let that power leak in the wrong ways.

The Milton Model is one of two systematic linguistic models developed by the co-creators of NLP. Milton Model language patterns were originally modelled from Milton Erikson, an acclaimed medical doctor, psychiatrist and hypnotherapist. His outstanding success in influencing patients to become well again was described as being 'artfully vague' - in a very systematic way. NLP's co-founders - Richard and his research partner John Grinder - studied these patterns, then replicated and systemised them.[2]

This model, when used precisely and elegantly, enables us to ensure that any communication is understood as applying personally to the listener, even when a group is being addressed, and can potentially bypass resistance and hesitation to new ideas and learning. This is important, because even though we are teaching a group, each member of the group is learning as an individual.

During a lesson introduction, Milton language patterns prime the learning, seed possibility, and open new channels of receptiveness.

We can teach students **ahead of time** what they need to know, so that when they become consciously aware of the learning content, it actually feels familiar to them, as if they are coming to it for a second time. So let's see how this works:

Learning to use language in specific ways and making small but significant changes to our language can have really impressive results with learners. Take Sue, for example. Sue works with children with hearing impairment and she participated in the original Durham Project (Chapter 3). Sue began to realise that her language was creating results in her pupils which she didn't want. One little boy was very nervous and a real worrier. She explained that previously she told him, *'don't worry, this isn't hard and if you get stuck I am here to help you'*. After the training, she changed her language and instead she said, *'I know you will do a great piece of work because you have loved this story and you already have lots of lovely ideas so you can really enjoy writing about them.'* She was delighted to report that the child's behaviour instantly changed and he immediately produced his first ever piece of totally independent writing. There was no panic, no delaying tactics and no pleas for help – a total transformation! (3)

Let's take a look at what Sue initially said to the boy, and notice a) how she inadvertently suggested some unhelpful internal states, such as worry, hard and stuck and, b) how by making herself available as his helper, she potentially undermined his sense of capability. The brain does not operationalise a negative. It understands consciously what a negative (don't) is, but it **can't do a 'don't**. The brain cancels out the negative and responds to the words 'worry' 'hard' 'stuck' **as commands**.

Now take a look at the language Sue used after NLP training. This time, you'll notice, a) she pre-supposed his 'easy' success (*'I know you will'*) – all by himself and, b) she pre-supposed and attached really helpful states by using words like *'great, loved, lovely, enjoy'*.

Sue **pre-framed** the session to enable the little boy to consider his own success possible, ahead of time, easily AND independently.

Now you can begin to see that in setting up a lesson there are a number of key variables to pay attention to, including:

- How to speak to each student and grab their attention in a way that means the learning applies each student personally, whilst speaking to the whole class
- How to presuppose successful outcomes so learners imagine their success
- How to ensure learners continue to be motivated by connecting their reality to their outcome • How to remove barriers and inoculate against anything that could get in the way of students' achievement So let's consider some of the Milton Model language patterns. We wonder what you will notice when you have adopted just one or two of them over the coming days as you set up your lessons. When you become aware of the ones that have the greatest impact on your class, you can then start adding more.

HOW TO SPEAK TO EACH STUDENT WITHIN THE WHOLE CLASS
Statements, stories, or questions that by design are generalisations that apply to everyone are known as Universal Quantifiers. The effect is that the listener feels they are being spoken to personally, even though they may be part of a large group. They feel that the lesson applies directly to them.

Here are some examples of statements that must be true for everyone - and therefore true for the individual. These are Universal Quantifiers:

- *I know you have had the experience of learning new things*
- *When you were little you learned to talk by copying other people*
- *As you are sitting in this room with your classmates*
- *When you came into school this morning each step brought you closer to this moment*

Similarly, we can still generalise and ensure a statement applies to the student by offering an alternative, where if one thing isn't true the other must be. Like this:

- *Some people learn quickly and some people take a little more time*

- *I don't know whether you speak French already or are just beginning to learn a new language*
- *You, as a boy or a girl...*

Remember, this is about being 'artfully vague' – on purpose!

HOW TO PRESUPPOSE SUCCESS

Once we have everyone feeling that they are being spoken to personally (because our Universal Quantifiers match their experience) we can go on to presuppose that the learning will be fun, easy and they can do it. If we simply tell the students that it will be fun, we risk rejection of what we are saying. The magic here is in presupposing the outcome in a way that the student is swept along with the flow, as we assume the desired outcomes are *a fait accompli*.

Presuppositions are probably one of the most useful patterns for teaching and learning, especially in setting up a lesson. There is a big difference between asking, *'are you going to learn something today?'* which requires a yes or no answer risking the likelihood of a negative response, and asking, *'what are you going to learn today?'* This latter statement presupposes that you will learn something; it's just a question of what.

There are a number of different types of presuppositions. Here are some:

Numbers – used to list the events that will happen, for example:

- *The **first thing** you will notice is how easy this is...* (pre-supposes you will notice many things after this and that it will be easy)
- *The **second part** of the task deepens your understanding further* (presupposes that there is a first part to the task and that you will understand in different depths)

In the examples above we have been explicit, and now it's your turn to work out what is being specifically presupposed as the Presupposition Patterns are expanded.

Awareness – presupposes a realisation that the event has happened already: It's not a matter of whether you have learned something or not, but merely a question of have you noticed yet!

For example:

- *You may have started to **become aware** of how much you have learned already*
- *I don't know if you will **notice** how fully you understand straight away, or as you do the practice exercise*

Timescale - presupposes an event is happening by linking it to a time scale. For example:

- *Over the **days to come** and more examples become available to you*
- *By taking **a few minutes** to reflect on your new skills you can understand even more*

Time verbs and adverbs – time processing words presuppose action over a period of time. For example:

- *As you **start** to use these patterns you can enjoy your new skills*
- *Do you want to ask any questions **before** completing your project?*

Choice – gives the feeling of a choice whilst presupposing the outcome. For example

- *Will you begin to use these language patterns immediately or a little later?*
- *It doesn't matter whether you complete the written or oral part of the quiz, it's fun to answer the questions*
- *Do you want to clean your teeth or put your pyjamas on first, before you go to bed?*

This last one is a favourite with all parents overcoming the bedtime blues!

Real skill in using these language patterns comes by adding one to the next and the next so the presuppositions are stacked one on top of the other. This works because before someone has had time to consciously negate or cancel one statement, you have moved on to another and another, so that all your students can accept at least one or two of them.

HOW TO ENSURE LEARNERS CONTINUE TO BE MOTIVATED BY CONNECTING THEIR REALITY TO THEIR OUTCOME

If all our students arrived for class ready and up for learning, enthusiastic and knowing that they could easily learn, then life would be easy. Unfortunately, life isn't like that, so we need to help a little. If we want our students to be enthusiastic and motivated we want to convince them that:

- They **can** do it
- It's **worth** doing and they want to do it
- It's **interesting**
- It's **enjoyable**

Of course, just telling them doesn't work, so we can use our language to influence how they approach the learning. This is how: By making a connection between two parts of a sentence so that the first part is equal or equivalent to the second part, we can take anything that is happening in the room, or true for the student, and attach it to something that is useful for the student and the learning. This allows us to pace the student's experience and connect it to something we want them to experience by assuming a connection exists – even if it doesn't. Here are some examples

- *I know some of you may have found equations boring in the past, that's OK **because it means** you like to be challenged with new learnings and are a fast learner*
- *Some of you didn't get enough sleep last night, but **that just means** you can relax more easily whilst learning new things*

You may have noticed that there are some other presuppositions added here for increased effectiveness!

CAUSE AND EFFECT

In a similar way, we can also pace what is happening and connect it to something that we want our students to believe. So:

- *The fact some of you have your MP3 with you **can cause you** to really want to pay attention to the music we are using to learn the new*

Spanish verbs today
- Sitting comfortably in your chair **makes it easy** to enjoy listening to Josh's presentation

As you use some of these patterns, you can begin to construct introductions which directly impact on your students' motivation and learning at both a conscious and unconscious level. This means you get to presuppose success, fun, great learning and anything else that you want to build into a great learning experience.

Take a moment to compare these two lesson introductions:

INTRODUCTION 1
'Hello everyone, it's really nice to see you here on Wednesday morning. I know that you woke up this morning and are looking forward to the lesson and eager to learn. Although some of you look tired I don't want you to miss out on any of the important things we are going to learn today. So sit up and pay attention. When you were a toddler you learned things really easily, I am sure you can do the same in this lesson. You have all got extraordinary brains and I know you are all looking forward to this lesson, which will be great fun.'

INTRODUCTION 2
'Hello everyone it's really nice seeing you here today on Wednesday morning. When you woke up this morning some of you were sleepy and some of you were wide awake; either way you may not have noticed just yet how easily you can relax and have fun in this class. I don't want you to enjoy too much paying attention to the important things you can learn today. When you were a toddler you learned lots of things just by playing and without really having to think about it, which means that today learning is easy because you have an extraordinary brain that takes in more than you realise.'

The first introduction is perfectly nice and encouraging, but does contain elements that a student could object to or disagree with. For example we don't know for sure that they were looking forward to the lesson or eager to learn. By taking the same content and applying some universal quantifiers, presuppositions and links, the second introduction becomes more impactful and improves the chances of agreement and success for the teacher and the students.

For example:
'Some of you were sleepy and some of you were wide awake' – Universal Quantifier.

'You may not have noticed yet how easily you can relax' – presupposes they can relax but may not have noticed yet.

'Which means that' – a link connecting two things together which may or may not be true but it feels like it is.

It's useful to go back now and read some of introduction 2 above, out loud. You may notice that as you read, you naturally emphasise certain words and parts of the sentence that you want the person to take notice of such as 'easily', 'relax' and 'enjoy', so you become systematic about the key messages you can embed in your language to give the command or suggestion.

Rather than giving instructions directly, you can embed instructions within a longer sentence. When you do this, you can often deliver instructions much more effectively and gracefully because generally the listener doesn't consciously realise that such directives have been communicated, for example:

*"As you think about your career to date, you can begin to **realise how useful this learning** is and look forward to a brighter future."*

HOW TO REMOVE BARRIERS AND INOCULATE AGAINST ANYTHING THAT COULD GET IN THE WAY OF YOUR STUDENTS' ACHIEVEMENT

Giving direct commands can create resistance in members of your group. When we embed a command or a suggestion or a question within a longer sentence, the student is more likely to accept the statement. It will also make more impact at the unconscious level when it is marked out in some way at the same time. Marking it out simply means a change in voice tone or tempo, raising or lowering the volume of your voice, or using a gesture. This is called Analogue Marking because it sets the statement apart from the rest of the sentence for special attention. Your students will not usually notice this marking consciously. In fact, they will respond more fully if they don't consciously perceive it.

Experiment with examples like these:
- *I notice that in my class people are able to **listen carefully and thougthfully** to the instructions*

In a similar way, questions, like commands or suggestions, can be embedded within a larger sentence structure that sounds like a statement:
- *I was wondering whether you can **let yourself relax and enjoy** this*

Negatives

Although negatives exist in language, the brain doesn't process negation at an unconscious level. In order not to do something you, have to imagine doing it in the first place:

- *Whatever you do, don't think of the colour blue right now!*
- *So you thought of the colour blue, right? Well, we can use negation to send the brain in the direction we want it to go, as in the following examples:*
- *We are not sure whether we should share the next section of the Milton patterns with you; we don't want you to have too much fun learning them!*
- *Don't think of creative ways to solve this problem too quickly!*

We are wondering whether now would be a good time for you to go back to the opening paragraphs and see how many patterns you can easily identify straight away, or maybe you prefer to wait until you have finished this chapter?

Here is an example of a practical lesson with a typical introduction, followed by an alternative utilising some of the patterns discussed, and maybe some we haven't discussed yet:

The teacher displays the following:
Aim: The students will be able to change a lightbulb

Objectives: The students are familiar with the equipment The students can use equipment safely

The students can safely remove the spent lightbulb

The students can safely replace the lightbulb with a new one

The students can test the light bulb is working effectively

The students can store away the equipment used and safely dispose of the old lightbulb

The teacher says:
'Now settle down everyone. Today we are going to learn to change a lightbulb. You will need to learn how to do this because everyone has to do this at some time in their lives. It's important that you learn to do this safely and don't damage yourselves or anyone else during the process. These are the objectives for today [reads off the list]'

The next example is provided by a Teaching Excellence student. Here is his 'upgrade':

'As it is Monday 12th June, today's lesson might fascinate or surprise you because as you settle in you can begin to relax and learn the most effective, simple, easy and enjoyable ways we can change a lightbulb. You may not have realised yet just how much you have already learned about electricity in the last few weeks, though I am wondering just how your imagination will light up any dark recesses of your brain with a clarity and sharpness only you can imagine. In the past some people may have felt that this was difficult, but they have not had your advantages of being taught by me! The bright future dawning before you means that you will never have a spent lightbulb casting darkness and gloom in your home again!'

When you compare the two introductions, what are the main differences you notice? Which introduction do you think will engage the learning brain fastest? It may be useful to highlight the patterns in the second paragraph.

Remember, the more you stack the presuppositions the more the students will engage in the process and begin to build generative learning. In order to understand the sentence you must accept most of it. So, as you are reading this book today, learning new things about NLP, which ideas for more effective teaching have already sprung to your mind? And whilst enjoying understanding how to change what you say in the classroom during this time, you can begin to relax and easily take in all the information because learning NLP is easy. The learning becomes one big process which allows you to gain trust and credibility as you build upon success.

MOTIVATION
The eternal cries from students -*'what are we doing this for?'* and *'why are we doing this?'* - are legitimate questions and you can be sure that, *'because it is on the syllabus'* is not a motivating answer!

People are motivated in many ways, sometimes by the process, which is enjoyable in itself, or by the result or outcome which is rewarding. Sometimes, we can be so motivated by the outcome we are prepared to put up with the pain of doing something that isn't pleasant.

Think about the story of two bricklayers. Asked, *'what are you doing?'* the first answers, *'I am laying bricks'*. The second answers, *'I am building a beautiful house'*.

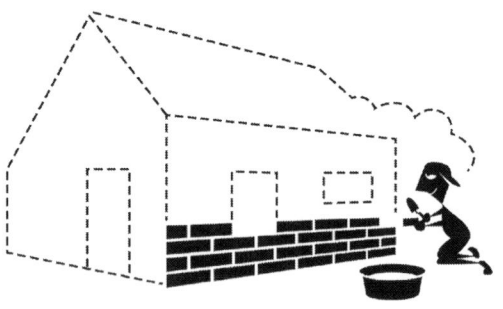

Which bricklayer is likely to be more motivated to lay bricks carefully and work until the job is done?

NLP provides us with a motivational tool in the form of Well-Formed Outcomes (WFO). Unlike the ubiquitous goal setting and SMART targets we find in mainstream management theory, having a well-formed outcome actually takes people a long way towards achieving their goal in the first place. It brings it nearer, and it makes it realisable, it has good feelings attached to it, so the person wants to do it, can imagine doing it and therefore is well on the way to getting there.

THE CONDITIONS FOR A WELL-FORMED OUT COME :
1. It is stated in the positive What you **do** want, rather than what you **don't** want! As we said earlier, negatives do not compute operationally

– we do what we 'don't want' (eg., *'don't think about the colour blue'*). If we say *'I don't want to fail my Spanish exam, it translates in the brain as 'fail my Spanish exam'*. However this next sentence is stated concisely and has a time reference, *'I want to pass my Spanish exam in June next year'*.

2. It is under the control of the person setting the goal
You can only achieve what you are responsible for. *'I want you to give me a good mark'* is not under the student's control, but *'I will work conscientiously so that I earn a good mark'* is under their control.

3. It is based in reality and is represented in at least three of the representational systems
You can test the goal ahead of time by predicting what you will see/hear/do/touch/feel (maybe smell and taste) when you achieve it e.g., *'It is June and I am sitting my Spanish GCSE exam. I feel well prepared, confident, capable and excited to demonstrate my ability. I can see myself smiling after the exam is finished and hearing myself say 'that went well'.*

4. It is ecological ...
...In that it doesn't challenge your existing values and there will be no negative effects on friends or family. Moreover, it should maintain anything that is helpful or wanted in the status quo. So, for example, expecting a teenager to stay in all weekend to catch up on their homework isn't reasonable because it challenges what is important to them, as they are likely to value friendships and their social life above homework.

A more reasonable example to work towards is, *'I know how to balance my studies and revision with friendship needs as well as making time for playing football.'*

Whenever a student asks *'why are we doing this?'* it is an opportunity to help to create a well-formed outcome with him/her. This does not necessarily have to take a great deal of time. Just notice the difference in the sensations between the next two sentences:

'When you complete this module you will be well on the way to passing your exams and will be able to get a good job'

Or

'Imagine the great feeling you will have after completing this module and being well on the way to the day you pick up that certificate and see how pleased everyone is and how fantastic you feel knowing you can get that perfect job [car- house – travel, etc]'

―――――――――― **SUMMARY** ――――――――――

During this chapter you have explored some of the Milton Model language patterns to set up the learning for engaged, motivated learners who can succeed. By using the patterns described, we don't know if you will notice straight away or after a few lessons, just how easily your students engage with your teaching as you use these skills.
How will you apply your new knowledge of well-formed outcomes in your next introduction to a lesson?

―――――――――― **REFERENCES** ――――――――――

1. Dr Seuss, 1990 Oh the places you'll go, Random House
2. Patterns of the Hypnotic Techniques of Milton H. Erickson, R. Bandler and J. Grinder
3. Durham Project) Kate Benson and John Carey 2006 The Durham Project, META Ltd

―――――――――― **ACTIVITIES** ――――――――――

Activity 1

Review the second lesson introduction earlier in this chapter. Here are some of the patterns you may have already noticed:

- Everybody woke up this morning (otherwise they wouldn't be here)
- The alternatives cover everyone, you were either wide awake or sleepy
- The presupposition is that you'll relax and have fun but may not have realised it yet
- The person doesn't process the negative 'don't' and only does the embedded command 'enjoy paying attention'
- Toddlers learn easily and you were one, so this is linked causally to the student's current ability to learn easily, which is also linked to

the fact they have an extraordinary brain and can learn even if they don't realise it

Use the patterns you have learned here now to change how you set up your next lesson. Many teachers find it surprising that even the smallest change can produce dramatic and instant changes. So write down 4 sentences using presuppositions and an example of each of the language patterns covered in this chapter to give you're students the suggestions that:

- They **can** do it
- It's **worth** doing and they **want** to do it
- It's **interesting**
- It's **enjoyable**

Activity 2

Look at your scheme of work and select 3 objectives. Create 3 well-formed outcomes to 'sell' the objective to your learners. Over to you now - have a go at using your new introduction and notice what happens!

CHAPTER 13

Keeping the lesson on track

Scan this to see the videos

'Flaming enthusiasm, backed up by horse sense and persistence, is the quality that most often makes for success' [1]

Dale Carnegie

In this chapter

- Spinning the 'prayer wheel'
- Building Confidence with Competence
- How to praise effectively
- Giving feedback for great results

At the end of a workshop, a lady asked for help with a problem she was experiencing with a group of students. She was in charge of a computer workshop to which a group of students brought their assignments from other classes to work on in her session.

Her complaint was that instead of getting on with their assignments, the students were playing computer games or going on the Internet.

Asked, *'are they doing this **all** the time?'* she replied, *'no, they're all right when I'm watching them or standing next to them, but as soon as my back* *is turned they stop working on their assignments'.* We asked her, *'what are the specific instructions you give to the students?'* She replied, *'I've told them time after time that I don't want to see them playing games on the computer when they're supposed to be doing their assignments'.*

There is a big clue here; the students are following her instructions exactly and doing precisely as they are told. **They are making sure she doesn't SEE them playing on the computers.**

'But I didn't mean that!' she cried.

Of course she didn't mean to give this instruction, and the moral in this tale is be careful what you ask for, because you will probably get it!

This is an example of how powerful language is, how easy it is to get a result **you don't want** and how easy it is to change the outcome. Once this teacher realised that the students were responding literally to her instruction, we worked on this alternative instruction:

'As you have arrived on time with your assignments and are ready to enjoy working, this means that when you have completed your assignments and I have checked that you have done them thoroughly, you can feel really great and use the time left to play on the computers if you want'. She insisted that it couldn't be that simple, but as she discovered in the next lesson – it really was!

LISTEN AS YOU SPEAK

It is crucial that you hone the ability to listen to what you are actually saying, *as you are speaking*, rather than consider speaking and listening as two separate activities. People say the opposite of talking is listening, but it isn't. The most important time to listen is when you are talking! A valuable NLP teaching skill involves learning how to plan, utilise and adjust your language at the same time as you are speaking.

And it's not just the words you say on the outside that matter. Internal dialogue is also language that influences the mind of the thinker, whilst the spoken word influences the mind of the receiver. As teachers, we must use language precisely because, as we are about to demonstrate, language has great power.

Now that you are familiar with presuppositions, we're sure you realise why we avoid presupposing things will be more difficult than they need to be, or presupposing that some kids are going to fail, or presupposing that they are not smart. Hearing something like, *'if you were intelligent you would be able to do this'*, will almost certainly render a child demoralised, believing themselves to be unintelligent at the very least (if not stupid), because that is what is presupposed in the sentence. This is rarely what is intended of course. What we want to do is the opposite, so that every time a student succeeds they feel clever and have good feelings about their success, so their confidence grows in line with their competence.

Ask any group of adults, *'who can't sing? Who can't paint? Who can't do maths?'* and you will surely hear a story of how a teacher once told a member of the group something negative which grew into a lifelong belief, haunting them and preventing their success in that particular area. We term this a *post-hypnotic suggestion* for a learning difficulty, despite this usually not being the teacher's intention. Simple ignorance about the power of words, or a lack of training in listening to what you are saying when you speak, is the culprit. Really listen to what you are actually saying, and you give yourself more chance to accelerate teaching and learning.

A client of Richard's believed absolutely that he could not read. He also had a vivid and unpleasant childhood memory of a teacher snapping a pencil in front of his face in frustration, and telling him, *'you'll never learn to read'*. And guess what? He didn't! For whatever reason, his unconscious mind accepted this as a command - pure hypnosis! Despite few teachers ever realising it, they have on the tips of their tongues both the process and the language of hypnosis. Suffice to say, with great power comes enormous responsibility for the educational well-being of learners, not just whilst they are in our classes but for the rest of their lives.

Learning to hear what you are saying and practising using the Milton language patterns outlined in the last chapter sensitises you to hearing the patterns in other people and in yourself. As you begin to hear the distinctions, remember that if you make a mistake or think you've said something silly, it's not the end of the world, you can just correct it. But keep doing it and you run the risk of doing a disservice to yourself as a teacher and to your students. For a start, you make your job harder than it needs to be, and we believe that making a teacher's job easy and enjoyable is a good thing! The more you learn to presuppose things are going to be easy and fun, the more you presuppose that kids are going to be self-initiated and will feel smart, and the closer they get to getting things right, the better they will feel.

SPINNING THE PRAYER WHEEL

A well set up lesson will of course increase the likelihood of students staying on track throughout the lesson and beyond. However, we can do much more than this. Often, teachers plan and prepare a lovely lesson, set the students up really well and off they go with the activities, learning away. After a little while the students seem to lose momentum and motivation and begin to wander off track. Sometimes, it's as if we cross our fingers and hope for the best until the end of the lesson! Whether your students continue to be enthusiastic and learn well throughout the lesson is not subject to chance; there are many variables and skills you can utilise to ensure that learning and motivation continue.

Think for a moment of a Tibetan prayer wheel. Getting it moving needs a lot of energy and a really good spin. If the wind is in the right direction, it will keep moving, if not, it stops and needs a really good spin again. However, given a little tap every now and again it will keep going with very little extra effort. A lesson is very similar, so here are some strategies to keep the prayer wheel spinning and the lesson on track.

The use and understanding of language changes as people mature. Younger children respond literally to language on a conscious level. For example, at a certain age, if you say to a child *'is the phone ringing?'* they just look at you and say *'yes!'* But when people reach a certain stage, they will respond by handing you the phone. As people grow up they do not process language literally on a conscious level, but people will still unconsciously respond to the literal meaning. As a child gets older, you can start to use questions such as, *'can you enjoy doing this now?'*

And of course the answer to the question is yes, but the command within the question is *'enjoy doing this now!'* Asking a question or posing a problem which is on the surface a statement of fact or a closed question but actually requires an action on the part of the listener is called a conversational postulate. For example, if we ask you *'do you have the time?'*, the answer is really yes or no, but most people will look at their watch and tell you the time.

Learning to be precise with your language is an essential skill for teachers. The language we use should take account of the different ways the conscious and unconscious mind processes information so that it is easy for a student to respond in a way that is helpful for their learning.

If students go off task it's often an uphill battle to get them back on track. The trick is to keep the momentum going by nudging the lesson in the right direction.

Praise is a great motivator and many studies show how effective it is in keeping students learning.[2] However, bouncing around the room scattering praise around - *'well done, that's fabulous, great terrific'* - in the hope of generating some enthusiasm may create some good feelings, but they are not necessarily associated with useful learning. The effect of this is to create confidence without competence. We don't want students to lack confidence, but neither do we want them to be confident doing something without developing their competence. Think of a brain surgeon who is very confident but not competent, or the young person who is confident in his driving ability but hasn't passed his test. Great teachers ensure that as competence grows, so does confidence.

BUILDING CONFIDENCE WITH COMPETENCE

There is a great deal of debate about lack of self-esteem in children today. Yet despite the concerns of parents and children, no one seems to be able to specify how to build self-esteem. It seems to be suggested that this is something you do first and then children will gain confidence. Well, no one has a bucket of self-esteem to throw over a child! Having a sense of self worth is a process, not a thing - we do not have it, we do it! It's simple - people have self-esteem when they do the right thing for the right reasons. Hence, learners build their self-esteem when they do the right things for the right reasons, and they have a sense of achievement when they overcome challenges and succeed in the task.

HOW TO PRAISE EFFECTIVELY

A recent study showed that children who are praised for effort rather than being praised for being clever, are much more successful.[3] This is simple; if you are praised for being clever, undertaking a new and difficult task may challenge your blossoming self-belief that you are clever, because if you fail it challenges this belief. If, on the other hand, you are praised for the effort you are putting in, your self-belief that you are the kind of person who keeps going and puts in effort is only reinforced by trying even harder. Although everyone likes praise in private, some learners find it hard to accept personal praise in a group situation, so a straightforward way to keep the prayer wheel spinning is through a running praise commentary. Adults do this naturally around very young children, like this: *'Oh look, Molly is putting the dolly in the pram; what a kind girl you are Molly, that's right, dolly needs to be strapped in to keep her safe. Well done Molly that's brilliant'*. Although people tend to stop doing this as children get older, it can have an amazing effect on students. When giving praise, the key is to link the praise with a specific activity, so each step tells the student to feel more confident as they gain competence. Then you can add language patterns to drive the learning forward, like this:

- *'Well that's fantastic, everyone has got the equipment set up in record time, which means that you will all complete the experiment and get fantastic data to put on your record sheets'*

- 'You're doing so well and I don't know whether you will finish the written part of the exercise or the group work part first, but either way it will make your grades really good when you have completed both parts'
- 'Now you have finished those equations you can check them against the answers and be determined to correct any slight mistakes and feel really good about getting so many right'

PUT IT IN QUOTES

When we quote someone else (or even ourselves) it increases the impact on the listener. This pattern can easily be used to let students know they are doing well, praising and inoculating against anything that may get in the way of learning. There is a report that says, 'praise passed on to another person feels even better than first hand' and when we stack these together it causes mild confusion, which means the learner accepts the comment on many levels.

Compare these two sentences:

'Mr Smith said you worked extremely well yesterday'

and 'I was talking to Mr Smith this morning and he said '2B are working extremely well'.

Now think about this: 'A wise man said, 'the more you practise using your language elegantly the more you will find that you do this naturally and the more your students will learn and more enjoyable teaching becomes'.

Using **'the more the more'** pattern illustrated in the paragraph above is an elegant way to spin the prayer wheel and builds propulsion for your students:

- '**The more** you learn about physics **the more** experiments you can do and **the more** the mysteries of science unfold before your very eyes'
- '**The faster** you learn the new vocabulary **the easier** it is to write great stories and the more fun you can have being creative'
- '**The more** curious you feel about discovering new facts **the easier** research becomes and **the better** your grades will be so that you feel proud of yourself'

Time for action

Many teachers use the word *'if'* without ever realising how they disadvantage themselves. *'If you answer the question, you get a sticker.'* Or even more unhelpfully, *'if you don't hand in your work you won't get a mark'*. *'If'* implies that something may or may not happen, so why dilute your influence with the possibility of failure when you could just as easily consolidate your influence by changing the word to *'**when**'*? Using time verbs and adverbs presupposes the task will happen, like this:

- *'**When** you hand in your work on time I will enjoy marking it and return it by Tuesday'*
- *'**Before** you get the answers right check through them again'*
- *'**While** you are here you can enjoy learning during our class'*
- *'**When** you continue reading this book you may notice how many more changes you are naturally making **before** you think consciously while you are teaching'*

GIVING FEEDBACK FOR GREAT RESULTS

When a student's learning isn't going so well, or you need to provide feedback of what to do next, it's helpful to have a way of redirecting the learning. We frequently hear encouragements such as, *'that's really great, but I want you to move on to page 7 now'*. The use of 'but', and the softer version, 'however', actually negates *'that's really great'* by directing the listener's attention to *'move on to page 7 now'*.

'But', and 'however' both have the potential to cancel what has just gone before, causing a separation within the sentence: *'You have done lots of good work today Jemima, but you haven't finished the exercises yet'*, leaves Jemima feeling like she has lots more to do and it's not good news.

'You haven't finished the exercises yet Jemima, but you have already done lots of good work today', has the effect of focusing on the good news, so Jemima is more likely to use the satisfaction of having done lots of work to motivate herself to finish the exercise. This is not the same as the famous 'praise sandwich', which doesn't cancel out the bad news, just leaves it squashed in the middle. Instead, this is about deciding where you want to direct someone's attention and then adding propulsion towards a goal. Try these:

- 'The last test didn't go so well **but now** you have had more practice this one will be easier'
- 'This question isn't quite right yet, **however** the other four are perfect'
- 'This essay needs a conclusion, **but** the introduction is fantastic'

So make sure you put your 'but' in the right place!

YES SETS
If a person acknowledges that a number of things are true, then they are very likely to believe the next thing you say is valid, whether it is true or not.

For example, you have this book in front of you (one truism) and are reading the words (second truism), you may have begun at the beginning or started somewhere else (third truism), and wherever you started you are learning how to use NLP to teach brilliantly (what we want you to do).

By determining that at least three things are true, we are more likely to accept the next thing as true. This useful 'yes set' pattern is often used in sales and because we are often 'selling' learning, it can be very helpful as a convincer for students, just as it may have been for you!

This is great pattern to remember when you need to get students back on track. Teachers are trained to notice mistakes and advise on corrections. However, pointing out when students are not on task isn't always useful. We know already that the students are not doing the task, and so do they. When we reverse the process and focus on what they **are** doing that's right and what is true for them, it enables us to move them from reverse gear and back into forward gear. So ask yourself, *'what is it that they are doing that is right?'*

Filtering for what is right rather than what is wrong, and using a 'yes set' enables you to pace the students' experience and lead them to a better place. For example, *'Ok guys, well done. You are all here with me today, sitting down and the room is full of chatter. You can see the questions in front of you, and as you finish talking to one another, you can now begin the next task'.*

This works better than just giving an instruction, because this way we maintain rapport and pace their reality, so it becomes much more likely that the students will follow our lead. It helps if you utilise the three main senses (see/hear/feel) and add the action (do) too, so what happens inside their minds goes something like this:

- *You are here and sitting down* - yes I am here and I can feel the chair
- *With me today* – yes I'm with you and it's today
- *And the room is full of chatter* – yes I can hear chatter
- *You can see the questions in front of you* – yes I can see questions in front of me
- *As you finish talking to one another* – OK everything else is true so this must be too
- *Begin the next task* – accepted as the next thing to do
- Off we go again and the prayer wheel is spinning once more!

OTHER VARIABLES
Although much of this chapter has focused on your language as a teacher, it is also worth mentioning that there are other non-verbal variables that are significant in keeping a lesson on track:

ROOM LAYOUT
Choosing and managing the room layout will influence the responses to the variety of activities you design for your students.

A classroom-style layout creates a state of passivity with attention focused on the teacher. The message could be translated as *'you sit, listen and absorb'*, with little opportunity to interact with anyone other than the teacher.

A horseshoe-style layout creates more opportunity to interact with the teacher and listen to/see the other students. This works OK, but the desire for contact with other students is often frustrated, so we can end up with the 'paper aeroplane syndrome', where missiles are used to connect across the room. If you like this layout, build in some opportunities to work together byw moving the chairs into the middle of the horseshoe.

Theatre-style works well with big groups, but isn't always practical if students need to write. It may also elicit states of vulnerability for some people.

A cabaret or chevron style is a very useful layout for active class engagement . Here, students are seated in groups (6 is a perfect number) around tables, with the end nearest the teacher kept clear so no one has their back to you. This allows the students to look and listen to you and work in pairs, threes or sixes without the disruption of moving tables. Schools are increasingly adopting this approach, which is drawn from active whole class management techniques.[3]

No single layout is correct all the time. It's a case of planning for the type of responses you want from your students and choosing the most appropriate layout to elicit this response. So if you want quiet reflection, cabaret is not the one to choose, but if you want group activity and discussion it may be the best choice.

Reception and infant teaching encourages the management of space and the states of little children in the classroom with story mats, quiet spaces, active play etc. However, as learners get older, it seems that teachers fail to recognise what a powerful influence the learning environment can have on students. Some environments are more challenging, such as computer rooms or laboratories, but experiment for yourself and notice what works for you and your students.

ATTENTION-GRABBERS
We're sure that you regularly consider how to make a dramatic point at the beginning of a class to illustrate the lesson to come. Using the same principle, it is a good idea to have a series of readily available props and resources to gain attention from the group if it is in danger of drifting. Putting peripheral posters on the wall reinforces learning, engages unconscious learning and can create interest or anticipation. You can utilise Power Point to sequence inspirational quotes or pictures relating to the subject. If you want your students to be quiet and reflective, use iTunes Visualisation, which creates patterns from the music and is quite dreamy.

One great teac her teaches Maths to engineers who complain they can't do it, dressing up in a magician's outfit to show them Maths tricks. Similarly, our NLP Education team have a range of outrageous props including wands and balls that giggle which we use to get students' attention and as anchors for states. One favourite prop is a black bin liner containing unknown items with a large notice attached with the instruction, *'Do not open this bag!'* Instant curiosity!

The key here is to be mindful of the significance of process in learning. Remember, great teaching is 20% content and 80% process.

SUMMARY

During this chapter you have explored ways to maintain and promote learning and keep the lesson on track. You have identified ways to motivate learners by using even more language patterns, such as yes sets and 'the more the more' patterns. You have learned specific ways to use praise to build confidence alongside competence. You have also considered some of the physical changes you can easily make to keep the lesson on track. So now you have read this chapter and reached the part of this book where you begin to really listen to and make changes to what you say to your students. Notice the impacts and enjoy the rewards!

REFERENCES

1. Dale Carnegie, 1936 How to win friends and influence people, London Vermillion
2. Elizabeth Gunderson Journal of Child Development Volume 84, Issue 5, September/October 2013
3. Robert Powell, 1997, Active Whole Class teaching, Stafford, Robert Powell Publications

ACTIVITIES

Activity 1

Prepare a new running commentary that has:
- A yes set pattern
- A 'more the more' pattern
- 2 time presuppositions

Use it tomorrow and notice what happens!

Activity 2

Collect together a resource box of attention-grabbers to keep with you and be creative about the different uses each object can have.

Activity 3

Draw a diagram of your teaching space or a typical classroom. Identify which areas and spaces you use for which activities and identify which states would be most useful to anchor in these places.

If you are working with little people in an infant school you will already be doing this to some degree. You will have an area for stories, maybe with a nice carpet to sit on, and an area for messy learning with water or sand. If you are working with older people, your space may be less defined. However, you can still manage the space. Where do you sit or stand when you are beginning or ending the session? Do you have a particular posture or place for setting homework? Where do you sit when the students are giving a presentation or working in groups?

You might like to create a curiosity corner or quiet thinking space. We're wondering how creative you can be, so map these onto your new plan and commit to testing it.

CHAPTER 14

Ending with new beginnings

Scan this to see the videos

'I like a teacher who sends you home with more to think about than homework.' (1)

Lily Tomlin

In this chapter

- Creating the desire for more learning
- Taking the learning beyond the classroom
- Stretch and Challenge through questioning
- Storytelling and Nesting learning

An experienced and wise teacher once said, *'my lessons have lots of beginnings and not many endings'*. There are times when even the best teachers come to the end of a lesson, exhausted and relieved, and manage to mutter something innocuous along the lines of *'well done class, you have worked well today, see you next week'*. When we give less attention to the ending of a lesson than we do to the beginning or to the lesson itself, we miss valuable opportunities because, rather than the end of a lesson bringing closure, it should be the beginning of even more. Similarly, any change of activity or shift in emphasis or process is a new beginning rather than an ending, and this can be where connections are made to deeper learning.

Perhaps you have heard of Hebb's Axiom: *'Neurons that fire together wire together!'*[2] Every experience we encounter, whether a feeling, a thought or a sensation, is embedded in thousands of neurons that form a network. As an experience is repeated, rehearsed or remembered, it becomes embedded in the brain's unique web-like structure and it becomes easier for the neurons to fire off and respond to the new learning.

The art and science of questioning is one way to fire and wire the neurons of our students' brains. A recent piece of research shows that teachers ask up to 2 questions every minute, up to 400 in a day, around 70,000 a year, or 2-3 million in the course of a career. Yet the majority of these are to check for understanding or are closed, process question such as, *'have you put your name on your work?'* or *'have you finished yet?'*[3]

It is more useful to use questioning for formative rather than just summative assessment; this is assessment FOR learning rather than OF learning. Summative assessment checks learning, often for external reasons, whereas formative assessment through questioning invites the learner to revisit their existing network of knowledge in a variety of ways, each time embedding the learning in a deeper and more meaningful (to their experience) way.

It may be useful to reflect on how many of the questions you ask in a day move the learning forward or are crafted to a specific end. A recent study found that finding a really great question was all that was needed to excite learners when they had the necessary resources available to them for research – in this case, the Internet. Questions such as *'why does hair keep growing on humans and not on animals?',* created hours of exciting enquiry amongst a group of 8-year-olds, leading them into genetics, insulation, evolutionary theory and much more.[4]

REPRESENTATIONAL SYSTEMS AND QUESTIONS
As you already know, people receive information about the world through the five sensory input channels – visual, auditory, kinaesthetic, olfactory and gustatory. Rather than each sense being given equal weight, each of us favours one or two over the others, although these **change according to the context**. Of course, there is considerable overlap in the parts of the brain responsible for processing our senses,

but one or the other usually dominates a particular experience at a particular moment in time. This is known as your sensory preference. In the classroom, this knowledge has major implications for building sensory-rich questions that connect the neural pathways to support, generate and embed learning.

Do you **see** our point? **Hear** what we are saying? **Catch** our meaning? Does this make **sense** now?

You may very well **see** what we mean, but not **hear** or **understand** what we are saying, and it may not make **sense** to you! Teachers will generally ask the question that best suits their preferences. Do you have a favourite saying? Do you ask your class to *'listen up'* or *'look at me'*? Do you say, *'am I getting through to you?'*

We have observed some teachers respond to students who don't understand something by explaining it again in exactly the same way as the first, second or third time, enunciating more clearly and speaking more slowly, as if this will push the learning into the student's head by an act of willpower! Instead, listening to how a student understands or pays attention is vital to ensuring that you communicate in a way they understand. If a student says, 'I don't know what you are saying', you have a number of choices; you can find a new way of explaining it in words, or you can change to a different representational system and say 'picture this' or 'let's walk ourselves through this'. (Caution - this is not the same as 'learning styles' theories, which are erroneous, as we discussed in Chapter 1)

Experiment with these examples:

- 'What technical adaptation to the presentation would you like to ***see*** Leanne?'
- 'How does the pace of this presentation ***sound*** to you?'
- 'Which musical rhythm ***feels*** most engaging, do you think?'

These sensory-laden questions enable Leanne to continually revisit and enrich her neural map of the topic, each time strengthening her connections within.

Recognising this natural variation in representational systems and learning how to utilise this provides you with an advantage, which means a teacher can connect all the representational systems together to quickly move the surface knowledge to the deep structure networks.

STRETCH AND CHALLENGE THROUGH QUESTIONING

The Meta Model is the inverse of the Milton Model introduced in Chapter 12. It was developed by Richard and his NLP co-founder John Grinder to identify and bring to the surface the limitations in a person's thinking and their model of the world. Its normal application is in relation to problems people may be having in their lives. As people describe their experience, they delete, distort and generalise their experience, which means their understanding, in the moment, is relatively superficial and on the surface. The Meta Model reconnects language with experiences, and can be used for gathering information, clarifying meanings, identifying limitations, and opening up choices, so it has a very relevant application in education for deepening learning and wiring together the synapses. (See later in the book for more explanation and information on how to use the Meta Model to resolve problems.) The NLP Education team have created a model for combining the use of the Meta Model with Blooms Taxonomy for effective questioning to enhance learning. Many teachers will be very familiar with Benjamin Bloom's work to create a scheme of classification for categorising questioning and tasks from lower order thinking (mastery) to higher order (developmental) thinking.[5] Blooms explains that the type of question asked directs the student into the type of thinking they do around a topic. For example, if we only ask questions around knowledge and comprehension, such as what, where or who (lower order thinking) we are likely to limit their thinking to this level:

- *What is....?*
- *Describe*
- *Why did...?*
- *Explain...*

However, if we ask questions that push the thinking towards developmental thinking (application, analysis, synthesis and evaluation) we direct the students to higher order and creative thinking:

- *How would you use…?*
- *What is the relationship between…?*
- *What could be changed to improve…?*
- *How would you prioritise…?*

Perversely, evidence shows that more higher order questions are asked of young children at school, while the higher the level of education, the more lower order questions are asked of students. Improving the quality of questions and increasing the number of higher order questions is a simple and effective way of improving the quality of learning without the need for greater resources or time on the part of the teacher. Here are some examples of Meta Model questions mapped against Blooms Taxonomy:

Knowledge	• How do you know?
	• Where did you find this out?
Comprehension	• What does that mean?
	• Always?
	• So what will that mean for..?
Application	• What would happen if..?
	• If that is true, what else could that mean?
	• How will you know when the solution is reached fully?
Analysis	• What is this similar to?
	• How is this different to..?
	• What is the exception to this pattern?
Synthesis	• How does this change what you know about x?
	• If you were to do this differently, what different results might you get?
	• What makes this a great answer?
Evaluation	• Now you know the options, what will you decide next time?
	• What would have made this easier from the start?
	• What did you do that made the difference?

For a detailed list of Blooms Taxonomy combined with Meta Model questions, see Appendix C.

Generative Learning

As a topic or session is concluded, you have an unprecedented opportunity not only to embed the learning, but to connect it to other areas of your students' lives now and in the future, so that the learning becomes generative. The founders of NLP observed that Milton Erickson didn't simply fix one problem in a patient; he wanted to create change so that every part of their lives improved as a result of this one small change. In this way the change or learning became generative. Imagine a snowball at the top of a mountain. You squeeze together a handful of snow and begin rolling it down the mountain. By the time it reaches the bottom it is huge. This is what we should be aiming for with any learning we have taught.

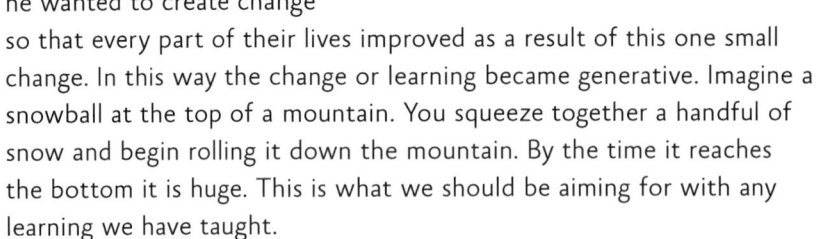

Milton Erickson used the skill of being 'artfully vague' to achieve this, and we can do the same in class. By doing this, we allow the learner to complete the details for themselves in ways that are helpful for them. While you look at the next few phrases, notice which of the patterns you recognise

- *'You've worked well and heard many new ideas today. There are things you have learned here that you are already aware of, and others, maybe not yet. For sure, you will come to see those new ideas as extremely useful in apositive way.'*
- *'Over the coming days and weeks you may notice new understanding of this topic emerging as a direct result of beginning to put things together here.'*
- *'I don't know exactly when you will notice changes in your project work, which group of ideas today sounded most exciting and which ones might yet surprise you.'*
- *'And now, as you look at some of the things you have learned today, you might get a sense of how your mind can continue these processes, which we have begun here in a meaningful way.'*

When we say *'extremely useful in a positive way'* we are not specifying how it's useful or what positive ways you will find to use this learning. We are being artfully vague, which means that in order to make sense of the sentence the student has to go inside their mind and find their own extremely useful ways to use the learning and the positive ways in which it can be used. The suggestion is personalised and meaningful to them, and because you are not imposing on their map of the world with your specific ideas, they don't need to resist what you are saying. In this way, the learning becomes generative and grows inside their minds over time, connecting with other learning, past and future.

By using time predicates like *days* and *weeks*, we are not saying exactly when the understandings will emerge, but we presuppose that they will. We are also artfully vague about how and what understandings will emerge. There is no actual causal link between gathering the things learned and sensing how your mind can continue these processes, but by linking the two things together one will naturally follow on from the other.

Temporal predicates, which are those that relate to time and the passage of time, such as *when, as, then, last, first, after, again*, all have what is called semantic density. They amplify or diminish feelings with great power and precision. So rather than saying *'number one, do this, number two do this'*, and simply listing your instructions, using temporal predicates allows you to increase the intensity of the feelings (or diminish them if this is your outcome) associated with the task. By enriching your language with a range of predicates you can intensify the feelings of curiosity, excitement and satisfaction for your students.

Here is an example from a Spanish teacher. How many patterns can you identify?

'Now that you have been learning to speak Spanish, before you become absolutely brilliant at it you will notice that you are beginning to use your brain in new ways, which may mean noticing how your brain becomes sharper in other ways too. The more you use your new language skills the easier they will become and the more you realise how smart you are although you may not have realised yet how easily you learned today. When you begin to pay attention to these things to practise, the more amazing consequences are in

your future. Because, as you gain in confidence with this new knowledge, I don't know how soon you will notice that people find you more interesting to talk to!'

You may have heard the advice for speakers to tell them what you are going to say, say it and tell them what you have said. Well, we can do more; presuppose what they are going to learn, remind them of how easily they are learning, and tell them how brilliant their lives will be now they have easily learned it!

STORYTELLING AND NESTING LEARNING
No self-respecting TV soap opera closes every storyline to the point where you are left feeling satisfied. Instead, they tease and invite you to return, often leaving a cliffhanger so you are slightly frustrated and want more. We can learn from this, because in essence teaching is more than education, it's the 'entertrainment', 'edutainment' business and you can preview the forthcoming attractions for eager minds!

A little chiding and teasing about what is coming up creates curiosity and a sense of pleasure. Rather than giving a message that *we are teaching you this and now it's finished*, connect the learning you have just completed to lots of other things that are to come. Even something as simple as saying, *'I am going to give you a problem to solve tomorrow and I don't know how fast most of you will be able to solve it'*, means the students ask, *'well, what's the problem; could you tell us what it is?'* You can say, *'I could, but then we won't have so much fun tomorrow...'*

The connections to what comes next should elicit curiosity and excitement. For example, your cliffhanger could be *'there's this guy I know who took this one equation and made one million pounds from it; now we will get back to that tomorrow'*. They do it on TV, so let's do it in class.

Suspense and curiosity are at the heart of storytelling. Children are automatically caught up by suspense stories, so we can make our lessons into mysteries and intrigues. Think about the classic story opening for children - 'once upon a time'... followed by words that fill the mind with sensory-rich experiences, holding open attention, crafting a story that elicits a myriad of emotional responses, each one connecting to each other. Good storytellers hold their listeners spellbound – that is to say, the listeners' minds stay open to the next idea and engaged in each listener's internal representation of the story. Each of us can learn to tell a good story and 'nest' the learning within the story.

When we do this, each piece of information or instruction is embedded inside a loop together with the emotional state created by the story. When the loop is closed, the information is nested within the story along with the emotional state. Much of this process is unconscious, and often the learner isn't aware of how the learning has taken place.

NESTED LOOPS

Richard pioneered the process of unconscious communication, and nested loops are at the heart of his work. Fortunately, we can now utilise these processes to make quantum leaps in the speed and effectiveness of learning. Nested loops work because the **conscious** mind is compelled to make sense of the information it is receiving, but it is the **unconscious** mind that has the ability to track many layers of input, and like any good story we wait for the conclusion before seeking closure.

Opening and closing loops is at the heart of storytelling, and there are many advantages to this process. Learning that is nested in loops captures the listener's attention and prevents premature closure.

When someone says, *'uh huh'*, this is the sound of a mind slamming shut! The person has closed down to learning and no further information will be taken in. The loops also connect or chain different states in the learner, so that one state automatically leads to the next and the next state. Rather than the learning being a step-by-step linear process, the learning becomes part of a whole process, where the learning is nested within and connected to a set of emotional responses.

- The story begins, create the state
- The learning and proces
- The story ends

A simple loop begins with a story, and the story continues until the teacher has elicited the emotional state associated with the story and anchored it. Then the learning, key points or steps to the process are embedded and the story is completed. The learner now has the totality of the learning captured along with the kinaesthetics of the story.

When we nest further loops, more than one loop is opened in sequence and each loop elicits a particular state. Once each loop is open, the key learning takes place and the loops are closed in reverse order so the learning nestles in the centre.

Hence the term 'nested loops'!

Nested loops can be very simple or develop complexity as you become more familiar with the process. Using nested loops is a powerful model of communication and requires some careful planning. It's important to line up all your ducks in a row first so you know where you are going with your teaching. However, like any other skill, regular practice makes it easier and easier. Once you have mastered the skills of nesting loops, imagine the possibilities! What if you opened a loop for each new topic? How about a whole syllabus? What if you opened a loop at the beginning of the year and didn't close it until the end of the year, or you kept the loop open for the whole time a child is with you? The possibilities are endless.

Here is a simple example:

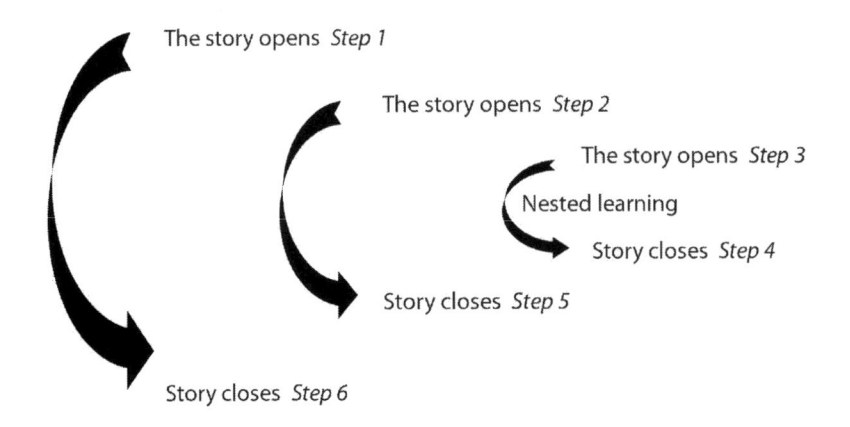

The story opens *Step 1*

The story opens *Step 2*

The story opens *Step 3*

Nested learning

Story closes *Step 4*

Story closes *Step 5*

Story closes *Step 6*

Story 1: I just saw on the news that a British guy Tim Peake has joined the space station and the news said he was the first Brit in space.
Story 2: That reminded me of being little and watching the first Moon landing. It was so thrilling.
Story 3: The closest I ever came to something like that was doing a bungee jump. I really didn't want to jump!
Nested learning: It can be very scary doing something for the first time. It can be really thrilling though when you take on the challenge and have a go. The challenge is just for you and it doesn't matter who else notices.

Now go back through the loops in reverse order:

Story 3: I never thought I would jump, but I did and the rush was fantastic
Story 2: I can still hear those immortal words *'a small step for man, a giant leap for mankind'*.
Story 1: Helen Sharman was actually the first Brit in space. She was a chemist from Sheffield and spent 8 days on the Mir space station. Do you remember her? I am sure she never forgot her amazing experience.

Of course, each nested loop is more than just one line and the story continues until the learners are in the state you want for them - curiosity, excitement, pride etc.

Nesting loops in NLP is regarded as an advanced skill and, like all new areas of learning, it's important to walk before you run, so if you are new to NLP we advise you to practise eliciting states and creating, stacking and chaining anchors first, and when you are confident and competent in these skills then move on to open a loop or two and build up from there.

SUMMARY

During this chapter you have explored ways to create deep and generative learning that continues beyond the topic and beyond the lesson. Sensory-rich language and Meta Model questioning skills enable you to move learning from the surface to a deeper level. You have discovered the Milton Model skill of being artfully vague for generative learning and have identified the use of cliff hangers and stories to excite and engage. And now you can begin to teach on multiple levels using the innovative and unique art and science of nested loops. We wonder which of the following exercises you will use to make tomorrow's lessons the easiest and most enjoyable ever!

REFERENCES

1. Lily Tomlin, actress and comedian, as Edith Ann (script by Jane Wagner)
2. Donald Hebb, 1949, The Organization of Behavior, New York: Wiley & Sons.
3. Steven Hastings TES 4 July, 2003
4. Dr Sugata Mitra http://www.hole-in-the-wall.com/Findings.html
5. Bloom, B. S et al, 1956, Taxonomy of educational objectives: The classification of educational goals. Handbook I: Cognitive domain. New York: David McKay Company.

ACTIVITIES

Activity 1

Go back to the set-up for your lesson you created in Chapter 12. Imagine how quickly and efficiently your students have worked and plan

5 closing sentences:

1. Tell them how brilliantly they have learned today
2. Connect this to the positive consequences for the next lesson
3. Give one distinct positive outcome from their point of view
4. Create one artfully vague consequence for the rest of their lives
5. Build a presupposition based on this lesson of how great the next lesson will be
6. Devise a 'cliffhanger' to tantalise them with for the next lesson

Use it tomorrow.

Activity 2

Devise sample questions for each level of Blooms Taxonomy and Meta Model challenge questions based on the story of Goldilocks and the Three Bears. We have given you at least one example to get you started, so it's easy for you to think of more now, isn't it?

THE STORY : GOLDILOCKS AND THE THREE BEARS

Goldilocks wanders into the house of the Three Bears. She tastes their porridge, finding one bowl "too hot," one bowl "too cold," and one bowl "just right." Goldilocks also tries out their chairs, finding one chair "too big," one "too small," and one "just right." Then she tries out the bears' beds, finding one bed "too hard," one "too soft," and one "just right." She falls asleep in Baby Bear's "just right" bed. When the bears return, they find that someone has been eating their porridge, sitting in their chairs, and sleeping in their beds. They discover Goldilocks in the "just right" bed and she runs away.

Cognitive Domain	Blooms Taxonomy Question: Example	Meta Model Challenge Questions: Examples
Knowledge	• Who are the main characters in the story? • •	• How do you know
Understanding/ Comprehension	• Why did Goldilocks prefer one bowl of porridge to the others? • •	• How **specifically** did you discover this? • •
Application	• How did the bears decide to have different porridge, chairs and beds? • •	• Why does size matter? • •

Analysis	• Why did the bears leave their porridge uneaten in their bowls and go out of the house? • •	• Is there a pattern here? • •
Synthesis	• What if the house had belonged to Little Red Riding Hood? Re-tell the story. • •	• What would you do differently next time? • •
Evaluation	• What does this story tell you about the state of Health and Safety training in Fairytale Land? • •	• Is it the same with every fairytale? • •

Extension activity

As you become comfortable with these skills and processes as you improve your experience in the classroom, the moment will soon arrive when you find yourself drawn to nested loops. Here is a process to begin the journey:

1. First select your topic
2. Begin by identifying 3 pieces of information you want to teach
3. Next create 3 anecdotes that create 3 states you want your learners to have as you teach your information. The stories may be things that have happened today, or may be drawn from your repertoire of anecdotes
4. Use the diagram in this chapter to map your nested loops
5. Have a go tomorrow

Some people find it a challenge to leave one story halfway through, so just use the absent-minded professor strategy. Your students probably won't notice and will just be pleased because they will think you have gone off the plot!

PART 4

TROUBLESHOOTING AND CHALLENGE

CHAPTER 15

Changing unhelpful beliefs and attitudes

SCAN THIS TO SEE THE VIDEOS

'No problem can be solved from the same level of consciousness that created it.' [1]

Albert Einstein

In this chapter
- Learn how to shrink a BIG problem down to size
- Discover what is really being said
- Use effective questions for change
- Changing beliefs and attitudes about learning

A student disclosed that he had a money problem, so the school counsellor asked him how he felt about this, if there are other things that worried him, how things were at home and did he have a part time job to help with finances? The student replied, *'why are you asking me all this stuff? I just need 30p for my bus fare, I left my wallet at home!'* Sometimes it helps to be specific!

Good teachers consistently devote their time and energy to supporting individual learners on a one-to-one basis, both to aid learning and to offer personal support. A listening ear and solid guidance go some way to helping learners, however we can do more. This chapter introduces you to the elegant and effective NLP Meta Model to help you to get to the core of a problem and create strategies to resolve difficulties. Using the Meta Model ensures that the concerns you address are the right ones and that your interventions produce lasting and beneficial outcomes. Elegant use of the NLP Meta Model as a guide to asking the right questions means that we avoid the sort of assumptions made by the school counsellor, and we can save a great deal of time and energy as we become more effective at helping our students.

The Meta Model provides a structure for asking questions to discover how a person is experiencing a problem. This model is systematic and meticulous, focusing on **how** the learner is experiencing a problem, rather than the **content** of the problem. Once again, the focus is on process, not content. Listening to the content of a problem, (that is, the detail of what the person is concerned about) draws us into their 'story' and why they have the problem. This gives us little or no insight into **how** to help to solve it.

Let's take exam anxiety as an example. Knowing everything about when the learner first experienced anxiety and all the subsequent times they felt that way doesn't provide the solution. However, we can help if we know that in order to feel anxious, the person goes through a sequence of steps (their strategy for getting anxious). We may discover that first they make a picture of themselves seeing the exam questions and not knowing any of the answers, then they associate into the picture and feel dread in their stomach and say to themselves, *'oh no, I am going to fail'*. Then they see a multi-coloured surround-sound movie of themselves getting their results and failing and they take the feeling of dread and mix it with abject disappointment. The chances are that if any of us were to follow this sequence we would have exam anxiety too!

Once we understand the process a person uses to feel anxious (or any other feeling they don't want to have) we can help them to change the feeling into something more useful, such as determination or relaxation.

The Meta Model is the inverse of the Milton Model (introduced in Chapter 12). The two models are two sides of the same coin. Where we use the Milton patterns to create great beliefs, states and strategies, we use the Meta Model to 'challenge' unhelpful beliefs, strategies and bad feelings. As we discuss the model you may find that you are already familiar with many of the patterns and can learn to use them in another helpful way.

When we use the word 'challenge' it is not to say that we go at the person aggressively. Quite the opposite, we use our questions elegantly, with finesse and with humour. When we use humour it gently chides a person into allowing the problem to diminish – it puts it into perspective – and it's hard to keep feeling bad when you're laughing. A useful metaphor is to view the problem as a huge rock, and we use the Meta Model to chip away at the stone to reduce its size and sort out what works from what doesn't, always working towards the outcome the person wants.

The Meta Model has three main functions:
1. To specify information
2. To clarify information
3. To open up a person's model or map of the world

To create their model or map of the world, humans delete, distort or generalise information. Each time we communicate with other people, we are presenting our map to them and to ourselves, and we are deleting, distorting and generalising information. This is useful, because it means conversations don't go on forever or become tedious. However, it can also be unhelpful. The function of the Meta Model is to find out what has been deleted, distorted, or generalised by the learner unhelpfully. If they delete, distort or generalise information in ways that are helpful, then leave them alone or, better still, reinforce the helpful belief!

Meta Model questions are used to gather and specify information about the experience the learner is having. This is not just information for you as the teacher; it also helps students to gather information about what they are doing on the inside that isn't working for them. The Meta Model allows you and the student to discover what has to happen for change to take place for that person specifically.

To specify the process of having a problem, we want to remove the biggest chunks of stone from our rock first, so we use a 'big chunk' question. Often, the best to start with is *'How do you know?'* In order to answer this question, the person has to go inside and think about it and as a result will often answer with a much more specific response than they might have done otherwise. Using our previous example, the initial statement could be *'I have exam anxiety'*. We ask the question – *'how do you know?'* and the person may say something like, *'Well, when I think about my exams I imagine I am not going to know any of the answers, and I dread the exams, knowing that I will be disappointed when I get my results'*. Now we have more specific information and we can continue with other questions to chip off the smaller pieces of rock until we have a clear and specified process of how the person creates anxiety around exams in him/herself.

Remember that the information we are seeking to discover are the deletions, distortions and generalisations the learner is making to create their map of the world. This is the surface structure of their world. We want to discover the deeper structure of their experience so that they can re-model their world in ways that serve them better. So the questions can be usefully categorised in the same way.

WHAT IS 'DELETED', OR MISSING?

When someone says, *'I'm scared'* / *'I'm worried'* / *'I'm confused'*, what is missing? A person has to be scared of something. Similarly, are they scared, worried or confused all the time? Ask them, *'What's scaring you?'* / *'When do you worry?'* / *'What specifically is confusing you?'* These questions prompt the person to go inside and find some more information. Two other things are happening, too. One is that feeling worried is a very big state and adding information puts the worrying in a particular context; by definition there are some things that are not worrying them, so this is now immediately more manageable. Secondly, notice the nature of the question. It doesn't say *'what are you confused about?'* it says *'when are you confused?'* Using an active tense – confusing - creates movement, unlike *'I'm confused'*, which implies being stuck in a state. Using an active tense – confusing - implies that things are fluid and can change. If you use a past tense – *'what **were** you confused about?'* – you can put the confusion in the past and imply that it is no longer happening.

COMPARED TO WHAT?

Sometimes students compare themselves to other people or compare one thing with another but miss out what it is they are comparing it with. This is called **comparative deletion** – *'he's better'* / *'this is worse'* / *'it's harder'*. Ask the student *'better than what?'* or *'compared to what?'* The student may then reply, *'he's better than me'* / *'this is worse than yesterday'* / *'it's harder than last week's maths'*. Again, you have helped the person to reduce the size of the problem and specified when and what it is that is limiting them.

WHO SAYS?

People often express as a fact something that is really just an opinion, using verbs that miss out the specifics about how, where and when. Notice the phrases *'it's hard'*, *'they are best'*, *'I am stupid'*, *'research says'*. What is missing here? Ask **'what** is hard', **'who** is best', **'how** do you know specifically' and **'which** research?' Once a student realises that it is just what they think about something, and isn't necessarily the absolute truth, it opens up the possibility of changing their point of view. In this way, *'I am stupid'* becomes *'I think I am stupid because yesterday I couldn't do the maths questions and my friend said, 'it's easy so you must be stupid'*. You may then want to go on to question the truth in this statement by asking, *'has your friend ever been wrong?'*

WHAT'S ALTERED OR DISTORTED?

'I have no motivation' 'His behaviour is bad!' 'I have anxiety', are all examples of taking a verb - the action to motivate, to behave, to be anxious - and turning it into a noun – an object. In NLP, these are called **nominalisations**. To test this, ask yourself *'can you put it in a wheelbarrow?'* If someone says, *'I have depression'*, or *'I have anxiety'*, we can't actually touch these things as objects (or put them in a wheelbarrow!), so we need to turn them back into processes which can change easily rather than be 'things that are static and hard to change. Ask, *'What is not motivating you?' 'How is he behaving badly?' 'How are you making yourself anxious?'* These questions create the possibility of movement and change.

The labels we attach to people such as ADHD or Dyslexia are designed as descriptions of symptoms or behaviours, but sometimes people can begin to define themselves by the term as if they are it. We challenge this in ways that enable students to see that they may have unusual or extraordinary ways of processing information. Ask them how do they do dyslexia or ADHD. Or you may find even more creative ways of challenging this belief, as this teacher did:

A young boy came into a teacher's class and said, *'I've got ADHD, Miss'*. She said, *'really? Where is it?'* He said, *'what you mean? I don't know where it is!'* As he did this, he held his hands out in front of him as if he was holding a parcel. The teacher said, *'Oh, there it is'* and pointed to his hands. *'Give it to me and I will put it under the table until the end of the lesson and then you can have your ADHD back'*. She mimed taking the ADHD from him and put it under the table. He smiled and said, *'you're mad, Miss!'* Then he behaved perfectly well all lesson and the next day came in and said, *'I left it outside today, Miss'*.

What she helped him to understand was that his ADHD was not a static object and he had choice in how he was behaving as a process.

Some teachers could do well to pay attention to the way they create nominalisations. 'Attitude, behaviour, motivation', are all nominalisations which are not a way to help a student to do things differently. Rather, this is just a way for people to convince themselves into a set of beliefs that absolves them of any responsibility. Next time you are in the staff room, just listen for some of the more common nominalisations and perhaps begin to challenge a few.

WHERE'S THE CONNECTION?

An interviewer once said to the musician Frank Zappa, *'You have long hair; does that make you a woman?'* Frank Zappa's response was, *'You have a wooden leg; does that make you a table?'*

We can distort information by linking two things together as if one thing makes another thing happen. *'You make me angry'*. *'When you look at me that way it makes me feel bad'*. The truth is, as the former US First Lady Eleanor Roosevelt said, *'no one can make me feel bad without my consent'*. Most students and many teachers often presuppose a causal link when there isn't one. Again, the way to challenge this is to ask, with a great deal of surprise in your voice, *'how do I/they do that!'* Young people use this pattern a great deal and of course little people do it in relation to magical thinking. Take the rhyme, *'if you tread on a nick you will marry a stick and a witch will come to your wedding'*. We are not going to challenge distortions that are natural in children or are useful and fun for them. However, as children grow up it may be helpful to them to see that two things may not be connected and they have more choices about how to respond to a situation or comment.

MIND READING

One young girl flounced out of the room in tears on hearing the teacher say, *'I have just spoken to your mother'*. The young girl wouldn't stay to listen because she had already decided that she knew what her mother had said. She took some convincing to listen to the actual response from her mother. We cannot know precisely what someone else is thinking, but we often distort reality and behave as if we can. Children are very good at this - *'You don't like me'*. *'He hates me'*. *'I know what you are thinking'*. *'You think I'm stupid'*. It's easy to challenge this by asking, *'how do you know that?'*.

WHAT'S THE CONNECTION?

Another misconception is that X means or is the same as Y. *'You don't love me, you don't bring me flowers anymore.'* *'You hate me – you gave me a C in my assignment'*. Simply ask how does X mean Y? Like this – *'how does me bringing you flowers mean that I love you?'* *'How does you getting a C mean I hate you?'*

WHAT'S GENERALISED?

Is it **always** true?
'Every student always wants to learn and always behaves beautifully in all my classes'. This is probably not true, even though it could help to choose to believe it. People can also make generalisations that are really unhelpful for their learning, such as: *'No one likes me'*. *'Everyone treats me badly and picks on me all the time!'* *'I always do badly in Languages'*. These patterns are **Generalisations**. The most obvious of these are known as **Universal Quantifiers**, which you learned in relation to the discussion on rapport in Chapter 12. Now we are considering them from the perspective of someone limiting their model of the world. You can challenge universal quantifiers simply by exaggerating the

statement, *'No one? Everyone? Always?'* Or you can simply ask, *'is there not one person who likes you? What about your mother, or me?'* **How** you ask these questions is just as important as **what** you ask. Reading these words on the page doesn't necessarily impart the tonality or smile that would accompany such a question; again, a little giggle and gentle tease maintains rapport, whereas a strong challenge may cause the person to reject your help.

WHAT HAS TO BE THERE?
Sometimes people assume that something is true before something else can happen. *'I can get on with my work when you stop picking on me'*, has a presupposition that you are picking on me. *'I can't answer the question because I am always wrong'*, presupposes that the person is always wrong. We have explored helpful presuppositions in the use of the Milton Model in the classroom. However, when you are working through a challenge with a student, the trick is to listen for any presuppositions which are preventing them using a better strategy. If you allow a presupposition to go unchallenged you are implicitly accepting it as true, so intervene as soon as you hear something being implied by the speaker.

WHERE'S THE CHOICE?
Try putting a tape recorder under your desk and playing back half an hour of you talking to students. As teachers we should, must, ought, have to, get them through their exams. They can or can't study, they might revise or they may not. These motivating words, known as Modal Operators, can imply possibility, such as *can, can't, might, may, could,* or can be words that imply necessity, such as *must, have to, should*. Listen to many teachers and parents and you may notice that the term *'you need to'* is the most common!

When a learner asks for help, the way they ask you gives you information about how to help them to move forward. If a student says, 'I can't do this' the question to ask is, 'what stops you?' If on the other hand they tell you that they 'mustn't do this', then the question is, *'what would happen if you did?'*

When a student implies they have no choice, either because they don't have the resources or some external factor stops them, your job is to provide the opportunity for them to explore either what's inside them that stops the process or what external factors are influencing them in their decision.

Now there is a lot of information here and it may seem to some that it is a challenge to know where to start, but it isn't really. It is more about listening to what is really going on and responding appropriately, rather than knowing which label or name of each pattern is which. Here's a transcript of a conversation Kate had with a student who was regularly getting into trouble for fighting. He had just had another fight when this conversation took place:

Kate: *Why did you hit him?*
Josh: *I had to!*
Kate: *You had to?*
Josh: *Yes, he called me a f****** b******.*
Kate: *Oh, so when someone calls you a f****** b****** you HAVE to hit him?*
Josh: *Yeah, that's right!*
Kate: *Even me?*
Josh: *Yeah, that's right!*
Kate: *OK, so what if I call you a f******* b******* in Japanese – would you have to hit me then?*
Josh: *Don't be stupid, of course not!'*
Kate: *Why not?* (asked in all innocence)
Josh: *Because I wouldn't know what you were saying!*
Kate: *Oh! You have to understand what I'm saying?*
Josh: *Yeah!*
Kate: *So what does it mean when someone calls you a f*****b*****?*
Josh: *They don't show me no respect.*
Kate: *(leaving the double negative aside...) So if someone doesn't show you respect you HAVE to hit them?*
Josh: *Yeah!*
Kate: *Have you ever called someone a f******** b******* and they hit you?*
Josh: *Yep!*
Kate: *What would happen if there were two guys you called f****** b*******s and one of them hit you but the other one, who was bigger than you, just smiled and walked away. Which one would you have more respect for?*

Josh: *The one who walked away, I guess*
Kate: *Oh really? So what are you going to do next time?*
Josh: *I'm going to say 'I could flatten you, but you ain't worth it'!*

This was progress, if not perfection! You might be thinking – what a long way around, why not just tell him not to hit people? Well, the reason is that he had been hearing that all his life and it didn't work because he hadn't worked out that he had other choices that still maintained his high value of 'respect'. All the other options had required him to give up his street belief about respect. This way, his values around respect were maintained, while the distortions in his thinking were challenged and allowed him to make a different choice in the future.

Now you may have noticed that some of these patterns overlap a little. What's important is that you go for the response that is going to make the biggest difference to the way the person perceives the difficulty they are having. When Josh said, *'I had to'*, the missing performative could have been challenged by asking *'who says?'* But by reflecting back **'had to'** he gained the information which showed him that X didn't mean Y and he could take a different course of action next time.

The effect of using the Meta Model is that the person goes inside themselves and carries out what is called a **transderivational search**. That is, they go and find some way to recover some deeper meaning to what they are saying and provide more information about what they are thinking. It's more thinking on purpose, isn't it?

When you read transcripts of people using NLP with clients or students, one of the things you may notice is that the practitioner doesn't always do a great deal of listening and there is a good reason for this. Take this situation: Eve came in to see her tutor and was obviously very unhappy and upset. She said, *'I hate school, I am always unhappy; no one likes me and they make me angry, teasing me. I am too slow and can't learn anything because I'm stupid!'* Her tutor's response was, *'you are not stupid Eve, you are very clever at some things'.* Because her tutor ignored the generalisations *'I hate school', 'I am always unhappy'* and the mind read *'no one likes me'*, it's fair for Eve to presume that these first three comments are true!

People are very experienced in justifying their position; the longer you let it go on, the more fixed their position becomes and the more they will convince themselves of their truth. When a student does this we need to go for the very first deletion, distortion, or generalisation, otherwise we are effectively agreeing with them. By challenging the very first statement we begin to cast doubt on this and all subsequent unhelpful beliefs.

When you create enough doubt about a belief and find enough examples of ways in which it isn't true, then the learner is able to find a new belief to support a better version of their model of the world. By asking the right question in the right way we can help the person to see what they have missed out or changed to be able to perpetuate a particular belief or behaviour.

Once you begin to use the Meta Model to specify exactly the difficulty the learner is having, this can often be sufficient for the learner to start to make changes in their internal behaviour for themselves. A learner may make a statement such as *'I can't do Maths'*, but when questioned the problem becomes *'I don't know how to multiply this number by that number in this equation; whenever I think about it I just feel sick'*. Now using NLP we would ask, *'how did you think about it? Did you make a picture or say something to yourself?'* The person then has to go inside and work out the process that they went through to make themselves feel sick and then it becomes easier to do something else instead.

Where this is not the case you at least have details of their strategy for the unhelpful thinking, and the pieces of the strategy that work and the ones that don't. You have chipped off enough rock to see precisely what is going on. At this point you can use the same processes you have already learned for installing, changing or modifying a strategy so it works for the student. There are more interventions and processes to use in the next chapter. Remember, people are not broken and they do not need fixing; they are just uneducated as to how to run their own brains and your interventions on a one-to-one basis are an extension of your teaching role - teaching your learners to run their own brains.

SUMMARY

In this chapter you have explored the elegant use of Meta Model as a way of making effective interventions with learners. You have identified the way people delete, distort and generalise information to maintain a belief or strategy and how to challenge these unhelpful assumptions in a supportive way to enable students to grow and learn.

REFERENCES

1. Attributed to Albert Einstein (1879-1955) Physicist & Nobel Laureate

ACTIVITIES

Activity 1

THE META MODEL INACTION

Here are some statements you may well have heard before from your learners. Think for a moment what you would have normally said, then have a go at asking different questions. Decide what is deleted, distorted or generalised in each statement and what would be an effective challenge to the statement to help the student think differently about the problem. Remember that some statements may have more than one deletion, distortion or generalisation, so think about which one you will challenge. There is a summary of the key questions to remind you below the grid.

Statement	Deletion/Distortion /Generalisation	Challenge
Everybody thinks I'm bad		
I know what's best for her		
You make me angry		
She hates me		

It's the wrong way to do it		
This is the way we should do it		
I don't get any support		
I need help		
I am always wrong		
I never get praise		
I can't do it		
I shouldn't go		
I am confused		
Dogs are bad		
This is the way we should do it		
I don't get any support		
I need help		
I am always wrong		
I never get praise		
I can't do it		
I shouldn't go		
I am confused		
Dogs are bad		

SUMMARY OF META MODEL QUESTIONS
- How do you know?
- Compared to what?
- How do you know when to...
- What specifically is (verb)...ing you
- Who says?
- When?
- What?
- How do I/they do that?
- How does this mean that?
- What stops you?
- What would happen if you could?
- What would happen if you did?
- Everybody? Always? Never? Nothing? All? No one?

Extension activity

Now think of some statements you, your students and your colleagues often make and practise challenging them with the Meta Model.

Activity 2

MODAL OPERATOR S ACTIVITY

Imagine that your manager has called a meeting. Read the statements in column one as if you are saying them to yourself and score yourself out of 10 as to how likely you are to go to the meeting. Now read column two as if your manager is saying the statement to you and notice if there is any difference in what you say to yourself and what another person says to you relating to your motivation. Which one is most likely to get you to the meeting? You may notice that you use this term more often than not to motivate your students, but of course they may use a different modal operator!

Say to yourself:	Your manager says to you:
I can go to the meeting	You can go to the meeting
I may go to the meeting	You may go to the meeting
I have to go to the meeting	You have to go to the
I should go to the meeting	You should go to the meeting
I must go to the meeting	You must go to the meeting
I will go to the meeting	You will go to the meeting
I am going to the meeting	You are going to the meeting

Extension activity

Create a similar exercise to the one above to use with your students around homework. This activity can create useful discussions about how your students motivate themselves and how they can feel good about getting on with the homework and feeling satisfied that they have completed the work.

CHAPTER 16

Timelines and other techniques for Motivation and Success

SCAN THIS TO SEE THE VIDEOS

"It always seems impossible until it's done." (1)

Nelson Mandela

In this chapter

- Timelines in the classroom – preparing for exams
- Bringing success into the present
- Spinning bad feelings into good feelings
- From stuck to motivated with a Visual Squash
- Swish for a change
- Visual Squash for a whole class

Over the years NLP has evolved a range of techniques to help people drive their own internal processes and make changes to how they think and feel. But the techniques are not NLP per se. NLP techniques develop over time as our skills improve and we find faster and easier ways to help people drive their own brains. Some techniques are no longer used because we have found better ways, but the fundamentals of NLP don't change.

Here we share with you some of the tried and tested ways to help your students to success. It is not an exhaustive list; it is designed to help you to begin to use your skills to create solutions for yourself. So these techniques are to get you started. The more you practise and build your confidence with this material, the easier it will be to find your own processes that work and you can begin to use NLP to improve the lives of your learners. We are sure that your creativity can find new and exciting ways to use these processes.

TIMELINES
Working with timelines allows you to support your students to unlock motivation and become self-managed learners. You can anchor the feelings of success and utilise the resources that are in the past, present and future. This enables learners to gain insights into the stages of their learning journey in relation to goals that are both short and longterm, and you can help them to install time-management strategies to help meet required deadlines.

We experience time in different ways at different times in our lives. Very young people have little concept of time – everything is very much in the moment. Think of how we explain to little ones that Christmas is coming and will be here after 2 sleeps. Exam dates in 6 months seem a lifetime away to a teenager, whereas for an adult it comes around all too quickly.

Often, young people are unable to put off immediate pleasure for long-term gain. In fact, there is evidence that teenagers lose the ability to delay gratification due to the changes in their frontal lobes during adolescence and in some cases don't regain this ability until they are in their early twenties.[2] Many students will choose a short-term benefit such as going out with their friends over the long-term benefit of passing their exams or graduating from college. One solution to this problem could be just to wait for them to grow up a bit, but this won't get them through their exams or motivate them to do their homework. The answer is to bring the pleasure of the success into the present state. Timeline work is an easy and rewarding process, useful for both one-to-one work or with a whole group.

Some applications of timelines in a learning context include changing the way the learner experiences things from the past, such as unhelpful experiences and decisions, so that they can experience what they want in their future in more resourceful ways. You can also use timelines to build propulsion into the experience of the learner, and timelines can also convince students that they are capable of achieving their goals and help them to build well-formed outcomes.

Timelines are a way of spatially organising time in our internal representation of reality. There is no way for our brains to conceptualise time, so we use space to represent time. The timelines that most people adopt can be described as either **Through Time** or **In Time**, although there are other cultural variations.

In time: This is where the sense of time is experienced as inside the body, (associated into the experience). Often, this is the perception that the future is in a line ahead of you, and the past in a line directly behind you. The present is experienced as 'within' you and is therefore known as **in-time**. This is the best state to be in to enjoy the moment. Being in time, you are also less likely to be aware of time passing, less likely to plan or stick to a plan and you may become side-tracked very easily.

Through time: This is where the sense of time is experienced as being outside the body (disassociated from the experience). Often, the timeline is perceived as laid out from left to right in front of you so you can see it. In this state, the past, present and future is 'available'. Being **through-time** is to be conscious of time passing, to be aware of the interaction of events, have time to attend an approaching lesson, to be able to plan, work to a plan, and multi-task.

By using the imagination to travel back and forwards along a person's timeline, we can create the experience of bringing future feelings of success into the present moment. This has the effect of making the gratification immediate. We can also travel along the timeline and gather resources that are necessary for the success.

PREPARING FOR EXAMS AND TESTS
A simple and easy way to prepare students for exams or upcoming tests is to take them on a timeline journey. Making elegant use of the Milton

patterns, allow your students to fill in the details of the experience for themselves while stacking positive suggestions along the way so it is perfect for them. You can experiment using the following process:

Have your students push back on their chairs away from their desks and close their eyes. Play some quiet relaxing music and weave a pleasant and relaxing journey into the future to a moment of success. Encourage the students to really appreciate the good feelings and amplify the state. Ask them to turn around inside their heads and look back at all they have achieved to get to this point of success. Mention here all the steps that lead to successful exams, like preparing a plan, organising time to revise, making notes, remembering and recalling easily. Take your students through each day and each exam, letting go of any doubts and moving on to the next confidently.

Next ask your students to move along their timeline inside their heads back to the present whilst gathering all the resources, skills and behaviours they have observed so they can bring them all back into the present with the feelings of success. As you ask them to open their eyes, explain that using your imagination in this way feels like remembering an experience and when we do something once it's much easier to do it the second time, even if it is in our imagination, isn't it?

Appendix E has a full transcript of this journey for you to use in your classes.

This process can be easily translated into a physical classroom activity, and this is often preferred by active and energetic learners. To do this, create a timeline on the floor across the room with three flipchart paper 'islands'.

Write NOW, EXAM and SUCCESS on the separate 'islands'.

Start with the group on NOW and create a great anticipatory state about the future for the students and anchor it with a sound and gesture. Devise a game with the students where they fill in the timeline with Post-It notes with all the activities and stages necessary to get success. Take the group to the SUCCESS island and build a really great state of what it feels like to succeed and anchor it.

(Check back to Chapter 11 for a reminder of how to do this). Have the group walk back to the EXAM island, taking the great feeling with them. Move them back to the NOW island while gathering all the resources they have from the future, bringing them into the here and now with the great feelings. Fire off the 'success' anchor in the present and connect it to the resources they have collected.

These two examples are designed for structured sessions. However, often a student becomes stuck or fearful in the middle of something else. In this situation, changes to the perception of time and success can be done conversationally to change the student's perception and feelings. By changing the tenses of the verb from future to present and from passive to active the experience of time changes too. Teachers tend to overuse the word 'will', which has the effect of pushing the experience into the future. It is more useful to push the resources into the past, so the student has them at their disposal and can bring the sense of achievement into the present.

Consider the effect of the following questions and statements:

- *What will you achieve tomorrow?*
- *As you leave class tomorrow what will you have achieved?*
- *Imagine yourself leaving the class tomorrow, now what have you achieved?*

The first question places the experience in the future. The second sentence places the experience in the future past and the third sentence brings the achievement into the present.

When a student is stuck or saying they can't do something it can be useful to physically move them away from the place where they are stuck and use a timeline conversationally to create a more resourceful state, as in the following example:

Ellen declares in the middle of the class that she just can't do the exercise. The teacher agrees with her, saying *'yes that's right Ellen, you can't do this yet'*. (Notice the teacher gains rapport by not arguing with the student or trying to convince them they can do it!) *'So come over here for a moment'* and the teacher leads her a few steps away from Ellen's seat. She then says, *'now just imagine for a moment how you would feel having completed this exercise; what a sense of satisfaction you now have, feeling really good that you have done it.'* (Building a feeling of confidence and success in the present) *'Just look back at yourself* (pointing at the chair) *and now that you have completed the task give the other Ellen some advice as to what she needs to do to succeed. What do you think would help first? After that what is next?'* Very quickly Ellen is finding the resources within herself to complete the task and it really only takes a minute or so. There are some other factors at play here too. By discussing 'Ellen's problem' in the third person, the student can disassociate from the unpleasant 'stuck' feeling while she thinks about the resources she needs to succeed.

It's worth stating that a person doesn't actually have a timeline! It's a useful metaphor for representing time to ourselves as a construct, so we are able to help our students overcome difficulties. Students find timelines great fun as well as a great resource. Once they understand the process a little, we often find that they begin to make use of the process for themselves.

PUTTING THINGS IN THE PAST
A similar process can be used to help students put in the past those experiences that have led them to believe that they can't do something, or are stupid, or will never be able to do something. Often, these beliefs come about because of a silly suggestion made by an unthinking adult with no intention of causing a lasting effect. However, sometimes they become limiting beliefs. If a student has failed in the past and believes they will fail in the future, it's a good idea to help them to understand that the best thing about the past is that it's over, and that just because they once believed something they don't have to now.

During a lesson observation, a very caring adult education tutor said to a group of nervous adult learners, *'now I know that you find exams difficult and stressful, don't worry though I am here to support you and no matter how hard you find it, it really isn't as hard as you think it will be'.* Even if the students had not been worrying, stressing and finding it difficult previously, they were now! The tutor meant well and really cared, but the meaning of the communication is the response you get! All this tutor needed to do was to put the past behind her students by saying, *'I know that some of you may have found exams tough in the past, but as you look back you can realise that it is over now that you are here with me you can find the experience easy and even enjoyable as you begin to learn how clever you are'*.

SPINNING BAD FEELINGS INTO GOOD FEELINGS

Many students have unpleasant feelings about school and college and some may become anxious or stressed by past experiences which they worry will recur in their lives. Neuro-Hypnotic Repatterning® (NHR) is one of the most powerful ways of changing long-held bad feelings into good ones. It works directly with the kinaesthetic, rather than using the other representational systems to change a person's experience. You will by now be familiar with this process from the chapters relating to state management.

To begin, ask the student to pay attention to the unpleasant feeling and notice how and where it moves in their body. Watch any hand gestures they make, as people often indicate with their hands where a feeling is and where it moves to. Notice the direction and ask the person to spin the feeling in that direction just for a moment so they become aware of the movement (often the feeling will intensify so only do this for a second or two). Next ask the student to take the feeling out of their body, put it in front of them and watch it spin, then begin to spin it in the opposite direction. Ask them to move the feeling back into the body and notice that the feeling has changed (often to the opposite feeling). Ask them to spin this good feeling faster until the student finds just the right intensity of feeling and starts to imagine carrying out the activity that they used to be anxious about in this new and comfortable state.

Here is the process illustrated:

There are a number of storybooks for younger children which use the NHR process in the story to help little people change bad feelings into lovely ones. Some of these books are listed in the bibliography.

Inappropriate behaviour can sometimes be a result of a lack of confidence or inability to deal with feelings. Here is how one NLP-trained tutor decided to work with a student whose swearing was getting very out of hand. The young man wrote about his experience and these are his words. When he first went to the college his literacy level was extremely low and he would not write anything, so we are reproducing his letter here to show you just how far a young person can progress personally and educationally with the right skilled teacher:

"At the beginning of the course of painting and decorating I was all right with my language but as the course progressed and I got to know people, they started taking the Mickey out of me and calling me names and I just started swearing at them... When Ivan [his tutor] took over he noticed me swearing a lot. One day he took me into his office and had a quiet word with me, saying I needed to calm it down or else I wouldn't get onto the next course and he helped me by saying change your swear words into fruits and vegetables. He did some stuff with me about standing in Wembley Stadium being Kaká [a football hero of his]. It made me feel really good and made me feel I could do lots more things than I could before. When my mates try and take the Mickey now I use the things that Ivan made me think about how good I am. It's working and I feel he has helped me to calm my swearing down. 5 weeks ago every other word I said was a swear word and now I hardly ever swear."*

FROM STUCK TO MOTIVATED WITH A VISUAL SQUASH

This is a great technique to help students to stop procrastinating. You can use this activity on a one-to-one basis or for a whole class. It can provide an alternative to the motivational speech teachers often feel necessary before an activity starts. You can experiment with this process in the following way: Have your students think about something they are really motivated to do and enjoy. Ask them to amplify the feeling (using spinning the feelings in the right direction) and notice where the image of the activity is in space. Suggest some of the submodalities of the representation, such as *'is it in colour'* and *'how big is it?'* Ask them to hold up their right hand and put the picture on the hand. Next ask them to make an image of the activity that they want to be motivated to do but aren't yet and put this image on their left hand. As they hold up their hands in front of them have them imagine pictures of all the steps they need to take to get to feel motivated about the activity. When they have all the steps laid out in sequence, have them slap their hands together and bring their hands to their chest to bring the good feeling inside.

SWISH FOR CHANGE

The Swish technique is very useful when people feel compelled to act in ways they don't want to. Try this for yourself so you have the experience and can help the students to change the way they feel and act. Make one image in your head of a behaviour or feeling you don't want to have and notice the submodalities of the image (see the list in the appendix if you want a reminder of the submodalities). Next make an image of the behaviour or feeling you do want and shrink it down to a small dark image and put it in the corner of the first image. Now shrink down the unwanted image to a small dark dot while you simultaneously bring up the wanted image, bright and bold so it completely covers the first image. Making a 'swish' sound helps!

This process can be adapted in many ways. Students can do this on their computers by creating images and manipulating them. Small children can put the images into balloons and send them off into space while making big bold pictures of new ways to be and pinning them to the walls. Here is an example of how activities can be adapted for younger children. Charlie is a 5-year-old whose mum thought he was school phobic. When Kate went to work with him, this turned out not to be the case; he just really wanted to play his favourite computer game in the mornings rather than get ready and go to school. He found the mornings very chaotic and he felt he didn't have any control over his little life, with everyone telling him what to do and what to eat and rushing him in the mornings. Once he was at school he settled very well, but the process of getting him there literally involved carrying him kicking and screaming. The first step was to encourage Charlie to draw what it was like in the mornings now. He said he didn't like that picture and so we screwed it up and put it in the bin. Then we asked him what he would like it to be like. Charlie decided that it would be good to get up 20 minutes earlier and have time to himself on his computer game, then he would feel ready to get himself ready to school. He felt that he was big enough to take responsibility for getting ready for school. Kate suggested he drew another picture. He immediately divided his page into 6 sections and drew each step of his perfect morning. It was bright, detailed and had timings on it. His mum agreed to leave him to his own devices for two weeks, even at the risk of being late for school. We colour copied the picture and laminated the sheets and Charlie placed them around the house to remind himself of his new strategy and the timings. The next morning Charlie was at school on time happily and with no fuss. Peace reigned again and continues to do so.

SUMMARY

During this chapter you have explored using timelines to motivate and engage learners by using the resources of the future in the present. You have discovered three other processes to adapt for use with your students to change states, feelings and behaviours and to boost motivation. We are sure that as you start to use the techniques of NLP you will create many more opportunities for your learners in the future.

REFERENCES

1. Attributed to Nelson Mandela President of South Africa from 1994 to 1999
2. Deborah Yurgelun-Todd (2007) Emotional and cognitive changes during adolescence. Curr Opin Neurobiol, Apr; 17

ACTIVITIES

Activity 1

Create a timeline with a group, adapting the method to suit the age group.

1. Start with the goal, and ask the students to create a poster and draw what success will be like for them (what pictures, sounds, feelings etc?). They all then stand with their poster and you ask them to 'look ahead' and imagine the future is in that space in front of them. Have them go and stand where the 'deadline' is (notice how many of them go a long way off!).

2. They can then place their 'success poster' in the place where they saw the deadline.

3. From the point where we have the present, ask them to consider bringing the deadline space closer and place the poster there. Ask them to notice the difference. For some students this is enough to get them wanting to make a start on steps towards achieving the goal.

4. Now have them walk to that space. Suggest that they are now reaching their goal.

5. Now ask them to go back to the present and look at the future again; the place on the timeline where their success poster is. Ask them what they need to do in the space that is between them and the poster. Let them suggest first steps. Use Meta Model questions to support their thinking at this stage and check for a well-formed outcome.

6. Now ask them to locate action steps on the timeline and anchor each 'step' to the timeline. Have them return to the present and re-connect with the goal, at each step looking back at the 'future past' and firing off the 'success' state to maintain motivation towards the goal. Remember: Build a state of success and confidence (or other required resourceful state) in the present and at each 'step' along the way.

Extension activities

What other whole class activities can you create around the techniques we have explored in this chapter? Which obstacles to achievement can you help your students to overcome by adapting and applying these ideas?

PART 4 - TROUBLESHOOTING AND CHALLENGE

CHAPTER 17

Strategies for Learning Difference

Scan this to see the videos

'Every child has an enormous drive to demonstrate competence' [1]

Buckminster Fuller

In this chapter

- Learning difference not difficulty
- Working with ADHD, Dyspraxia, Dyslexia, Autism and OCD
- How to teach to the symptom not the syndrome
- Explore neurological diversity

On every seminar we teach there are worried parents who want to know how to help children who have a diagnosis of a learning difficulty. The questions range from how to teach a dyslexic child to spell, to how to help an autistic child integrate into school, to general questions such as how to use NLP with Attention Deficit Hyperactivity Disorder (ADHD).

To address this vast subject completely will require another book. However, this chapter gives you some helpful ideas as to how you as a teacher or parent can help children with the proliferation of diagnoses now flooding the world of education. First, though, let's back up and discover what exactly is being talked about when we attach these labels to children, or to adults for that matter.

Discussions and concerns in schools often revolve around 'frustrating' or 'difficult' students. These learners are often identified as being fidgety, untidy, excitable, loud, attention-seeking, lacking in concentration, under-achieving, disorganised, or lacking motivation. Parents are often worried that their child doesn't seem to be doing as well as others and they are desperate to discover why this may be.

There seems to be an increasing desire to provide a label or diagnosis for children to explain away the behaviour, hence the list of syndromes and conditions seems to get longer and longer: Dyslexia, Dyspraxia, Attention Deficit Disorder, Attention Deficit Hyperactivity Disorder, Autistic Spectrum Disorder, Asperger's Syndrome, Emotional Behavioural Difficulty, to name just a few. The diagnostic process has advantages and disadvantages. Some children need the labels to afford them better learning support and they flourish, but others become limited by a label which can negatively affect their self-image and sense of identity. If you have struggled to learn something and, despite all your best efforts, you still can't do it, then having an explanation can help. However, it is not helpful if you have a label attached to you and people start to believe that things will always be this way and you can't learn new strategies.

In extreme cases, the label provides a smoke screen for lack of parenting skills or lack of creativity in teaching processes. It is also worth noting that in many countries, schools and colleges receive additional learning support to help manage the unruly child or perk up their performance statistics, which may provide some explanation for the explosion in diagnoses over the past few years.

Our approach differs from the norm in a number of key ways. Firstly, we prefer the term **Learning Difference** to Learning 'Difficulty' or 'Disability'. We prefer this term because, in our view, the problem is not a learning difficulty but a teaching difficulty. Humans are neurologically diverse and to some extent everyone is 'wired' differently. People vary from whatever the 'norm' is in widely different degrees. Differences, including learning differences, are to be celebrated and some learners simply learn and process information in an alternative way.

The onus is on us as educators and parents to discover how a child processes information, what strategies may work better for them, and to teach creative ways to overcome the hurdles and challenges each learner faces. It is much more helpful to think in terms of learning difference, recognising that humans are neurologically diverse and can learn new strategies and new skills to become exquisite learners in their own way.

Departments of Education in many countries put significant resources into supporting learners with learning difficulties, which is admirable. The problem is that support is often given to provide adjustment for the learner, rather than teaching an effective strategy. For example, some students who have difficulty reading are provided with a member of staff to read for them. This seems absurd, which is why our approach differs significantly from 'reasonable adjustment'. Our solution is to teach the student to read for themselves, rather than say if they can't read let someone else do it for it for them. Reading is not regarded as a high order skill. There are many examples of children and young people with many challenges who have learned to read and develop other mastery skills. At one time it was thought that children with Down's Syndrome could never read. This has fortunately been proved a myth and research shows that with the right interventions and strategies children with this genetic condition often access reading and move on to higher skills.[2] If a country can have a 98% literacy rate, it means many people with different brain wiring can achieve the foundation skill of reading for lifelong learning.[3]

There is a great deal of new research into neuro-diversity and the way brains are wired, which is very helpful to teachers in understanding and identifying how a student is failing to learn. There is conjecture as to why some people have brains that are wired differently, but it really isn't important for our purposes here. There is also much research into the neuroplasticity of the brain demonstrating that humans can continue to learn in adulthood.[4] So even if a person didn't get the help they required at school, it is never too late to start.

A further major difference in our approach, when using NLP to work with neurologically diverse learners, is to **teach to symptom**. This means that we identify what the learner can do and what the learner can't do yet as a means of finding a way that enables them to learn in a new way. The focus is on capability, not incapacity. As with all good NLP interventions, we start by asking ourselves and the learner some helpful questions, such as:

- What is the learner trying to achieve by this behaviour or strategy?
- What is his/her current strategy?
- Which bits of the current strategy work and which bits don't work so well?
- What can s/he do already that gives him/her the resources to achieve what s/he wants?
- What resources or skills doesn't s/he have yet that will help him/her?
- In what context would the current strategy or behaviour work to achieve something more useful?

We are often asked for guidance on how to work with children who have a learning difference such as Dyslexia, Dyspraxia or other 'disability' label. Our answer is, we will work with them in the same way as we would work with anyone else - applying the presuppositions and asking good questions to discover an effective strategy that works for the person.

Now let's take a look at some of common labels, what they mean and how we can help using NLP:

DYSLEXIA

According to the Oxford English Dictionary, the definition of Dyslexia is, *'A general term for disorders that involve difficulty in learning to read or interpret words, letters, and other symbols, but that do not affect general intelligence.'*

The term is commonly associated with spelling and reading while other factors such as directional and sequencing confusion, organisational problems, poor memory and visual sensitivity are also commonly associated with Dyslexia.

The difficulties a person experiences generally become the focus of attention, while the strengths and uniqueness of the person are missed. People with a diagnosis of Dyslexia often have excellent communication skills and a caring, empathic disposition. Some have high visual spatial awareness, good understanding of the workings of machinery, computers, circuitry, etc. Some are innovative, good trouble-shooters, creative and lateral thinkers, communicators and mediators. People with Dyslexia can be a great asset to an organisation and many are extremely successful in business. These skills and resources can easily be harnessed to overcome the challenges faced by a learner

A person with a dyslexic brain may have advantages that the rest of humanity does not. Certainly, they can cope with a degree of chaos that most of us would find daunting. Stress is often a part of the life of a dyslexic person. Constantly struggling to do tasks that others 'say' are easy, can cause stress and so dyslexic people learn to live with a level of stress others don't experience. It seems that they deal with moments of crisis much better than many of us. Winston Churchill (who many people believe had Dylsexia) was a supreme example of this. A further advantage is that a dyslexic may have no need to take notes and may be able to store their thoughts in wonderful vivid pictures in their head, creating a much fuller experience and great memory recall.

The key to helping someone who has wiring that works in a different way to the majority is to figure out a way to utilise the resources they have to solve the problem. If a person has auditory processing difficulties, they will have a great deal of difficulty in learning to read or spell by sounding out words. Most of us find this a challenge anyway, and it can be insurmountable for someone with this type of Dyslexia. On the other hand, they may well have fantastic visual spatial awareness, so the spelling strategy outlined in this book (Chapter 3) may be easy for them, especially if they link it to a really great feeling and a determination to succeed.

Often the difference between a poor speller and a dyslexic is stress. A poor speller may not be able to spell and doesn't necessarily care that much. A dyslexic may stress over their ability and hold a strong belief that because they are dyslexic they cannot spell, and it becomes a huge obstacle to learning for them. It makes sense that anyone who keeps trying to do something but just can't find a way to succeed could be stressed out. So it's a good idea to deal with the stress up front and use strategies to relax and remove any tension that could get in the way of effective learning. Once a person relaxes and any limiting belief is doubted and removed, the spelling or reading becomes simply a matter of the right strategy. This works both ways. Success in the strategy can change a person's beliefs about their identity.

Terry is a senior HR manager with a Dyslexia diagnosis and he was convinced that he couldn't learn to spell because of his Dyslexia. Kate persuaded him to suspend his disbelief just for the sake of an experiment, convincing him that the outcome didn't matter either way because we were just playing with strategies. Once he had learned to spell one word he realised that using a visual strategy was much easier for him. Whenever Terry wrote to Kate subsequently he signed himself 'Terry Restaurant' after learning to be confident in spelling this word after 40 years of using 'café' as an alternative!

Remember Louise, the lady we taught to spell in 15 minutes at a seminar (Chapter 3)? She had been labelled dyslexic many years before. The first word she chose to spell was 'administered'. She was a nurse and had for years avoided writing 'administered' in patient notes, writing 'given' instead. When she learned to spell 'administered' quickly and easily, she said, *'why haven't I been able to figure this out for myself?'* This is a fairly typical response - she believed she was stupid for not being able to work it out. When we responded that it wasn't her responsibility and it was just that no one had shown her how, a very big belief about herself also changed for the better.

Reading is often even more of a challenge than spelling for people diagnosed with Dyslexia. Light sensitivity can make the words dance on the page, reverse some letters and jumble others. Sometimes very simple solutions work well. For instance, tipping the reading material to a 45 degree angle (like the old school desks) helps reduce glare, as do coloured overlays. Certainly, black on white print is one of the most difficult to decipher, while blue on cream is much easier on the eye.[5]

Sometimes more creative solutions need to be developed. One lady reported that she felt as if she had two sets of eyes; one set inside her head and the other opposite her. One set was associated and the other was disassociated and she flicked between both sets of eyes, which made reading very hard. Using her NLP skills she brought both sets of eyes to the same side of the book so they were looking at the same angle. She could immediately read easily. She now runs courses teaching this simple technique and has a great deal of success with children using the simple instruction, *'before you begin to read bring both sets of eyes around this side of the table'*.

To summarise, if the problem is to do with an inability to learn something then ask:

- What is it the learner is trying to achieve?
- How are they not doing it?
- Are there parts of what they are doing that are useful and work? (We want to keep these parts)
- Is there a strategy that we know about that will probably work?
- If not, what strategy can we create with this person that may work? And finally, keep going until the person is in a happy place - and if it doesn't work, be tenacious and try something else!

DYSPRAXIA

The Oxford English Dictionary defines Dyspraxia as a *'developmental disorder causing difficulty in activities requiring coordination and movement'*. It was known as the 'Clumsy Child Syndrome' at one time. There are many overlaps within these learning differences and Dyspraxia is often associated with Dyslexia and Attention Deficit Disorder. Essentially, children with this label don't seem to be totally 'in' their bodies. They don't understand what to do and how to do it and a dyspraxic child may be seen running with feet splayed and hands flapping, shoelaces undone and buttons out of sequence. They may have difficulty tracking text and be sensitive to light, sound and texture. They are typically persistent and determined, empathic and caring, and have good auditory skills.

There is depressingly little practical help available to these children other than 'reasonable adjustment'. That term means making allowances instead of providing strategies that help them to get on with their lives and build on their numerous strengths.

Joe had a lot of difficulty co-ordinating his body and staying balanced. He described it like this, *'when I put my foot down I don't really know where it will stop'*. He had problems knowing where his body ended. Fortunately, he was a very persistent little boy and we designed a set of movements combined with strong visualisations to help him to know where the ground was and how to correct his balance when his foot hit the ground.

There is some evidence that promoting gross motor movements helps to develop fine motor movements such as writing, which is helpful for dyspraxic brains. Physical activities such as Brain Gym, which promotes a series of exercises claimed to improve academic performance, also seem valuable. Danny had a very bad accident which caused a significant damage to his brain. He was an amazing character who had overcome enormous difficulties before he came to us. He had learned to walk and talk again and was functioning very well. However, his writing was very cramped and listed to one side of the page. By using a series of BIG movements, in the form of shapes which crossed the midline of his body and practising infinity loops, Danny started to even out his writing. The infinity loop or 'lazy 8' (a figure of eight on its side) incorporates all the shapes and movements needed to write, so the exercises trained Danny's brain to make the *'write'* movements in the right proportions to make his writing clearer.

ATTENTION DEFICIT HYPERACTIVITY DISORDER

A worrying development over the past few years is the increased diagnosis of Attention Deficit Disorder (ADD) and Attention Deficit Hyperactivity Disorder (ADHD), especially in the USA. In 2011, 11% of children had a diagnosis of one of these conditions in the USA and there appear to be higher clusters in some US states. The number of children diagnosed increased from 9% in 2009 to 11% in 2011 and as the number of diagnoses grew, increasing numbers of children and young people were prescribed Methylphenidate – a central nervous system stimulant prescribed under various trade names including Ritalin. (6) On the other hand, in France the percentage of ADHD diagnosis remains at less than 5%. It would seem that French doctors prefer to view ADHD within a social rather than medical context.

Pamela Druckerman, a Paris-based journalist who wrote 'Bringing Up Bébé: One American Mother Discovers the Wisdom of French Parenting', observes that French parents love their children just as much as American parents. They give them piano lessons, take them to sports practice, and encourage them to make the most of their talents. But French parents have a different philosophy of discipline. Consistently enforced limits, in the French view, make children feel safe and secure. Clear limits, they believe, actually make a child feel happier and safer. Finally, French parents believe that hearing the word "no" rescues children from the "tyranny of their own desires."(7)

The definition of ADD and ADHD in the Oxford English Dictionary is, *'any of a range of behavioural disorders occurring primarily in children, including such symptoms as poor concentration, hyperactivity and learning difficulties'*. We are concerned that these 'conditions' have become a dumping ground for any child who has difficulty being in charge of their own mind.

This is not the place to discuss the medical profession's clinical decisions, but there is evidence that whilst bad parenting doesn't cause ADHD, good parenting can mitigate the excesses of ADHD behaviour.(8)
The routine that our Grandmother would recognise of regular bedtimes, plenty of fresh air and exercise, three meals a day, limited snacks and limited access to TV and new technology, especially at night, works well for lots of children. We are not advocating that this is the only strategy for a child with ADHD, but it would seem sensible to explore all alternative routes before administering a very powerful drug to a child.

Of course, all of these measures are frameworks to help with ADHD and ADD. However, NLP is the study of subjective experience, so our approach is to understand what is happening with a child on the inside. Typically, children with ADHD don't appear to listen to instructions, or respond instantly and sometimes fidget inappropriately in class.

Michael, aged 13, was asked, *'what are you thinking about when the teacher is talking?'* He replied that he was thinking about football, then rollerblading, then about a film he had seen. Observing him and asking him 'how' he thought about these things, it was clear that he made lots of pictures which flitted from one to another rapidly. By picking one picture and changing the submodalities so this image was big and bright and still, he learned to focus his attention on just one thought for longer and calm his thinking.

Children with ADHD often need strategies to manage their impulsivity. It isn't that other children don't want to get up and run around the classroom, it's just that the child with ADHD does it! Simple suggestions such as providing a timescale for sitting and listening, say 2 minutes, and then guidance as to what will happen next, *'then you can go and bring the yellow file from my desk',* provides a child with a short timeline so they can defer the impulse to act, knowing they are going to do something else in 2 minutes. Children with symptoms of ADHD have wonderfully creative minds that they just can't control. Teaching the NLP processes of managing the submodalities of their thoughts unleashes their creative talents and potential to be successful and happy adults.

AUTISM
Autism and Asperger's Syndrome are typically included in the term Autistic Spectrum Disorder.

The dictionary definition is, *'a mental condition present from early childhood, characterised by great difficulty in communicating and forming relationships with other people and in using language and abstract concepts'.*

The range of behaviours associated with Autism means that teaching to symptom becomes even more important. Many people with Autism function perfectly well, whereas others face many challenges and require constant care. Many children with profound Autism will repetitively bang their heads against a wall. The usual response to this is to pad the walls, which stops damage but doesn't do anything for the behaviour. We observed carers working with children on the Autistic Spectrum pacing and mirroring repetitive behaviours. This mirroring behaviour allowed the children to begin to establish rapport and connect with the carers.

If the carer mirrored the behaviour in a different way, such as tapping their hand at the same speed and tempo as the child was banging, the child would begin to respond to the adult. This seems to make sense; the child is doing something to achieve something and when the adult participates in this s/he is beginning to enter the world of the child and building a level of rapport that the child does not normally experience. From this point of connection, carers can begin to lead the child into better ways of achieving what they want.

Children on the Autistic Spectrum or identified with Asperger's Syndrome are often uncomfortable with change and new situations. Finding ways for a child to repeat an experience until it becomes comfortable can help a great deal. One very enlightened headteacher worked with the teacher and parents of a little boy with Autism, to create a miniature classroom at home, including a miniature whiteboard, desks and chairs. At the end of the school day, the little boy could go home and repeat the day by acting it out over and over. As he repeated the day he became familiar with his experiences and so he could relax and feel comfortable. In this way, as he integrated his experience from one day, he found that he could face each new day without fear and be confident that he was ready for a new experience.

Sometimes the problem is not with learning something new, but with inappropriate behaviour. In this case, we ask what is the person trying to achieve with this behaviour? It may be comfort or attention or escape. The next step is to find a way for the person to achieve this in a more fruitful way. Richard was asked to see a little boy with Autism. The boy spent a great deal of time in a cupboard under the stairs. His parents desperately tried to coax him out of his hideaway. Richard did the opposite. He made the cupboard the most comforting and cosy place with cushions and favourite toys. Then he sat down with the parents and chatted.

After a little while the door of the cupboard opened and a little later a giggle came from inside. The boy's mother said it had been years since her son had giggled. It was a question of finding a way for the little boy to achieve what he was after, and when he had achieved this he was able to move forward because now his strategy for finding comfort and safety worked.

Although we have used the usual labels for learning disabilities in this chapter, it is our opinion that learning difference is very individual and the only way to ensure success is to truly listen and observe the child and the family interactions. Here is a case study documented by Kay Cooke, a member of the NLP Education Team, which researches NLP in teaching and learning. It illustrates just how applying the principles and processes outlined here can swiftly and easily change the behaviour of a child. Kay writes:

James was 8-years-old, newly diagnosed with ADHD and was running amok. His mother ran after him. He led the pace. Parents and teachers imposed their rules. The little boy refused to be harnessed.

Mum 'told' him that playing on the laptop would be fun for him while we talked. He point blank refused, mum pleaded with him and the teacher rolled her eyes.

We intervened and told him about a really cool game for big lads on the laptop, but didn't think he would be interested – of course he was. Whilst playfully chatting, we elicited a state of curiosity in James (what would it feel, look, sound like?), then frustration (at not being old enough to play), and then finally, when James' full attention was in one place, we rewarded him with the game, holding his attention further with questions that engaged 'his' interest in the game.

James was engrossed until we noticed (calibrated) subtle non-verbal 'alert/alarm' signals. It was evident that these were minimal cues coinciding with his teacher detailing all the **'problems'** this child had. We clarified with James that he didn't like to hear what was 'wrong' with him and suggested that the teacher instead explained (re-framed) what she would like James to be doing instead (Well-Formed Outcomes).

Techniques we used during the meeting also included

- Respecting his map of the world and what was true for him
- Pacing his reality to build rapport
- Calibrating his responses to his environment
- Leading him through a chain of useful states that engaged attention
- Anchored the attention with rewards (that met his values)
- Directing his motivation towards what he wanted rather than away from what he didn't want (familiar to him)

When a teacher focuses on the 'difficulty in dealing with the situation', he/she becomes ineffective because the situation has become all about him or her. On the other hand, when a teacher makes the situation all about the individual learning requirements of a learner, s/he becomes both effective and helpful to the learner.

One grandparent said to us, *'they tell me my grandson has ADHD and poor memory processing, yet he can spell and pronounce every name of every football player (including complicated foreign names) in the Champion's League. How come?'*

It is not about finding out 'why', but following the clues and asking HOW does he memorise these names? What is his strategy for this, compared with his spelling list in class? What do the submodalities of his experiences reveal? Which states bring him the fastest results? Once we figure out 'how' a learner does something well, we get to the heart of their learning needs.

The way a person processes information and their associated behaviours are useful in some context, even if they are not useful in the context at the moment. For example, it may be unhelpful for a person with Obsessive Compulsive Disorder to wash their hands 100 times a day, but if the OCD is focused in the right direction then it becomes an asset. If you are a musician and your obsession is to practise for 7 hours a day you will become a very good musician. There are many examples of extremely successful people who channel their OCD into productive areas. Often the first thing we do with people with OCD is get them to make long lists of all the things they must do each day. On the list are activities such as recalling 5 relaxing situations, 4 happy memories, smiling 7 times before leaving the house. We utilise their OCD to promote their wellbeing and happiness.

We work with many parents and teachers who seem to prefer to bring in the experts rather than develop their own skills to help their child. One important message to parents and teachers is **you are the experts in this child**. By all means get advice, learn new ways of working with your child, but remember that ultimately it is in you they trust.

One family we met had two children with almost all the learning difficulty diagnoses between them. They had extra Maths and English tutors, specialist behaviourists, movement and balance classes as well as the usual extra-curricula activities. Dad had taken an NLP Practitioner course and decided to include this in their 'therapy' too. After only 30 minutes observing the children in the house with their parents it become very clear that:

- The only way the children could get attention was to 'have a difficulty', an emotional outburst or some other heart-rending problem. The rest of the time they didn't require any attention.
- The children thought they were broken and needed fixing and that it was someone else's responsibility to do this.
- The children thought that until they were fixed they would not live up to their parents' expectations of them.
- The children knew their parents were disappointed, worried and illequipped to raise them and needed experts to help them.
- The parents became the main focus of the intervention. We refused to do the work with their children for them and, with a great deal of support initially, we taught the parents the strategies to help their own children themselves. There were some key messages: Your children are normal. You are the experts in your children and they are your responsibility. Pay attention to them when they are doing all the right things and reward them for this behaviour. Lastly and most importantly, enjoy your children and have fun with them.

SUMMARY

The stories of the children and adults in this chapter demonstrate that the same processes we have explained in this book so far apply equally to **all learners**. The range of neurological diversity means each and every one of us has the capacity to understand and enter the reality of another person, however different they may at first appear to be, and can learn from the experience. When we look and listen and teach to the symptoms, great advances in learning can be made with all learners.

REFERENCES

1. Buckminster Fuller, Presentation to U.S. Congressional Subcommittee on World Game 1969
2. Buckley SJ, Bird G. 1993 Teaching children with Down Syndrome to read. Down Syndrome Research and Practice.
3. UNESCO Institute for Statistics (UIS) (statistical office of UNESCO and is the primary UN depository for cross-nationally comparable statistics on education, science and technology, culture, and communication covering more than 200 countries and territories.)
4. Rakic, P. (January 2002). "Neurogenesis in adult primate neocortex: an evaluation of the evidence". Nature Reviews Neuroscience
5. British Dyslexia Association http://www.bdadyslexia.org.uk
6. The MTA Cooperative Group: A 14-Month randomized clinical trial of treatment strategies for attention-deficit/hyperactivity disorder (ADHD) . Arch Gen Psychiatry 1999; 56: 1073-1086.
7. Druckerman, Pamela, 2012, Bringing Up Bébé: One American Mother Discovers the Wisdom of French Parenting, Penguin. Published in the U.K. as: French Children Don't Throw Food, Doubleday.
8. Centres for Disease Control and Prevention, http://www.cdc.gov

ACTIVITIES

Activity 1

Using your creativity and curiosity, find a person in your circle of family or friends who is particularly neurologically diverse from you; someone who can do something that you can't or has ways of thinking that are very different from you. Elicit their strategy for doing something inside their head that you couldn't do and try on their strategy and way of thinking. Admire the differences. What have you learned?

Activity 2

Ask this person if there is something that they would like to do better. Elicit their current strategy and compare it with your strategy. How might you go about teaching this person in a way that matches their learning needs?

Scan this to see the videos

PART 5

NLP FUN
IN SCHOOLS

This section provides real life action research and case studies by teachers, education managers and learning support staff who are applying NLP with their learners in the classroom, school or college. The case studies are written in their own words and from their level of experience, although we have edited the material for consistency and clarity.

The teachers have all had some NLP training. Some, including those who participated in the Durham and Northumberland projects, had just two days training before they began to make changes in the classroom. Other teachers have completed the NLP Practitioner for Education or the Master Practitioner for Education and Teaching Excellence programme. It is evident from the case studies that even a small amount of NLP training can deliver real results and impact for teachers and their learners. Some of the following are single strategy case studies, while others are more indepth studies demonstrating a range of NLP skills applied to the subject area.

The chapters are organised by age group so it is easy for you to find examples that apply to your learners. However, many of the examples apply across the age range and you may want to read beyond one age group and use your creativity to apply the experience in your own practice. A further section relates to education management. Each case study indicates the level of training of the teacher.

CODING SYMBOLS

Between 2 and 4 days training

NLP Practitioner

NLP Master Practitioner and Teaching Excellence

CHAPTER 18

Early Years: Under 5-years-old

Teachers and Learning Support Assistants in Early Years Education have many approaches they intuitively use which are closely aligned with NLP. Their focus on pleasurable states and enjoyment is an important lesson for all teachers. We have not as yet had many teachers working in this age group qualify in NLP, but the short case studies below from the Durham and Northumberland projects show their enthusiasm for the subject and learning more.

CHANGING SUBMODALITIES TO OVERCOME ANXIETY AND CREATE HAPPY STATES

Changing the internal experience using submodalities and visualising outcomes works with even very small children.

Erica Tait teaches at Malvin's Close Primary Academy in Blyth, Northumberland

Research Plan

During our NLP training, I was particularly fascinated with how visualisation techniques linked to anchoring could have such a positive impact upon a person's emotional state and their own perceptions. Therefore I wanted to see whether I could initiate such strong responses within my own practice in the classroom environment.

Action

After speaking to her parents after school, it was identified that A was getting really upset and worried at home for no apparent reason that the parent could see. It was evident that she had no coping strategies for dealing with her emotions after specific events at home and school.

I chose a time in the classroom where we would not be disturbed by other children and decided to use the Submodality Comparison Checklist to gain a greater insight to A's own feelings and perceptions when she got upset. I felt it was vital that I didn't ask her too many questions about why she was upset, instead focusing on an approach to cope with her feelings in difficult times. First of all she thought of a sad experience. She said she could see a room straight in front of her eyes, and that it was very dim with 'pointy bits'. She also used her arms to represent something heavy pushing her down. After that we focused on a positive experience and her face immediately lit up. She said she could see a photo of her friends which was yellow and bright. She looked up to her left slightly when she was speaking to me. She also said there were giggling noises, which made her laugh. I brought the picture closer to her face and she immediately laughed, which gave her a bit of a shock! We then discussed the benefit of the feeling and how she could use this picture/feeling when she felt that she couldn't cope with a sad feeling at home or at school.

Impact

For the rest of the week she caught my eye and looked at the direction of the picture and smiled. Two days later her mum came in to tell me that she had changed at home in the evenings. A had even told her mum that she had her own picture that made her feel warm inside. A week later she even managed to sort out a disagreement with a group of friends by saying, *'I can help us; I like it when we are happy. I know I make them feel warm like friends can'*.

NLP has enabled A to express her emotions much more at home, and has given her the confidence to tackle new or uncomfortable situations in a positive way as opposed to how she coped before.

As a teacher I have become a great deal more confident when dealing with difficult children or situations, and I believe this is solely due to the experience I have had using NLP methods.

SMALL CHANGES IN LANGUAGE TO CREATE A BIG IMPACT

Laura Holland teaches at Mowbray First School, Choppington, Northumberland

Research Plan
I became very interested in discovering the impact I could have by introducing some small changes in the way I spoke to my pupils. The child referred to as P is a 5-year-old boy in my Year 1 class. I had begun to notice that P, who had been diagnosed as having Type 1 Diabetes at the end of his Reception year, was lacking motivation towards his written work. As a result, the work that he was producing was of a poor quality in comparison to other pupils of the same ability.

Through my first experience of NLP I became aware of how the use of my own language when responding to his work was impacting on his attitude towards his writing in independent tasks. He responded well to visual rewards such as stickers but the verbal feedback was not having the same effect, even though I felt that I was responding in a positive way. I hoped that changing a few words around would encourage a more consistent and positive attitude towards learning.

Action
I am sure that many practitioners in the primary sector will be familiar with the concept of 'Two stars and a Wish' as a child's technique for self-assessment.

Previously, when responding to P's work, I would always start with the positive aspects, for example; whether he had achieved the success criteria, good content or use of vocabulary. I would follow this with *'but' (your handwriting is untidy, you haven't put your capital letters in the right place, you have no full stops etc)*. Learning about language techniques through NLP showed me how phrasing the language in this way and using 'but' following the positive language was in fact erasing all the praise and left the focus on the negative.
I changed the order of the phrases around 'but' and adding 'and' such as: *'You missed out your full stops and forgot to use a capital letter for the proper nouns but your handwriting is excellent and you have used some really creative story words...'*

Impact
I found I had a different child in my class; one who was motivated and eager to produce good work, and who took pride in what he did. I

became more self-aware of how I used language to assess the work of other children and made a conscious effort to ensure that I made use of 'and' and 'but' in a more constructive and positive way. This impacted on all children with regard to their motivation and pride in how they responded to and presented their work. 'And' and 'but', are small words that have proved themselves to be powerful and influential tools in the classroom. Through my research project, I have seen the way in which they can motivate children to learn and take pride in what they have done, which only serves to boost their confidence and make them eager to achieve well.

LANGUAGE PATTERNS WITH CHILDREN WITH LITTLE ENGLISH LANGUAGE
Changes in language impact on very young children even those whose first language is not English.

Julia Quinn works in the Foundation Stage Unit, Framwellgate Moor Primary School, Durham

Research Plan
After the first 2 days of NLP training I decided to focus on a little boy, who I will call G, who had quite severe behavioural problems. He understood very little English, was extremely bright and had been moved about a lot. He had only been in our school for a couple of months. My focus was on helping him to settle and be less excitable, while not damping down his natural exuberance. At the time of the research, his English speech was not very clear. I wanted to see if he could be helped by NLP techniques and more one-to-one attention.

Action
I helped him to imagine a boy who was really good friends with everyone, and made his daddy happy every day (he is extremely close to Dad who brings him to school). I also used stickers with him and he really WANTED those stickers! I had thought perhaps he was too intelligent to be 'bribed' but I was wrong. I made it more specific and worked on him producing 'desired states' by saying what the sticker was for, for example, sitting down properly, crossing legs, not hurting friends etc., and he understood that too.

Impact
We all worked extremely hard to praise G at all times and to be aware of our use of language when working with him. G improved considerably.

MUSIC AND STATE MANAGEMENT
A number of Early Years teachers focused on the use of music and anchoring. Here is a summary of their projects:

Joni White works with Reception children at Framwellgate Moor Primary School, Durham

Research plan
Creating positive learning states is very important to me as I work in the Early Years age group. This is a time when children should be developing good learning strategies and an enjoyment of learning and school life. Pupils are developing curiosity and a thirst for learning without fear of failure, feeling safe and secure enough to make mistakes and gain from all activities they encounter. To achieve these aims I planned a five-step process:

a. Assess the pupils' current state of mind at key moments throughout the day. Identify times of the day where the classroom state could be improved.

b. Trial pieces of music at different times of the day for different purposes. Consider factors such as pace and rhythm of music, volume level and whether the music has words.

c. Record the 'feeling' of the state of the classroom during the different pieces of music.

d. Reflect each day upon which pieces of music were successful at which points during the day and consider why.

e. Create a bank of music that is suitable for key points during a day and record it on planning.

Action

I used my laptop computer as the images which appear on the interactive whiteboard are also very useful in creating an atmosphere. These images move and rotate in accordance with the music being played. The success criteria for the project were that:

- Pupils would have a positive state of mind ready for learning
- The level of pupil noise would be lower
- Pupils' learning would be encouraged

A positive response from the pupils on how they felt about different pieces of music would also be considered. The timescale for the project was initially one month. To implement my project I began by looking at key times in the day when pupils' state was not appropriate for learning. The key times I identified were:

- Children entering the classroom in the morning
- Children returning from outdoor activity
- Children returning from lunch
- Children tidying the classroom
- Children getting changed for PE
- Children preparing for home time

I began to find particular pieces of music caused a different response from the ones I anticipated. One fast piece of music I selected for tidying up caused a frantic state of mind. I had thought the piece would make the children tidy up quicker and be ready to begin work. Instead, it made them tidy frantically and when they sat down they were still very unsettled and not engaging with the learning for at least the first 5 minutes of the lesson.

During one handwriting session I decided to look at how music would affect the engagement of the learner if it was played while they were working. I chose a classical instrumental piece as I didn't want the music to disturb the children. I chose handwriting as I decided it wasn't a task that needed a great deal of active concentration in comparison to something like addition, where children need to count and often calculate out loud. The music really seemed to help the children to focus upon the task, and it really helped them to carry out their task more quickly. As this had succeeded, I used it the following week in the same lesson.

I am currently in the process of putting together all the most useful music tracks I have onto one CD with a note beside each track regarding the influence the music 'should' have. I will regularly use this CD with my new Reception class.

Impact
The improved 'state' of the class after the use of music has had the most influence upon my keenness to change my approach, and I intend to feed back to all of the staff in our school on the benefits of using music in the classroom for changing pupils' state. I believe this is something I would like to investigate further to consider other learning which could be influenced by music.

USING ESTABLISHED MUSICAL ANCHORS

Louise Lightly teaches at Wansbeck First School, Ashington, Northumberland

Research Plan
When deciding upon the focus for my learning I thought about the issues I felt were causing disruption within the classroom for the children, as well as thinking about which times of the day I felt most stressed out by the children's behaviour and the lack of routine.

Action
I decided to trial a piece of music at tidy-up time at the end of a session in order to aid the children to tidy up quietly, co-operatively and responsibly. I wanted the music to act as an anchor which would tell the children that it was time to tidy up and encourage them to do so in a positive way. I discussed with the children what they felt good tidying would look like in our classroom. They said many of the things I hoped, such as *quiet, sensible, quick, no silliness*. I then introduced them to my chosen piece of music taken from the Disney film, The Sorcerer's Apprentice. We discussed what this piece of music made them feel. We used this piece of music for the first week of the trial

and to begin with the children responded well. However, after a few days the children went back to their old ways of not tidying up quickly or sensibly. We then tried music from the Harry Potter films and the children said they would be able to do 'magic' tidying. However, I found that when I played this music many of the children got over-excited and this resulted in a noisy and distracting atmosphere.

I spent some time discussing my learning with my colleagues and the nursery teacher suggested I trialed the tidy-up music my colleagues used in the Nursery class.

Impact

The first time I used this music I didn't discuss it with the children; when they heard it they recognised it as the nursery tidy-up music and instantly responded to it. I believe that this is due to the strong anchor created during their time in Nursery - the children still related the piece of music to tidying up.

I intend to use this music in September with my new Reception class. I am now working more closely with the Nursery team to ensure continuity in the music we use within Foundation Stage classrooms. This is something which I am hoping to discuss implementing throughout the rest of school.

CREATIVE USE OF SPATIAL ANCHORING IN THE CLASSROOM
Rachael extends the range and scope of anchors for tidying up, home time and conflict resolution.

Rachael Coull teaches at Northburn Primary School, Cramlington, Northumberland

Research plan

My focus is on the use of anchoring and the impact this has on behaviour.

Throughout the project my aim is for the children to become more aware of expectations in relation to behaviour at specific points in the Nursery session. Because of more explicit expectations and increased consistency between staff, it is hoped the children's behaviour will improve, which will offer them greater opportunity to access the curriculum.

During my morning Nursery class, since the January intake the behaviour of some children had become increasingly challenging, especially at times where it was necessary to gain whole class attention and calm in order to carry out a routine task such as home time or tidy-up time.

Action

Initially, I pinpointed two particular times where the class was not as calm or organised as I would have liked. I already use a countdown technique in order to get whole class attention when they are in the middle of play. Although this worked for the majority, there were still some children who consistently did not follow this routine and would carry on playing or chatting, making it a more lengthy process than it needed to be. The other main time was home time, which had become a pretty stressful occasion – trying to give out pictures, asking the children to remain seated and calling out their names to dismiss them. I decided to carry on using my countdown technique as this was already partly successful so I set about designating a specific spot to stand in when I wanted to gain the class' attention.

I chose one spot inside and another outside (which became the "tidy-up time spot"). The more I used this technique, the quicker the children reacted and the less I had to say. After a couple of weeks of using the spot outside I would put my hand in the air, say *'five'* and the children began to run to where I was standing and sit down on the floor, ready for their tidy-up task.

As this anchor became embedded, I watched other staff use the same technique but in random positions and saw it to be less successful, with some children taking a long time to respond and some not even coming to the spot. As I made my intentions explicit to the other staff, they began to take on this concept and also saw the benefits, also introducing their own ideas. One day, because the children had spilt water on the area we usually stop at, I stood a couple of metres away and used the same technique and the children still responded quickly, however instead of coming to sit in a group, they all came and sat in a perfect circle. I later discovered that the previous day, the TA in my class had gathered the children in that spot to play some ring games – they had in fact created their own anchor, which we continued to use successfully for that purpose.

As for home time, I decided to anchor the experience with music – initially making my intentions clear to the children, telling them what behaviour I would see and why before turning on the music. This process was a little more gradual and I never fully established the "ideal golden silence", however this time proved to be a lot calmer than previously. The children were able to receive their pictures more quickly, hear their names being called more easily, and the parents were visibly impressed, commenting on the calm and peacefulness as they entered Nursery at home time, and the staff felt less stressed.

As these anchors became embedded, others followed, including the "rant and rave chair" - a stool which I only sat on when I was "feeling a little bit cross!" and needed to talk to the class as a whole. I was unsure whether this particular anchor would have as much effect as the others because only on rare occasions does the class need to be addressed as a whole in relation to behaviour. However, after only using this technique a couple of times in a four-week period all I have to do now is sit on the stool in front of the children, their faces drop and there is silence as one child asks, *'are you feeling a bit sad?'*

A further anchor which came about throughout this project as a team effort, was to help deal with children in conflict situations as and when they happened. The anchor came in the form of 3 chairs placed in a triangle formation. The two children sit facing each other and the third chair is for a member of staff to mediate between the two. Again, this technique quickly became embedded, with some children at times going to get their own chair when they realised they had done something wrong! The main benefit of this technique is that the children appear to calm down more quickly after an incident and, through structured questioning and discussion, are able to resolve conflict. I found that children were increasingly able to own up to what happened and seek a resolution acceptable to themselves, meaning they did not quite as readily go and do the same thing again.

Impact

Throughout the project there has been a great positive impact on the staff and children. Routine tasks throughout the session are carried out in a more focused manner and the children's behaviour at these times has improved. Along with this, staff are able to deal with situations in a calmer manner and are more explicit about the reasons for doing things and this has made us as a team more focused on what we want to achieve and how.

CHAPTER 19

Primary and Elementary School, 5 to 11-year-olds

SUBJECT-SPECIFIC TEACHING STRATEGIES
The Primary education sector provides a wealth of experience and good practice in applying NLP. It was difficult to choose from so many really excellent projects, so here is an inspiring selection:

A WHOLE CLASS STRATEGY FOR SPELLING
This project demonstrates how NLP can be applied to spelling with amazing results in a whole class situation and has made the Durham Project famous around the world

"Maybe with NLP techniques we can have parents queuing up to send their children to our school"

Headteacher

Andrea Pearson and Kelly Field work with Y4 at Framwellgate Moor Primary School, Durham

Research Plan
Spelling had always been taught in a structured way throughout the week and I felt the attainment in spelling could be improved by implementing simple changes in the approach, and using the ideas put forward during our NLP course.

Some children struggle when learning spellings so strategies need to be found and employed which work for them. I felt I was doing my utmost to support the children and if my approaches did not suit particular learners, they needed to be changed or adapted.

Within school we worked closely together to ensure that ideas were used with all pupils, including those with special educational needs, and we were able to discuss ideas and plans.

We had the full support of the Headteacher, including time given for analysis.

The aims of our project were to:
- Find more effective approaches to teach spelling
- Ensure pupils would learn and retain spellings more easily

We planned a 3-week project using the weekly spelling activities as a focus. We decided to make small changes each week to the structured approach, and to test the children each time so we could measure the impact. The spellings would be scored out of 8, and our success criteria were:
- To improve the full mark score
- To improve the 'more than 5 out of 8' score

Action
WEEK 1 - BASELINE
- Spellings were given as usual. A spelling test was carried out and the

results were used as a baseline for the research.

- Spelling pattern was 'i before e'

WEEK 2 - START OF PROJECT
- Spellings were written on the right hand side (from the children's point of view) of the whiteboard with the spelling pattern written in a ***different colour***, eg., chan**ge** / **ge**rm
- Children copied the spellings in their spelling logs using coloured felt tips to show the spelling pattern
- Children worked in pairs, spelling out letter by letter - 'spell change... c..h..a..n..g..e..' - other child jots down spelling
- Children wrote spellings in handwriting books (joined script)
- Children used Look, Cover, Write, Check sheets and wrote **'ge'** in a colour. Children encouraged to look upwards to recall the 'look' of the spelling - 'can you see the word?'
- Spelling test

WEEK 3
- Spellings were written on the right hand side (from the children's point of view) of the whiteboard with the spelling pattern written in a different colour. The children all moved seats during the spelling session to allow all a direct ahead view to the whiteboard.
- Children were given fragranced felt tips to record the spelling pattern, eg., giant engine
- Because the children with special educational needs did not seem to be responding to the changes introduced so far – ie., their scores were not particularly changing - they were given spellings on cards with the target blend highlighted in textured materials (net, corrugated card, bubble wrap, string, and fur)
- Spelling test

Impact
Below is the data illustrating the changes in the pupils' spelling scores, and there are a number of conclusions we have come to as a result of the project and analysis of the scores
- The evidence has proved so overwhelming that this strategy can make a huge difference to a child's ability to memorise spellings
- An awareness of eye accessing cues, where to place the spellings, how and where to ask children to visualise words etc., also improved their ability to remember spellings.
- The extra time element involved when using these activities is minimal (with the SEN (special educational needs) group being the exception, but it would be manageable).
- Because they were changing the pen within each word, the children were more focused when learning spellings.
- This will have an impact on the teaching of spelling within our school. Many of the problems some children had retaining new spellings will be addressed.
- The added effect will be a much more open and flexible approach to the teaching of a range of primary curriculum content.
- The use of test results and observation gave the most appropriate forms of evidence with which to analyse the effect of implementing these approaches.

	% Full Score	% Over 5 correct
Week 1	18	46
Week 2	66	81
Week 3	71	92-5

VARIATIONS IN THE TOTAL NUMBER OF CHILDREN ARE BECAUSE OF ABSENCE

	Week 1	Week 2	Week 3
	No of children	No of children	No of children
8	5	18	20
7	5	2	1
6	4	2	3
5	4	0	2
4	2	0	0
3	2	0	1
2	1	2	0
1	3	0	1
0	2	1	0
Total children	28	25	28

SPELLING SUCCESS IN THE NETHERLANDS

Here is a practical and detailed case study of using the spelling strategy as a whole class approach over a longer period of time. Notice in the transcript the language Riejan uses to enthuse her learners.

Riejan Smits is a teacher in The Netherlands specialising in intervention work with children who are not reaching their potential

Research plan

In September 2010 I started with a new group of students; 9 children in group 5 (age 8 and 9) and 12 children in group 4 (age 6 and 7). The previous year was a troubled year; 31 children in one classroom and an inexperienced teacher who received no help with her teaching.

The spelling results of the children in my group were dramatically low. 80% of the children got an E score. In the Netherlands we use standard testing. The results are shown as A-B-C-D-E scores. A and B are good scores and should be accomplished by 80% of the students. C score means you have to examine the results and make a plan to get the child to an A or B score. D and E scores are very low and you can have no more than 5% of the children in that score. For the D-E children you have to make a repair plan and show it to your director. You can imagine that I was in a shock when I learned the results of this spelling and I wanted to raise the results. Learning to spell correctly is an important part of our language education.

Together with my director we aimed for an improvement of 40% in the spelling results in this year. I wanted a higher outcome but my director wanted a more realistic outcome. The results of the spelling test were unacceptable to me. I wanted to teach the children the right strategy for spelling and have a lot of fun while learning. I also wanted them to feel successful, capable and proud of their achievements with spelling (and all the other learning of course).

The elements of NLP I built into the plan were: Go into the right state, go first, inoculate against failure and/or negative beliefs, nested loops, trances, timelines, anchoring, Milton patterns.

I have already taught my children a lot of NLP techniques, so I can tell them to go into a state of curiosity where they feel comfortable, and they will. I use timelines to make sure the kids are in a state of trust in the future, showing them how, when and why we are doing things.
The kids love this stuff; flying over the timelines, building strong powerful beliefs and feeling good about themselves. I also use the timelines for other subjects such as Maths, History, Drawing, Planning and much more.

At the start of the new school year I told my children that I had been to school again myself and that I had learned a lot of very useful tricks and magic to make learning easier, funnier, faster, more successful, and that I was ready to start sharing that information with them. (Getting them into the right state, I was there already - the Milton patterns are there, you will recognise them):

..."I know for a fact that children are very quick learners, so let's start with the first secret - we are going to be excellent spellers and we will make the best cheating list possible; the cheating list that no one will discover, because we will make the list inside our minds. We are going to be like magicians... are you ready? Let me tell you what my plan is - we have to learn 20 words, every 2 weeks, so we have 10 days for 20 words. Piece of cake! At the end of the 2 weeks we will exactly know how to spell the 20 words because we practised the strategy I learned from Richard Bandler every day. He is a doctor and knows how our minds learn... He is always investigating how he can make learning easier and whenever he finds out, he tells it to his students and they tell their students, so it is like a stone you drop into the water. So my plan for the next two weeks looks like this (drawing on my digital board):

Day 1 Today we will read all the 20 words, so we already are starting to know them. Then we will categorise them and we will learn the first strategy:

The Perfect Spelling Strategy

Richard Bandler is a smart man, for example, if I want to become a great singer, it would be a great idea to go to a teacher who sings beautifully herself, wouldn't it? Do you think it's a smart idea to go to a singer who sings out of key? Don't think so. Richard went out to ask really good spellers - how do you spell so well? And he was amazed and glad because all good spellers said, *'well it is very easy, if I want to spell the word "natuurlijk"* (the spelling problem is uur; you spell uur, but you say uu translation: of course) *'I just look in my mind and there is the picture of the word'*. And Richard noticed that all good spellers looked right above. So I have put all the 20 words on the digital board and I will show you with each word how I do it, because I'm a great speller too:

Natuurlijk
This is too small, I will make it bigger...

Natuurlijk

This is better. Now I change the spelling problem into a beautiful colour...

*Nat**uur**lijk*

So, that looks really awesome. We are going to do this together! Make a picture of this word. Close your eyes when your picture is made.

Open them and do it again.

This is cool. Close your eyes and see the picture.

Open your eyes and make a picture, make sure it is a bright picture and close your eyes. Now, as you sit still and watch the word in your mind, you can all point to the first letter of this image, point out the 'a', the 'l', the 'r'. Excellent!

Wow, I think we are so good. Now, here comes the magic; you can make the picture smaller:

*Nat**uur**lijk*

and smaller:

*Nat**uur**lijk*

so you can copy the word into our book. Compare it with the picture in your mind, compare it with the picture on the board. And that's the famous cheating list. We are so going to be THE best spellers ever! The spelling category was - eer, oor aar, uur (eur). You spell the r, but you don't say it. We took all the words of that category and practised them. Then I got back to my timeline on the digital board.

Day 1 Making pictures in our minds and practice with your neighbour

Day 2 Practise in your book - you can work in pairs and you can work with colours

Day 3 Practise on the computer

Day 4 Hand in your book after you have checked the words; you will win a sticker if you have all the words correct

Day 5 You make a test for someone else in the classroom with a maximum of 10 words. You will work in pairs. And you may work with a lot of different children.

Day 6 Make the practice exercises in your book

Day 7 A small test of all the 20 words

Day 8 Practise the words you weren't really sure of yet

Day 9 Practise on the computer with other children; make a game with the words or look at the back of your book. All the words we have to learn this school year are there, so you can learn ahead and gain an advantage!

Day 10 Test successfully made!

Oh, I have to finish my story; Richard told me that it is really important to reward students after they did a great job! So what would you like me to give to you after we worked really well? Would you settle for some sweets? Okay, deal!

Let's go to work.

I also use visual and kinaesthetic anchors. All the children have a table illustrating these on their tables and they use it very frequently. I have added a picture of it.

The kinaesthetic anchor for this category is with the thumb on their noses and three wiggling fingers in the air; the words with eer, aar, oor, uur are making fun of you, but we know we have to spell them with three characters! And by using the three fingers it is made into a visual and kinaesthetic anchor.

Picture strategy list:

Impact
The children loved the new way and are still very enthusiastic. I was very surprised at the motivation of the children. They are studying without me telling them, because they like to. They want to be better, they motivate others and they are inventing new games and ways of practising.

In the longer term, I have continued with this strategy. The children are happy with the yellow strategy form and they use it when necessary. Even if they are sick on day 10, the test day, they want to make the test when they are back at school!

Because we trained on the picture-making technique for a lot of weeks, it is now into the system of most children. When they encounter a difficult word they will make a big picture of the word on the computer or in their "thinking book".

After 10 weeks we had a standard spelling test. 21 children did the test and

- 19 children got an A score!
- 2 children scored B. These two are diagnosed with dyslexia.

I danced on the table (I really did!) and bought them some sweets because they did an excellent job! In February there will be another test and my children are learning and studying of their own free will!

My Director was happy. Now he wants to know more about NLP. He was not very interested, now he wants me to give a workshop on NLP and teaching. My colleagues are asking a lot of questions and are applying NLP techniques in their classes too. It is contagious! Even the academy for teachers wants to know more!

So the improvement is overwhelming; 21 children did great, that is 100%.

SPREADING THE STRATEGY ACROSS THE SCHOOL
Naina demonstrates that managers have a vital role to play in passing on NLP techniques to staff.

Naina Chauhan is Deputy Head/SENCO (Special Educational Needs Co-ordinator) at West Thornton Primary Academy, Croydon, London

Research plan
I began my journey of introducing NLP to my school in the back of my mind (or the forefront...). Kate's words played back again and again: *'NLP is about elegance ... it's the smallest intervention that makes the biggest change'.*

Action
The set up of a new SEN (special educational needs) learning zone in the school in the autumn term brought with it new opportunities. I had asked the teacher in the room to try out the NLP spelling strategy on C, a Year 6 (age 10-11) child who was experiencing difficulty with reading and writing and was displaying dyslexic symptoms. After going through the Durham Project findings with her, the teacher set off enthusiastically. She was to see this child each afternoon and spend 20 minutes with him on spellings and reading.

Impact
His Salford Reading score[1] at the beginning of term (Sept) was 6.1 years. As the weeks went by, I was kept informed of his progress and of the fact that not only did he seem to be improving in spellings and reading, but he had grown in confidence as a consequence of his successes. His reading score increased by 1.7 years in just 5 weeks! The strategy was working and now was being introduced to others by this teacher... Bingo!

─────────────── **REFERENCES** ───────────────

1. Salford Reading Score: A reading test widely used in UK schools, which calculates the reading age of a child.

COMFORT AND FUN TO IMPROVE READING

Helen recognises the importance of reading for the ability to access subjects students love to learn.

Helen Keay provides SEN (special educational needs) learning support at Framwellgate Moor Primary School, Durham

Project plan

The focus for the teaching project was my work with a Year 6 [age 10-11] pupil with a Statement of Special Educational Needs.
The pupil had reading difficulties and no interest in learning to read. The pupil showed an interest and ability in Science and Numeracy, but the amount of progress she could make in these areas was considerably restricted by her difficulties in reading. The pupil is dependent upon another individual to verbalise the written text. The aims of my project were to find a more effective and positive approach to reading with pupils throughout the school and to implement a more consistent approach enabling pupils to learn and enjoy. I planned to work for 3 weeks on an individual reading programme based on the Year 6 pupil's stage and interests.

Action

I withdrew the pupil from the class to work in a small room used as a story room for Nursery age pupils. The room was decorated with the Nursery children's paintings of zoo animals. Comfortable rocking chairs and music to aid accelerated learning, chosen by the pupil, playing in the background created a relaxed atmosphere. The pupil remarked how it was "just like home".

I implemented this for 15 minutes in the morning and 15 minutes in the afternoon for 3 weeks over a 4-week period (due to a holiday week). I used the Oxford Fuzz Buzz reading scheme introduced to the pupil in September 2005. These books are enjoyed by a large number of pupils throughout the class.

The annual assessment carried out in May 2006 using the Salford Reading Test gave the pupil's reading age as 5.7 years. After the 4 week project period the assessment was repeated and the pupil's reading age had increased to 6.1 years. The pupil's interest in reading had also increased dramatically and is now at the stage where she is asking to read.

Impact
Employing new strategies has been beneficial to me, giving me a greater awareness of the environment in which children learn and its impact on the learning achieved. The result from this reading project has been shared throughout the school. I feel I will be able to continue using this approach throughout the school with all pupils showing reading difficulties. This will enable those children to develop stronger reading skills and increased confidence and ability whilst learning in a relaxed, calming and soothing environment.

TEACHING READING – EYE ACCESSING STUDY OF DIFFERENT READING STRATEGIES
Zoe highlights an important lesson in flexibility for teachers teaching reading.

Zoe Ryan is a Foundation Stage teacher at Bedlington West End First School, Bedlington, Northumberland

Research Plan
I decided to look at how young children develop their early reading skills. As a teacher working with young children, it is very noticeable how some children can be stronger at developing their reading skills using phonetic strategies, whereas others may find it easier to learn a 'sight vocabulary' and a look-and-say technique. Through the NLP training we were given an insight into how people's eye movements can give an indication as to their thought processes. It was emphasised that the model given would not apply to everyone in the same way but could possibly give an insight into which memories or skills people were using. I decided to try to use the eye accessing cues with children demonstrating a significant strength in either phonics or look-and-say reading strategies.

Action
I highlighted six children who had a strength in either using a phonetic approach when reading/writing or who used a look-and-say-approach,

focusing on using words they had previously memorised. I ensured there was a mix of boys and girls so that I could observe any differences between genders. I worked one-to one with each child, observing their eye accessing cues to see if any patterns emerged. I needed to position myself so that I could observe while still interacting with the child. I gave each child a set of pictures for CVC (consonant-vowel-consonant) words. Initially we talked about what the pictures might represent and I then encouraged the children to write the words beneath the pictures.

A is a child who employs a mainly look-and-say approach.
When selecting the letters she needed to write, A was observed to look upwards to her right for the majority of the letters, and she also closed her eyes at times. These eye accessing cues seemed to indicate that she was visualising the letters before writing them. She needed no help in remembering the letter shapes.

B is a child who employs a mainly look-and-say approach and has an excellent sight vocabulary.
When selecting the letters she needed to write, B was observed to look directly upwards, while for some of the words she did not stop to think, just writing the words straight away. These eye accessing cues seemed to indicate that she was visualising words she was unsure of and writing others from memory without having to visualise individual letters.

C is a child who employs a mainly look-and-say approach, with a reluctance to attempt to use sounds to blend words.
After deciding what each picture represented, C was reluctant to attempt to write and needed encouragement to write anything. He was observed to look directly upwards and then, with encouragement, would write the appropriate letters. When unsure he could be observed to look upwards and then immediately downwards and to his left as though he was searching for reassurance.

D is a child who employs a mainly phonetic approach.
When selecting the letters to write, D was very confident and wrote many without hesitation. For the few sounds he was unsure of, D was

observed to move his eyes directly to his left and then down to the left. These eye accessing cues would suggest that he was auditorily remembering the sounds and self-talking.

E is a child who employs a mainly phonetic approach.
When selecting the letters to write, it was observed that E made very clear, almost exaggerated eye movements. He would initially move his eyes directly to the right and then immediately to the left. This pattern continued throughout, with him looking down to the left on one occasion. These eye accessing cues would suggest that he was mainly auditorily remembering the sounds and occasionally self-talking.

F is a very confident child employing a mainly phonetic approach.
F was able to write all the relevant sounds without giving any eye accessing cues. She could have been using strategies, but was very confident and wrote the words without hesitation.

On reviewing the results there seemed to be a clear indication that the children who had a strength using look-and-say were visually constructing the words. They could 'see' the letters and were then able to write them down. The children who have a strength phonetically were hearing the sounds or remembering the sound and then transferring the sounds to the letter shapes.

This would seem to strengthen the argument for a varied approach when helping children learn to read, using a combination of strategies encompassing visual, auditory and kinesthetic. So children can see, hear and physically manipulate the words we are helping them to learn.

Impact
The findings from this research have influenced my approach to teaching reading. It has shown how important it is to use a variety of techniques to include all learners. Using a primarily phonetic approach may not work for our visual learners looking at the shapes of words, and a look-and-say approach doesn't necessarily give the auditory learner the stimuli needed for them to progress.

CREATIVITY AND CONFIDENCE IN FRENCH LANGUAGE WHOLE CLASS TEACHING

David Hicks is a peripatetic French and Music teacher working in a number of schools in South East England

Research plan

To work with a Year 6 class (age 10-11), helping pupils become more creative and confident to spell and understand French words, so they achieve with more ease.

- A measurable goal of either improved scores in the test, or evidence of more interest and excitement about using the new strategy.
- Use of sensory-based material, including submodalities of the visual, auditory and kinaesthetic representation systems.

Action

Using the Milton Model, I began by using truisms and inoculation to introduce the exercise:

'Ok folks, today we are going to look at a great way to learn how to spell some new French words really easily' [Here I also used analogue marking with the embedded command of spelling words really easily]

I used presuppositions and more embedded commands as I carried on:

'Now as you get more used to using this technique you will find that it becomes so easy to use and it's also a fun way to learn new spellings so you'll get really good.' I gave each pupil in the class a list of 8 French words to learn:

SOURIS / CINQUANTE / HARICOTS / POISSON / ÉTAGÈRES / ARAIGNÉE / IMPERMÉABLE / CHEMISIER

I used submodalities of the representational systems to help pupils create a powerful visual anchor:

'Now let's take the first word – souris. I want you to - in your mind - give each letter a different colour, perhaps make it bright and really vibrant... It

can even sparkle. Now I want you to make the letters 10 times bigger... and now double the size again... Now I want you to project these letters onto a huge cinema screen... and then [using voice inflection to further induce an hypnotic state] imagine a mouse rock and roll group playing your favourite song... Now listen to the music for a few moments... and now let go of this image and file it away in your head [as I used my arms to indicate 'visual construct' up to the right].'

I used the same technique for the next word – **cinquante**. In addition to the visual cue of the word on the cinema screen I suggested they imagine 50 of any things they liked. I suggested they could be still or moving about - like 50 peas rolling all over the screen, or 50 stick insects, etc. For this word I also have a physical prompt that I use with the pupils, so in addition to the visual submodalities - colour / shape / size / brightness - I introduced a kinaesthetic element into the exercise.

I then gave pupils time to carry out the same process for all the other 6 words.

I changed focus for the next part of the lesson, and worked on sports using the verb faire - to do, where we used movement to perform the sport and then we sang my 'sport song'. Before I ended the lesson I reminded pupils of the exercise for their homework task, and told them to replay the process at home before the next lesson (a couple of days later).

Spelling test
At the start of this lesson, before I tested the pupils on the 8 words, I helped the pupils access the visual anchor by saying: *'Ok so now we are going to do the spelling test as usual, but this time I want you to look up to where you stored the picture in your head* [but this time I pointed up and to pupils' left] *and you'll see how easy it is to see the picture back in the cinema...*
Number 1: **'souris'**
Number 2: **'cinquante'**
etc

Impact
I logged two separate results from these tests:

1. Number of errors in the word spelling

2. The meaning of the word in English

The results were very interesting: In comparing previous spelling test scores across the class, there was a small but clear decrease in the number of spelling mistakes with the words, but a massive improvement in comprehension of the words:

- 6 pupils - the scores were generally unaltered
- 2 pupils - the scores were worse
- 23 pupils showed a 2 or 3 point improvement in their scores
- For comprehension marks, most pupils returned 100% full marks, in comparison to an average of 40%.

Pupil feedback from the exercise:

- It was really fun to imagine all the pictures
- I kept seeing different things on the cinema screen
- I felt I got better
- I knew I was getting the right answer
- It was a different way of learning stuff
- It was a bit difficult at first – I didn't know what was going on
- Once I got into it, it was cool
- I was able to shut my eyes
- I liked making pictures

CREATIVE USE OF NLP FOR CREATIVE WRITING

This project focused on using NLP for story writing for 8-9-year-old children. There are many ideas to try out from this project.

Riejan Smits from The Netherlands completed this fascinating project for her Teaching Excellence certificate

Research plan

In the language textbook we use, the children must write stories, and they don't normally like this assignment. They find it hard, they don't know how to start or how to end. I wanted them to write a short story, to enjoy writing it, and to read it in the classroom. One of the goals this school year is writing a short text using core words. The core words are - sun, storm, raindrop, lightning. I wanted the children to write a short story in which they had to imagine that they were a raindrop, a storm, thunder or the Sun. The story must have a beginning, a middle and an end.

I also wanted the children to experience that writing a short story could be done in a short period of time and that it was fun to do. One of the new rules in this assignment was - you can help each other for 10 minutes and then you will have 3 more minutes to finish your story. I wanted to find out for myself how the results would be if I used a completely different approach to this, using the techniques learned on the Teaching Excellence course. So, instead of writing in a book, the children were given coloured paper filled with shapes. There were no long instructions; instead, there was a short list on the whiteboard of what to do, using words as well as drawings. In circles on the whiteboard I wrote:

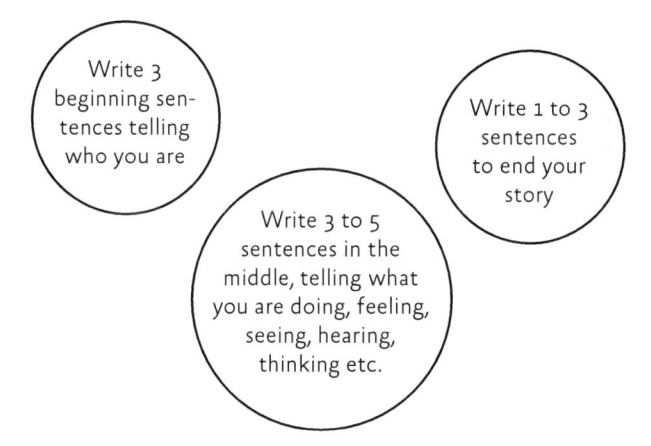

- Write 3 beginning sentences telling who you are
- Write 3 to 5 sentences in the middle, telling what you are doing, feeling, seeing, hearing, thinking etc.
- Write 1 to 3 sentences to end your story

...'You can start with a mind map while the music is playing'
[it was hip hop, so they could think quickly!]
'You can write a few words for a short sentence, you can use adjectives and nouns to make a longer sentence.'

Action
In order to inoculate against failure, I told them that I had developed a beautiful form with a lot of shapes so it would be easier to write a

few sentences, and that they could determine for themselves in which direction they wanted to write. Because there were no lines on the sheet of paper, their creativity would get bigger, so the story would flow easier out of their heads onto the paper. For a relaxing state I put on our Mozart CD. In previous lessons we had worked with Mozart and the children knew that his music helped them to concentrate on their projects. I read a study about classical music used in education, and one of the findings was that when listening to Mozart, your brain will become smarter! I told this to the children and they were willing to try it; at first there was a lot of giggling, but they now really love working with classical music.

I used Milton patterns to put the children into a relaxing, creative state, using phrases like, *'the new form will make it easier, the music will help you, no lines makes it easier to write'*.

After the instruction, which was short and simple, the children chose the sheet they wanted and started writing. The mind map was done on the same sheet and some children used their Thinking Book.
I introduced a Thinking Book after the Teaching Excellence course. I thought the name was well-founded and it is a nested loop they can use for a very long period. I talked about it with a colleague and she is using one too. It's great - they use it to think, to make notes, and they make pictures in it so they remember more. They love the book. I have written their names on the front of the book in gold; the magic is working!

Impact

The children loved the new form. They really liked the fact that there were no lines on the sheet, so they didn't feel restricted or limited. Because there were more shapes, they could write a beginning sentence and then if they chose go to the end and back to the middle part without worrying; the shapes placed the story and kept them focused. All the children wrote a story. After 10 minutes I stopped them and asked them to read the stories of the other children in the group, helping each other and asking for help if they wanted or needed it. 3 minutes later everybody returned to the project, finished their task and then asked me if they could read them to the children of Group 4.

We did and we loved the stories. Now there was another advantage: Group 4 did not need any instruction, they had seen it with Group 5 and they understood how it worked, so that afternoon Group 4 did a similar project, writing an answer to a letter (a textbook assignment). I have translated a few of Group 5's wonderful stories below:

I am the sun
I am nice and warm
And I shine

I am up in the sky
Everybody likes me
I am yellow
I am happy
I shine high

And then it was this way far
I am a human being again
It was excellent to be in the sky
Me and the sun lived happy and long
Will you tell granny I said high

I am a sun
And I shine beautiful
And when it rains
I'll become a rainbow
One day something happened
A cloud appeared
And I saw it It was the lightning
And I went away
I was sad
And the lightning disappeared
And I was happy once again

I am a storm
I can be very dangerous
Accidents can happen

Sometimes big clouds appear
But it is possible that other things will happen as well
Many times lightning comes frequently
It is very dangerous for animals too
There I go...
Flowing and flowing
Further and further

I am the sun
I would love to be the sun
I would live many adventures
And I want to shine like a super happy human being

No cloud can hold me back and everybody shall think I am good
I shall be famous
Everybody shall lay down in my sunlight
Thus shall it feel to be the sun
To see the land

This is how I feel and have a happy life, me being the sun
I shall look upon every person as if he is a god
Whether it is summer or spring, I will shine all day

All the children read their stories, either from my "confident spot" in the classroom or from my "reading chair".

These two chairs are anchors in my classroom. I told the children that the chair on the **right** is my reading chair, and when you sit on it, reading out loud is so much easier. The "confident spot" is in the middle, **right** in front of the digital board. When I want some extra confidence, I will stand on that spot. I trained and practised it with the children and the spot is doing its job very well!

After the assignment we evaluated the task. The children's comments included, 'the shapes are fun to write in', 'it was easy', they were proud and asked me if we could do this more.

I was amazed at the results. The story of the storm was made by a boy who normally didn't finish this kind of project. He would normally say; 'this is too difficult, I don't know any words, I'm no good in story writing'. This time, he just started and completed the job and was so proud! In the afternoon, he took his mother into the classroom so she could read his story.

CHAPTER 20

Primary and Elementary School, 5-11-year-olds

CREATING POSITIVE LEARNING STATES AND OVERCOMING CHALLENGES

This chapter provides case studies of teachers working one-to-one and with their groups to create readiness to learn and happy learners. Milton Language patterns with a hearing impaired learner

Sue Fraser works with hearing impaired children at Durham Gilesgate Primary School, Durham

Research Plan

The aim of my project was to determine whether I could impact on the level of engagement and attention of the children in my group by altering my language patterns to include those of the Milton Model. Initially, I aimed to concentrate on our language patterns at the opening of each lesson and also at the point of introducing the children's independent work. The timescale set for this project was less than 3 weeks in the classroom. Would there be a discernable difference within such a short time frame?

Action

The project was implemented by planning the opening of lessons in detail. This included the manner of delivery (awareness of personal state) and the use of embedded commands and suggestions, quotes and positive language. The introduction of the children's individual work was also planned in the same way. Initially these two points in each lesson were the focus, however I soon found that the patterns were becoming more natural and I could incorporate them quite readily in to the rest of the lesson. (The more I practised, the more automatic it became and the more impact I could see!) The impact of the change of language patterns was observed on day one. An 8-year-old hearing-impaired boy in my group is very nervous and a worrier. I had previously constantly told him, *'Don't worry, this isn't hard and if you get stuck, I am here to help you'.* In the light of what I learned about the way language can lead the brain I realised that I had been inadvertently telling this little boy to worry because the work was going to be so hard he would need help. So, of course, he did! As soon as I stopped using that language his panic vanished and his behaviour changed. All I needed to do was say, *'I know you will easily do a great piece of work because you have loved this story and you have got lots of lovely ideas, I am sure you will enjoy writing about them'.*

Impact
The child immediately produced his first ever piece of totally independent writing. There was no panic, no delaying tactics and no pleas for help – a total transformation. I have continued to find that the atmosphere in lessons has been more relaxed and more positive.
The children seem to engage in the lesson and maintain concentration for longer. They are definitely happier to have a go at tasks independently. I have developed skills that have enabled me to analyse my own state and use of language patterns, and to work on changing these to help achieve desired outcomes in pupils' learning. This will be an ongoing process, but in a very short time I have observed very positive changes.

CREATING HAPPINESS AND HARMONY FOR A CHILD WITH MULTIPLE CHALLENGES

Catherine Bennison works at Walworth School, Newton Aycliffe, County Durham - a special school for 4-11-year-olds

Research Plan
The 8-year-old pupil on whom I focused presents with multiple challenges including communication difficulties, being verbally and physically abusive, extremely low self-esteem, self-harm, absenteeism, recent deterioration in all of the above. The school was wondering what to try next. I planned to utilise state management (my own, that of my support assistant, and the pupil's), and Milton Model language patterns to improve the behaviour of this young boy (A). Because of a number of circumstances I only had one week in which to create any

change, and this makes the results all the more remarkable. A presents with a complex set of needs, including:

- Severe speech problems which make him very difficult to understand, so he shouts to compensate
- Communication difficulties causing A to often say the opposite of what he actually means, but he has no problems with receptive language
- Being verbally and physically abusive towards adults - swearing, kicking, spitting, hitting almost daily
- Extremely low self-esteem, referring to himself as 'thick' and 'stupid'
- Trying to self-harm
- Until 18 months ago he received 2:1 tuition and has only been in fulltime education for a short while, even though he is in Year 4 [ages 8-9]
- His situation had recently deteriorated for reasons outside school control leading to his violent incidents becoming more serious and a number of fixed-term exclusions
- He will seize any opportunity to absent himself from school
- He always tries to disrupt at some point of the day
- He tries to avoid completing independent tasks Because of his behaviours resulting from those needs, other children in our class had become very resentful of him and often expressed the wish that he wasn't in our class. Recently, his mother had told us that she felt she was at the 'end of the road' with him.

Action
Given this very complex situation I agreed the following with my support assistant:
- That we used to have very positive attitude in class and we needed to get back to that
- It was very important that the staff team should be happy and smiling with relaxed body language, at the beginning of the day. We would use the smiling and body language as an anchor throughout the day
- We had stopped playing music as part of the beginning of the day routine and we both felt it was important to start again - anotherpart of the anchoring process: music, nice activity, smiling adults positive atmosphere
- That we were using too many negatives like 'don't', so we decided

to use Milton Model language patterns to presuppose success and be less confrontational
- That we needed to use rewards more than negative consequences, e.g. instead of, *'if you don't finish your work you will miss your choice-time'*, we could say, *'I know you are going to be able to finish this and then you can have a great time at choice time playing with the cars'*.

We decided to pilot an NLP-based approach for one week and then evaluate its success with regard to A. Our success criteria would be that A would get fewer MIRs (referrals for seriously unacceptable behaviour), complete his independent tasks, and there would be fewer incidents of class disruption.

Research Diary
MONDAY
- A good start to the day - A welcomed into the classroom.
- The first challenge came when he refused to read. Used Milton presuppositions to defuse the situation and it worked!
  'I know you can read really well and you will be able to read this book quickly then we will be able to go and change it and you will be able to choose another book'.
  The rest of class applauded when he finished reading - a major breakthrough; they would have jeered before. Their behaviour mirrored our adult behaviour.
- A was challenging again at lunchtime. The Milton Model worked again:
  'I know you wanted to go to computers but you will have a really good time in the quad and this afternoon we will make time in class for you to use the computer.'
- Overall, a good day with A on full points; the first time since before Easter.

TUESDAY
- Taxi driver informed school that A had problems at home.
- I feared for the worst but remained positive and managed my state.
- Lots of smiles when he arrived in class, even though he immediately switched the lights off and hid behind the door. Chatted to him about football, and he got his colours out and sat at his table and completed

his picture.
- Refused to participate in whole class activity during Literacy but he was again talked round by reminding him of the fun he would have at choice time and after a few moments he rejoined the activity.
- On full points again at the end of the day.

WEDNESDAY
- Classroom observation visit from A's Educational Psychologist during the Literacy lesson. I managed my state really well. Lots of smiles and enthusiasm, even though I was feeling quite anxious and imagining a worst-case scenario. I engaged in lots of positive interaction with A, reminding him how well he did in yesterday's Literacy lesson, how much fun we were going to have at Forest School, and how many points he had this week already.
- The Educational Psychologist was very impressed with A, saying that it was the longest she had seen him participate. She commented positively on how well he was able to recall yesterday's learning, and the fact that he was able take turns when answering questions.
- A absented himself later in a tag rugby session that none of the class team were involved in, but was able to talk to me about his behaviour (usually puts he hands over his ears and shouts '*blah! blah!*'). My use of the word 'talk' is important in this context because he normally shouts.
- Mixed behaviour at Forest School.[1] The Forest School Leader was not familiar with the use of the language patterns. A absented himself at the end of day as he was going to his taxi.

THURSDAY
- Small problem in Numeracy; not buying in to whole class activity as usual. But unusually, very short lived, approximately 3 minutes, then back on track after I used the Milton language patterns again to great effect: '*Remember how proud you were on Tuesday when you got full points in Numeracy. I know you can do it again. You are doing so well and you have already given me some really good answers and I know you are going to really enjoy lunchtime when you go to computer group.*'
- Unfortunately absented on return to class after lunch.

FRIDAY
- A difficult day for A because it was unstructured (whole school involved in activities around football World Cup day). Did voluntarily come and sit next to me in class during first lesson while colouring a picture but found outside difficult. Lots of 1:1 support needed, but didn't absent himself or become abusive.
- Didn't look as happy. Unstructured situations are going to need more thinking about.

Impact
- A finished the week with a Gold Award for the first time this year!
- His peers were much more tolerant and supportive of him; a massive change from before half term. • He was able to complete all independent tasks for the first time in weeks, and took a pride in his achievements.
- His general demeanour improved - not as noisy, more prepared to listen, less frustrated with himself
- Managing my own state worked really well because by the end of the week I felt much less stressed and much calmer.
- Everyone in class benefited, e.g., ASD children had a much calmer, less anxious week (much less screaming)
- Showed us that more work needs to be done. Even though he had a better week he still managed to absent on several occasions and this needs to be addressed.
- Also showed the importance of a whole school approach - when other staff became involved (tag rugby and Forest School) A's behaviour deteriorated because they were not using the same methods.
- This variation in A's behaviour illustrates the effectiveness of the NLP-based approach in that, when it was used by the staff, his behaviour was so much better and he looked much happier. An unexpected though very welcome by-product was that the whole class was more supportive and forgiving, and happier.

REFERENCES

1. Forest School offers learners regular opportunities to achieve and develop confidence and self-esteem through hands-on learning experiences in a woodland or natural environment with trees.

WORKING WITH A CHILD DISPLAYING SEVERE ANXIETY

Helen Watson, teacher of children with Specific Learning Difficulties

Research plan

I was already using Milton Model to good effect to help with confidence. I had been aware for some time that there were children coming to me who had anxiety issues that I might be able to deal with even more effectively.

Until now I had helped to remove this anxiety by equipping them with more effective strategies (e.g. NLP spelling strategy) and using Milton Model language to encourage success and build confidence. This had been working well, but I see many children who have severe anxiety around school and around tests and I felt there was more I could do.

The question I wanted to ask was: How effective is the Meta Model in uncovering the exact nature of the anxiety and then how can I use other NLP techniques to effectively remove this anxiety?

My main aim for my own professional development was to see how I could use more NLP, firstly to make what I already did more effective and consistent, and secondly to help with a wider range of problems. My main aim for the pupil was that they could confidently overcome their anxiety and achieve their potential.

I decided to focus on one child (G) whose mother had asked me to help her with "low confidence " and "panics" and the fact she was "too scared" to do the AR Test (an online reading test used by her school).

G is a good reader. However, because her progress at school from one level of books to another is determined by her performance in this online multiple choice test, she is on a low level of books given her reading competence. Importantly to her, all her friends are on a higher level and this is affecting her confidence.

Plan of action
1. Goal setting
2. Use Meta Model to uncover problem
3. Use submodalities to change the picture
4. Anchor this picture with breathing

Action
1. GOAL SETTING
At the first session we determined that her goals were to get all the questions right and move up to a higher level of reading book.

2. META MODEL QUESTIONS TO UNCOVER THE PROBLEM
I had a list of Meta Model questions as a prompt so that I could slot them in as needed, eg., *'how do you know?' 'who says?'* G explained to me that after she had read her graded school reading book the test asked her a number of specific questions about what she had read. I had also spoken to her mum and done some of my own research into the Accelerated Reading Programme (the basis of the test) before the session. G said that she needed to get 100% to move up a level, although other sources told me this was 80%. G was only getting 40% - 60% so she not moving up a level. In the last year she had made very little progress up the levels.

PRACTICAL ACTIVITIES TO ASSESS HER READING COMPETENCE AND COMPREHENSION
We spent about 15 minutes reading a range of texts that she had brought with her and it was obvious to both of us that she read well. We also spent some time doing a comprehension exercise where she had to read a page and then answer questions. She had a good understanding of the text.

FURTHER META MODEL QUESTIONS
Firstly - having asked her questions about the mechanics of the test and established that she thought of them as important, something she

wasn't good at and scary - I did a lot of questioning around how she perceived the tests and also got her laughing at them. Then we began to address her feelings when she sat down to do a test. She described it as a 'funny feeling' in her stomach. We explored this 'funny feeling' and she decided it was like 'fluttering butterflies'.

3. USING SUBMODALITIES TO CHANGE THE PICTURE
She described the colour of her butterflies and what they were doing. We discussed why we get butterflies (good stress) and how sometimes when we are very bothered by something the butterflies are too lively (bad stress).

4. ANCHOR THIS PICTURE WITH THE BREATH
We then practised calming the butterflies down with a deep-breathing technique. We did all the above in one session and 3 weeks later G returned. In her mind she was coming to concentrate on some traditional comprehension exercises to help with her homework. In my mind, we were going to see how she had got on with her AR Test.

Impact
Mum reported that G had gone up "a couple of stages" in her reading books. She was no longer worried about the AR Test and had been getting 90% - 100%. I could see how much more confident G looked and how when she talked about the tests now she was looking forward to doing more so that she could go up yet another level. G reported that she had *'done pretty well'* and that she *'felt amazing'*. When I asked her casually *'and how were the butterflies?'* She said that she had felt them starting to "flutter" as she sat down to do her test and then *'as soon as I did what you said'* (breathe slowly and deeply) *'they settled down'*. The Meta Model allowed me to uncover the problem and the associated pictures quite quickly. The use of submodalities meant we could change that picture. We were then able to anchor this new picture with the breathing and G could get it back quickly whenever she wanted.

PLAN FOR FUTURE ACTION
I shall now use Meta Model more with intent to uncover the problem and use the ideas of submodalities. I had been told that children love submodalities and this experience has proved that to me. The breathing

technique is a good anchor and I now feel more confident to explore other anchors.

SIMPLE LANGUAGE CHANGES FOR BIG IMPACT:
Yes, Yes, Yes!

Emma demonstrates that just one simple language change can make a big impact.

Emma Loader teaches at Corbridge First School, Northumberland

Research plan
My focus is both leadership development and enhancement of my teaching by using NLP techniques within the classroom. In particular I was interested in the use of different language patterns to enhance pupils' behaviour, motivation, attitude and results.

After learning about the concept of using certain language patterns to influence pupil attitude and learning within the classroom, I decided to try to adopt one particular language pattern, the 'yes' set, within my everyday teaching, to see if it had any effect. I began by focusing on a particular child (A), who had problems concentrating on a task for very long without adult help and would get emotional and grumpy if she found the task hard.

Action
For one week I used my usual teaching methods so that I had a 'control'. A's concentration varied from day to day – sometimes only on task for 5 minutes at a time, but on two days managed to complete the task and stay focused for 15 minutes without adult intervention. On 3 out of the 5 days, A cried during the task, saying that she couldn't do it even though, when I checked her understanding, she did have a clear idea of what was expected.

During the second week, I implemented the new language pattern and gave A three facts (for example: *'you have a pen, you have your book, you* have space to work') and then I would utter a final command such as 'and now you are going to get on without my help until you have finished the work'.

Impact

I noticed that although the time that A sat and concentrated did not really improve, the standard of her work did. A had had problems with handwriting prior to me using the language pattern, but afterwards it was much neater. Also, the quantity of work that she produced was greater than under my existing teaching methods.

I decided to try this influential language with the whole class. Therefore, before I sent the children off to do their work, I would use a 'yes set' first. I noticed that the children were far more focused, the volume in the class was quieter and the work they produced of a better quality. The class also seemed calmer and more certain of what was expected of them. As a result, I have started using this language pattern in my everyday teaching and am still reaping the benefits today.

I WONDER...
Stephanie demonstrates how another language pattern can impact on a child in this extract of her project.

Stephanie Kidd teaches at Coulson Park First School, Ashington, Northumberland

Research plan

There is one boy in my class who has a high ability across all fields however, despite his intelligence, he responds badly and becomes very upset when he gets a question wrong or finds something difficult.

Action

Usually I encourage him to have another try, but it can take a substantial amount of time until he is willing to do so. The child recently volunteered an answer that was incorrect and he quickly became upset. Instead of asking him to try again I rephrased my speech and engaged his curiosity by saying *'I wonder what would happen if you just read that question again'*. The child's head came up; he read the question again and volunteered another answer, still incorrect. I used a similar phrase, *'I wonder if you would get a different answer if you read it just one more time'.* He read it again, volunteered a different answer and got it right. The whole process took a matter of minutes and the child's self-esteem was left intact. I also began to make use of presuppositions that imply the children would achieve and that seemed to instill a greater level of confidence in a number of the children.

Impact
Although there have been no major differences to the way my classroom runs there have been small yet significant changes. Children seem to be more willing to try as I invoke their curiosity and embed in them the belief that they can and already have achieved. As I continue on the learning curve that is NLP and as implementation becomes more natural, I feel there will be more of these changes.

SPATIAL AND CLASSROOM ANCHORS FOR QUIET ATTENTION

Nicola Hurst teaches at Northburn Primary School, Cramlington Northumberland

Research plan
I decided to put the space available in my classroom to better use. My school has a signal that when an adult raises their arm above their head they want all pupils to follow suit and stop talking. I have used this throughout my time at the school with varying degrees of success. Some pupils follow it to the letter, whereas some raise their arm and continue chatting to their friends. My new anchor was to be that when I stood in a particular spot in my classroom it meant that I wanted everyone to stop what they were doing and focus on me. I began to do this without explaining to the class what I was doing.

Action
The spot I chose was near the classroom door and at the opposite end of the room to where the whiteboard is, so that the pupils were not used to me standing there at all. The first time was rather successful! I stood in the spot and didn't say anything as I observed the class. Some

pupils sitting close to me realised I was nearby and, slowly but surely, they began to stop what they were doing and waited for me to speak. The rest of the class picked up on the atmosphere and halted their activities. Once every single child was paying full attention to me I gave further instructions but did not explain why I had moved to elsewhere in the classroom. Once the class began work again there was a very calm atmosphere. I had succeeded in getting their attention without having to say a word and this undoubtedly had a positive impact on the response I received from the class. I was also in a positive state, as I had not been met with resistance about the arm signal and neither had I had to raise my voice.

I continued to use this anchor and after a few more times I overheard a pupil whisper *'shhhh, Miss Hurst is standing in the corner'*. The pupils had successfully linked my action to what I wanted from them. As time progressed, we got to the stage where I wouldn't even have to reach my spot on the opposite side of the classroom for everyone to put their full attention on me. The atmosphere was altogether calmer and made for a much more positive learning environment.

A few pupils in my class swing on their chairs and I would normally say *'stop swinging on your chair'* or *'don't swing on your chair'*. I adapted how I asked pupils to sit appropriately on their chairs into commands such as, *'please place all four chair legs on the floor'*, without addressing a particular child or halting my teaching flow. As time progressed, I changed the spoken command into a signal where I raised four fingers on the same hand to my shoulder height. The few pupils who habitually swung on their chairs then checked that they were sitting appropriately and, if not, adjusted their seating accordingly. This then meant the teaching and learning within the lesson could continue without undue interruptions.

Impact

The spatial anchoring has exceeded my expectations. My classroom is calmer and more settled, without the need to raise my voice to get pupils' attention. I no longer get a half-hearted response when I want them to halt their activities.

The impact of the spatial anchoring on myself was that I found my classroom management was smoother and I was in a more positive state when communicating with pupils. The classroom was more productive because over time there was less time spent waiting to get all pupils' attention. Pupils' behaviour and motivation appeared to have greatly improved over the length of the project.

READY TO LEARN
Metaphors and anchoring create a classroom of engaged learners ready for story time.

Julie Newton teaches at Corbridge First School, Northumberland

Research plan
To be successful learners, children need to be in an appropriate emotional state to access the learning opportunities provided. After the first part of my NLP training I focused on my pupils' readiness for learning, particularly at the beginning of whole class teaching sessions. I felt that as the year had progressed the children seemed to take longer to settle when coming to the carpet so, as a starting point for my research project, I decided to collect observational evidence to confirm my initial thoughts.

Action
I asked my teaching assistant to help me do this over one week and then together we evaluated what we had seen. Before beginning the research, I had expected that any planned interventions would probably be focused upon 2 or 3 children. However, in reality our observations showed that the unsettled state of the class could not always be put down to these pupils. Children illustrated their un-readiness for learning in several ways, for example, by distracting others by inappropriate behaviour, being distracted by others, talking, and fidgeting. It was also interesting to analyse my reactions to specific incidents and consider the type of impact (i.e. positive or negative) this may have on a child's emotional state.

After considering different anchoring techniques that we had discussed during our training, I decided to use 'carpet places' but with an additional feature - 'magic'! I told the children a story about a class, just like themselves, which became the most fantastic class ever, embellishing the story with lots of colourful details and helping the children to visualise what it would be like to be in that class. Part of the story explained that the reason this class was so amazing was that their teacher had been given some magic powder that, once sprinkled on the carpet, helped the children sit smartly, gave them extra thinking power and helped them to listen and learn. However, the powder only worked if each child sat on his or her special 'magic spot'. The children were enthralled by the story and when I asked them if they would like to pretend that they were the class from the story the reply was resoundingly positive! The next day I brought in some 'magic powder' and the children were mesmerised as I sprinkled it onto the carpet and then gave them each a 'magic spot' to sit on. Once on their spots I praised the children and told them how smartly they were sitting, how much extra thinking power they had and how ready they were to listen and learn.

Impact

The 'magic spots' have been a great aid to teaching and learning within the classroom. Children are much calmer, focused and receptive to learning at the start of whole class sessions and a quick wave of the magic wand is a great visual aid to remind the children of what is expected of them. Also, if a child has had an incident at playtime that has been upsetting, going to sit on his/her magic spot seems to have a comforting effect. The system of seating is easily adapted - if children need moving around this can easily be done by just getting hold of a bit more of that magic powder and giving the carpet a quick sprinkle!

CHAPTER 21

Secondary and High School 11-to-15 year olds

Secondary and High School teaching is the area that can most benefit from NLP in the classroom. The good practice in learning approaches of the Primary sector is sadly not always transferred to the next stage of a child's learning journey and we hope that the good practice we share here is implemented by many teachers in the secondary sector.

CREATING ENTHUSIASM FOR FRENCH GRAMMAR

Emma Volpe was an MFL teacher at the former Allendale Middle School, Northumberland

Research plan

After discussion with colleagues and the course leader I decided to focus my project on using positive language and reframing with my Year 8 (ages 12-13) French class. This is a mixed ability class with students ranging from Level 2 to Level 5. There are 13 girls and 15 boys, including two pupils with an Autistic Spectrum Disorder diagnosis. There is a good relationship among the students. I chose this class because I was about to teach a difficult topic (le passé compose) including complex grammar, which can de-motivate the less able.

I wanted to see if, by using NLP techniques, I might be able to create a more positive learning environment which would help students approach challenges with vigour and result in a higher level of achievement and increased motivation. I decided that my focus was going to be using the Milton Model language patterns. I wanted to see if by changing my language I was able to create a more dynamic and positive learning environment.

Action
Being aware that the starter activity of a lesson is a key area to the success of the lesson as a whole, I focused on using language to frame the lesson positively. For example:

'I know that you have been eager to talk about things that have happened in the past...'

'You may already have noticed...'

'I know that you are curious about/ have been wanting to use...'

This particular topic is all about recognising patterns, making links, etc. and this depends very much on helping the students "notice what they notice".

'What would it be like if...'/ 'You know it's like...'

Although I had initially thought that I would concentrate on one particular class, once I began to question my own language techniques it was almost impossible not to employ the patterns with other classes. I also focused on a particular boy who had begun to lose confidence in the subject. I spent some time with him setting short-term goals employing NLP language patterns. I kept a track of this particular student's positive state and participation over three weeks by using a scale of 1-4, with 1 as positive and 4 as negative.

Impact
There is no doubt that over the course of a few weeks a more positive learning environment was created as a result of the project. The class was less fragmented in its focus and responded well to the language patterns I used. The students responded to the challenges with enthusiasm and I received positive verbal feedback from them. They were proud of their achievements and more engaged with the subject. It was particularly pleasing to hear this from male pupils, as raising standards and improving motivation amongst boys was one of the key areas of focus for French within the school.

The language used stimulated curiosity and made the learning experience more inclusive. The one student that I particularly focused upon responded beyond expectation, gaining 10/10 in a vocabulary test (the target had been 8). The pleasure gained from his success fuelled his motivation and his participation in whole class discussion increased enormously.

MOVING FROM A CHILD WHO 'DOES NOT WRITE' TO A CREATIVE WRITING ENTHUSIAST

This is an extract from an extremely thorough piece of research by Jacinta.

Jacinta Fennessy is a teacher in Austria

Research plan

As the Learning Support teacher, I was assigned a Grade 5 student. K, aged 11, is Austrian, his mother tongue is German and he was learning through the medium of English. He had been at this school for one academic year and he had attended international schools in other countries before the family returned to Austria in June 2009.

K had a very good vocabulary in English and he was able to articulate his ideas orally with fluency. He read fluently at grade level. However, K did not write. He used all sorts of excuses to avoid writing, e.g. the teacher wants him to write only in sentences, the teacher will only accept cursive-style writing, the teacher will only accept written work in pen, problems with his pen/pencil and, especially, he can't remember the ideas – this immediately after expressing them orally.

K's mum was becoming extremely frustrated with him because, despite all his parents' efforts, K would simply not complete homework assignments, ever!

I met with K three times a week, each time for 30 minutes. Over the first couple of weeks I established that K could actually write, with intensive sentence-by-sentence support, having reassured him that any style of writing, or indeed a mixed style of writing, was acceptable, using any type of writing tool. It was slow, intensive, laborious and emotionally draining - for both of us!

Here is an example of dialogue to initiate some writing from K prior to considering NLP intervention:

Jacinta: 'What did you do at the weekend?'
K: 'Well, actually, nothing really.'
J: 'So, you stayed in bed all weekend?'
K: 'Well no, I did get up.'
J: 'Great. Write that down.'
K: 'Well, actually, I don't remember what I did.'
J: 'Remember Friday after school - did you have an after-school activity? Did you go straight home?'
K: 'I went to M's house. Well, actually it's an apartment' [several sentences about going to M's house] J: 'That's interesting. Write that down.'
K: [taking his pencil in his hand and aiming at the page] 'But.... the problem is... I can't actually remember what I said first' etc. I wanted K to write his ideas without the endless procrastination, to feel good about writing, and to begin to trust that the ideas he expressed orally were valuable and acceptable and perfectly valid for his written assignments. It was evident that this was critical for K's wellbeing, for his self-esteem and for his confidence. I felt that, despite all our efforts to get K to write, something was interfering with this and that making him feel good about writing was the key to unlocking his block.

Action
November 10th, my notes: *He looks zoned out, pale and is always yawning – even at the beginning of the day. How to make him feel good about writing?*

ELEMENTS OF NLP USED
• States, kinaesthetic anchoring, verbal pacing and leading using truisms and conjunctions, future pacing
• Milton Model: Embedded commands, analogue marking
• Presuppositions: Subordinate clauses of time, commentary words, change of time verbs, adverbs, awareness, tag questions

Session 1
STATES

As we walked to my classroom one day, K said, *'I don't know why, but I feel my teacher really hates me.'* [She'd just told him off because he had forgotten to hand in his homework again]. By using the Meta Model questions to establish what exactly he meant by that, it became clear that he really felt that his teacher and his parents were very unhappy with him when he didn't write up his assignments. Further, when we addressed his claims that he couldn't remember what he wanted to write, we reached the stage, again through Meta Model questions, that he had no difficulty remembering events, information and appointments, but that he didn't feel good about writing. His stated goal, therefore, was to write up his work at school and his homework at home in the time given. To be able to do this he felt he needed to feel good about writing. This would look like this: K sitting at his desk/table, writing. He would feel happy, proud and relieved. Writing his ideas would definitely make his parents happy and his teacher would be relieved. The shouting would stop at home. He wouldn't have to stay in during recess to do the writing.

ANCHORING

I asked K to think about a time when he felt very happy, proud and relieved at having done something challenging. He smiled and said, 'that's easy', then described his first time diving from a rock into the sea. Noted - eye accessing cues:
- Down left when describing the feeling
- Up left when describing what he did and what the scene looked like
- Middle left when he talked about the sounds he heard

He described the event and the feelings of this, the happiest moment in his life.

I asked K what would happen if he could have that same feeling when he started to write his ideas in class and when he did his homework. He looked incredulous and shook his head. *'Imagine'*,

I said, *'having that same feeling when you write. Would that be amazing, or what?'* He nodded and replied, *'that would be amazing'*. I asked what he had to do to get the feeling and he immediately said he could get the feeling by thinking about it. I told him to think about the experience again and make the picture brighter. He said, *'it's very bright already. The sun is shining off the sea, the sky is blue.'* I told him to hear the sounds and he described the sound of the waves against the rocks and the clapping of the people watching who were waiting to dive. I told him to make that clapping into a tumultuous applause.

He nodded and smiled. I told him to now get the feeling of pride, relief and happiness as strong as you can, and continued:

'You are sitting here with me and learning about focusing on writing assignments. You are curious and interested in how to focus so as to do your best and write your great ideas. While you are listening, you are aware of how fantastic it is that you have interesting ideas, and as you think about writing you get the feeling of happiness, pride and relief that you got when you first dived off the rock into the sea, and you realise how easily and confidently you can write your ideas. Luckily, with your great intelligence, you will quickly realise how easily you can focus and how much fun it is to write your ideas.'

End of session 1 (30 minutes)

Session 2

I decided to anchor the feeling to the writing tool (pen or pencil). I revisited the memory of the experience that provided the feeling to be anchored, got him to get the feeling and describe it. I asked him to make the picture brighter, hear the sounds more loudly (the clapping, the people still waiting to dive). I told him to make that into a huge applause and add triumphant music. I continued: *'Now make that feeling more intense, stronger ... an amazing feeling of relief, pride and happiness. There is a lovely feeling of excitement as you think about how good you will feel using your skills and intelligence as you focus and do the best you can do, enjoying yourself and having a fantastic time, didn't you? Now pick up the pencil - when you feel the pencil in your hand at the start of a writing task, at school or at home, you will get this same feeling of pride, relief and happiness and you will begin to focus on the task and start writing your great and interesting ideas.'*

BREAKING THE STATE:
'What lesson have you got after this?' / Music / A little interaction about the instrument he is learning...

'Now pick up the pencil to write. Got the feeling?'

Smiling and nodding. Involved in the writing task (comprehension exercise from his class)

Noted:
Smiling – great memory for detailed answer to question number 3 on the writing task.

Writing – needed to be reminded of the feeling.

Asked for clarification re whether he should write in sentences or bullet points.

Needed clarification re meaning of 'extract'. Noticed struggle so I intervened by commenting on the amount of writing he had done and reminding him of the 'feeling'. He consciously revisited the feeling.

Did it!

Session 3
My target today was to give K the opportunity to write something of his own choice, set off the anchor and see what happened.

We had a discussion about why he was yawning today. He and his parents and brother stayed up late watching Universum, an environmental programme in German about birds of paradise. He told me a bit about the programme.

Then I gave a similar talk as I had done during last session, ending with: *'...you will now focus on the task and start writing your fantastic and interesting ideas about the Universum programme you watched last night'.*

Noted:

- 8:52 began to write
- K asked one question about the word for programme
- 9:00 (5 lines written)
- K asked how to spell New Guinea
- 9:05 (10 lines written in a focused way)
- 9:10 (15 lines written)
- K tells me about "an emerald green bird puffing up its chest". I tell him this is a beautiful description.
- 9:15 I tell him it is time to finish, that the session is coming to an end. He tells me he has to finish the sentence first.
- No prompts from me!
- No avoidance from K!
- K told me he wanted to show the piece of writing to his class teacher. She smiled broadly and told him excitedly that this piece of writing was amazing and that she was proud of him. She looked towards me in disbelief.

Session 4

This session was focused on preparing K for the homework assignment for the coming week. After reviewing the assignment and dealing with any problem areas in terms of what he needed to do or the terminology used in Maths and Unit of Inquiry, I decided to check with K about the effect his work completion during the last session had on his teacher.

'Can you remember what Ms. J looked like?' 'Yes, she was smiling; she got a bit pink and glowy'. 'What did she say?' He recalled that also.

When asked how he thought she had felt, he said she probably felt very happy and relieved. He said she probably felt proud of him and thought he was intelligent and able to write.

EFFORT AT FUTURE PACING:
Me: *'She likes what you did. When you write your ideas, she is happy and proud of you. She looked radiant and beautiful when she saw what you had done. As you continue to write your ideas, she will be happy and proud of you and you will be happy, proud and relieved every time you hold your*

pencil/ pen in your hand to write your amazing ideas. You will be using your wonderful intelligence, writing your great ideas and doing your very best, won't you? Who else will feel happy and excited and proud of you when you do your best and write your ideas?'

K: *'My Mum and Dad.'*

J: *'So when you hold your pen/pencil in your hand and begin to write your homework, you will use your wonderful intelligence to write your ideas confidently, you will focus on the task, you will feel comfortable, proud, relieved and happy to have these interesting ideas, to be able to write your ideas so well, and you will feel an extra glow of happiness because your Mum and Dad are feeling so proud of you and are so happy for you and for the way you focus and the great work you are doing, won't you.'*

Discussion about when he is going to do the homework.

He decides he will ask his mum if the time he has chosen is convenient for her to be available to support him if he needs it. I suggest that he takes control. Choose when, where and set the time. Then take his pencil in his hand and get the feeling and begin to write his homework. I ask him if this is something he is able to do now. He says, *'I can take control.'* We discuss the procedure if he gets stuck on an item – move on to the next item. Get everything done that he can do by himself first. Then go back and ask for help from his mum or dad. If they are not sure, then wait until he can get help from his teacher.

Impact

K loves to talk. He is also very analytical and has a talent for detail. He is open and pretty honest with me because I have worked closely with him for a few weeks and I have acted on all the information he has provided so as to remove unnecessary demands.

Asking questions to establish his goals would seem pretty similar to the types of dialogue we had during the preceding weeks. Asking him to remember a time when he had been extremely happy etc. would have been new to him, but his response was immediate and his choice was unique. His description of the event and his feelings were detailed and seemed true to his experience. Associating the feeling from this with writing seemed like it might be a step too far, but, amazingly, K was curious enough to go along with the request.

During Session 2, when we had time to test the anchor, I noted that initially K was smiling, focused well and was writing easily. As he became challenged by the need for clarification, he began to get fidgety, but he responded immediately when reminded to *'feel the pencil and get the feeling'*. He asked for clarification and was back on track. Next time he needed clarification, he just asked and continued. Towards the end of the session, he seemed to struggle. Again, with a reminder he was back on track and finished the task. This was the first time that K had written an assignment without intensive prompting.

Outcome in the longer term

K has experienced success by changing the feeling he has when he writes. He has felt better about himself, he has written his ideas in a focused way and he has received some amazingly positive feedback, which was spontaneous and honest. This has happened because he has gone from endless procrastination and writing only when prompted, coaxed and threatened, to producing a page of writing without the need for continuous intervention.

He has accepted responsibility in a positive way and actively planned for the next opportunity to set off his anchored feelings. This needs to be generalised to his homework assignments at home and to his work in the grade level classroom. That will be the focus of our sessions in the immediate future. His grade level teacher has said, 'Now I believe we are going to crack this!'

IT'S GOOD TO TALK IN SCIENCE TEACHING

NLP achieved more than expected for Joanna and Helen and they applied every bit of their short training to great effect.

Joanna Dobson and Helen Fuhr teach at St Benet Biscop High School in Bedlington, Northumberland

Research plan

The main aims of this project were to improve pupil behaviour and achievement by using specific NLP language and communication strategies, and to give pupils strategies for voicing their ideas and build confidence in their own ability, allowing them to take more responsibility for their own learning.

Assessment of the success of the strategy is based on subjective assessments of students' behaviour and achievements and objective tests in results gained in mock GCSE tests or levels achieved in coursework and project work. A longer-term aim will be to assess the improvements in behaviour and attainment of all students in classes where NLP strategies have been implemented. The project is also designed to improve attitude and motivation for pupils in relation to their personal learning, research skills and standard of homework.

Action

As this was a joint project, we decided to choose a student we both teach. We chose the focus student because she was already on report and was seen to be having difficulties in other subject areas. We produced an NLP lesson assessment sheet where we could record information about the student's focus and concentration, work rate, communication with staff and pupils and her tendency to distract others. We also gave the student an overall mark for her compliancy in lessons; 4 being fully compliant and 1 being refusal to follow directions. We focused on the use of the use of language in lessons. Commonly used phrases such as *'why...'* questions were changed to more positive phrases such as, *'can you explain how you came to that conclusion?'* and *'what is it that you don't understand?'* Language was used regularly to elicit more thoughtful responses from students, for example, *'I like that answer, can you tell me more about your thoughts on this?' 'You have made an excellent start on this task, what do you think you could do to improve this piece of work?'* To make the research more valid we decided to monitor four other students in the same classroom using the same assessment criteria. We have observed positive effects in a number of other students and examples have also been included below.

Impact

The impact of NLP strategies has been far more wide reaching than we had anticipated. A Year 10 (age 14-15) class which we focused on initially was a Foundation Science group with abilities ranging from C to F grades. Confidence and motivation were key areas to target throughout the student group. Since the NLP input, our focus student has met all the objectives set out in the project. Her work rate and concentration have been consistently excellent and the level of work she has produced both in lessons and at home has been of a consistently high standard. She has contributed well in lessons and has maintained her focus during tasks.

The effect on three of the additional four students studied in this class has been rather more dramatic:

Student 1 is an extremely quiet student with very little confidence in his ability. He very rarely contributed voluntarily to class discussions or offered answers to questions without prompting. With regular encouragement and use of NLP language he has shown a great improvement in his contributions in class, demonstrating a significant level of understanding. With more difficult topics, he was encouraged to explain his ideas to the class and was able to confidently describe a biological principle to the whole class using a diagram on the board and the correct scientific language.

Student 2 is a quiet student with poor concentration levels. He very rarely contributed voluntarily to class discussions or offered answers to questions without prompting. With regular encouragement and use of NLP language he has shown a great improvement in his contributions in class, also demonstrating a significant level of understanding. During a recent class debate on Human Impact on the Environment, he showed a remarkable level of understanding of the topics discussed and was able to give a sound, reasoned argument for his opinions. He was focused and on task throughout the lesson. He became increasingly animated during the discussion and delivered his opinions confidently and enthusiastically. He obviously enjoyed the lesson and left the class smiling and still offering his opinions and ideas!

Student 3 appears to be a confident student in everything but his academic ability. He can be disruptive and cheeky and is easily distracted by his peers. He finds working to deadlines difficult and rarely completes timed tasks in lessons. Homework is also an issue and is rarely completed. I felt that Student 3 lacked confidence in his own ability and was frightened of failure. He did not expect to do well and so underperformed regularly. Using NLP strategies with lots of positive reinforcement and praise appears to have had a marked effect on his performance and behaviour. Over the weeks of the project, he became more focused in lessons and was encouraged to participate at every opportunity, offering his own ideas and opinions. At first, he found this difficult and gave the usual response of shrugging his shoulders and muttering *'don't know'*. Gradually, he grew in confidence and started to contribute more in lessons and complete written tasks. The breakthrough came after he completed a mock Biology GCSE paper. He achieved a C grade, having been predicted an E. I used the opportunity to reinforce the positive messages used throughout the project and he was obviously delighted with his performance. Since then, he has continued to contribute well to the class and has produced 2 homework tasks on time!

The use of NLP strategies has become an inherent part of my teaching and I have seen improvements in students in other classes where I have used specific language or strategies to solve problems. I have therefore extended the project to include some examples of the effects observed in students from other classes and year groups.

The following two examples are from Year 9 (age 13-14):

Student 4: A very likeable student who tries very hard in lesson but has a severe confidence problem and is afraid to tackle anything new. Extremely concerned about tests and exams and loses all concentration if faced with a test. Using NLP strategies with lots of positive reinforcement and praise appears to have had a marked effect on his performance and confidence. In a recent lesson, we were drawing graphs and interpreting data. He drew the graphs then pushed the paper aside and said he couldn't do the work. Below is a transcript of the conversation:

Student 4: *'I can't do this!'*
JD: *'Who says you can't do it?'*
Student 4: *'It's all wrong. The graphs are wrong.'*
JD: *'I know you can answer this question.'*
Student 4: *'It's not right.'*
JD: *'Can you tell me what is wrong with your graphs?'*
Student 4: *'No'*
JD: *'Neither can I!'*

Student 4 checked the graphs again, broke into a smile and proceeded to finish the task completely. When we reviewed the task, he was able to explain and describe how he had completed the task confidently.

He still finds test situations extremely stressful but NLP techniques help to calm him down significantly. I decided to use an NLP Anchoring and Visualisation technique to help overcome his fear in exams and improve his confidence. Before every assessment and particularly before his mock SATS test, I have used a whole class relaxation technique to allow the students to calm down and focus, asking them to visualise themselves completing the test successfully and seeing the grade they want to achieve written on the front of the paper. This has not only helped this student to remain calm during test situations, but has also created a relaxed, calm environment, which has helped the other pupils in the class to focus on their work. Student 4 is now aware of how he reacts to test situations and knows he needs to deal with this problem. He is gradually learning how to cope and use strategies to help him calm down. Interestingly, the rest of the class obviously benefit from this technique too and now ask for the relaxation technique to be used before they do any end-of-topic test!

Student 5 is a very able student working in a Triple Award Science class with many gifted and talented students. He has decided that he does not fit into this very able group and has convinced himself he is going to fail. I have worked on positive reinforcement together with peer teaching to encourage him and help him to regain his confidence.

The first signs that the strategy may have been having an effect were seen in homework completed and handed in on time. This is a major improvement for this student, who had struggled to complete any homework since September. An 8-week project was given to the class in April and the work he handed in was excellent, showing a very good level of research and understanding. I have also used peer teaching with this student. He is an extremely good mathematician and will complete any tasks involving scientific equations very quickly. I have then used him to peer teach other pupils and he has obviously enjoyed this role and has gained confidence from it.

NLP has made us more conscious of the words we use when talking to students and we both feel confident enough to be able to guide students into reaching their own conclusions when dealing with various issues. Building rapport with students is very important and being aware that each individual interprets and sees things completely differently has made us inquisitive to research NLP further. Through our discussions, we have observed that NLP enables students to engage and contribute usefully to lessons. Students have been able to explain themselves more clearly and are able to problem solve and bring themselves to suitable and workable solutions through guidance and communication with the teacher. There has been a significant improvement in the levels of confidence shown by pupils in the classroom and this has led to increased motivation which has manifested itself both in improved contribution and work rate in class and improved quality of homework.

We have also shared our experience with both our mentor and an Additional Support Teacher at school and they are both planning to incorporate our ideas into their own teaching. In addition, we are planning teaching sessions in September to extend these ideas to the wider school community and in this way we may be able to target specific pupils across the curriculum to gain a deeper understanding of the effects of NLP strategies used in a wider context.

STATE AND LANGUAGE TO BUILD CONFIDENCE IN OUTDOOR PURSUITS

Ian McDuff teaches at Astley Community High School, Seaton Delaval, Northumberland

Research plan

My particular interest is in developing my mentoring skills in terms of pastoral support by the use of NLP techniques, specifically to develop my use of language to engage disaffected pupils. I decided to use the skills I developed on the first 2 days of the NLP course during a 3-day outward-bound course with my tutor group. I targeted one pupil with low self-esteem who often struggled to feel part of the group. This off-site programme would be a challenge to him due to his levels of physical ability and his limited social skills. My aim was to evaluate how this pupil initially coped with his new surroundings and the challenges he was going to face. I was looking to consider any changes in his behaviour and the behaviour of other pupils within the group.

Action

During the 3-day programme, a number of team-based activities took place. These involved splitting the 22 pupils into typically 4 groups and setting each group a challenge in competition with the other 3 groups. The pupil who was the focus of my study, T, would typically be the last to be chosen if pupils made team selections, so to avoid this, the teachers chose groups.

Initially, T was reluctant to take an active role within the group. It appeared that he was afraid of 'letting the group down' or of his team failing due to his lack of ability. However, these being group activities, his weaknesses were balanced out and the team he was involved with was fairly successful.

My first intervention came following the first set of challenges. I discussed with T the emotions he felt during the tasks and how these changed when successes were achieved. I made sure that I emphasised that he was part of the success and without his participation the team may not have succeeded.

Building upon this initial discussion, throughout the remainder of the 3 days I focused on setting T mini targets. These were sometimes part of team events and at other times individual challenges. When it appeared that T was about to give up or walk away from a difficult challenge, I reminded him of his prior successes *'Remember what it felt like when you did...'*

'How do you think you will feel when you achieve...'

'You can't do this ... yet'

'Just suppose you could do this...'

In most instances T fulfilled the tasks set out for him.

Impact
There was a noticeable change in the attitude of other members of the group towards T. They were aware of his physical limitations, but as they saw he was trying to succeed and trying his best, they began to offer their encouragement. This had a further positive impact on T. It was clearly apparent that he felt more accepted into the group by this encouragement. He felt part of the team, a valued player. Without the NLP training, my mentoring of T would not have been as successful.

This has demonstrated to me that the use of simple but effective questioning techniques can dramatically affect the behaviour and attitude of pupils. Seeing the success with an individual pupil over a period of 3 days, I continue to use positive questioning within the classroom environment and it continues to demonstrate a powerful means of influencing pupil behaviour and attitude.

On returning to school, T has become more confident. Other members of the teaching staff have noticed this too. He appears to have lost a lot of his negativity with regard to school. His attendance level has also improved

VOICE TONE AND BODY LANGUAGE IN FOOD TECHNOLOGY LESSONS

Michelle Whall teaches at Astley Community High School, Seaton Delaval Northumberland

Research plan
Shortly after the first NLP session I noticed there appeared to be pupils within a particular class upon whom other pupils modelled their behaviours. These pupils seemed to have an influence over the

behaviour and mood of the rest of the class, and other students appeared to be taking quite overt behavioural cues from these influencers. Often, these behaviours were low-level distractions such as giggling, pen tapping, whispering and chair-rocking. However, on occasion these influencing pupils would seem to take cues from me and would 'shush' their fellow pupils or discourage them from other distracting behaviours.

This was a Year 9 (age 13-14) Food Technology class of 30 pupils whom I saw once a fortnight for the last lesson on a Friday. Since I saw them so infrequently, my rapport with this class was not a strong as with other classes. A considerable amount of time was devoted to classroom management and I seemed to spend a lot of the lesson repeating instructions over and over and consequently not making much progress with the curriculum.

I thought it would be of benefit to harness the influence certain pupils had in a positive manner using NLP techniques, hoping that these pupils would positively influence the rest of the class. I also wondered whether the behaviour of some of the influencing pupils might improve, since these pupils had frequent demerits.

Action
LESSON 1
I identified 4 pupils who appeared to have influence over the behaviour of their peers and arranged the class into 4 groups (the room has 4 static clusters of work spaces), each with an influencing pupil. These influencing pupils were seated in a position in which they had a clear view of me at all times (something which the static seating in the Food Room precludes for the majority of the pupils, which possibly contributes to the low-level disturbances in this class). The pupils identified as having influence were not told the reason for the seating plan and neither were the rest of the class. The first thing I experimented with was the tonality of my voice, which I have always thought a little high-pitched. I ensured that when I gave commands I lowered the tone of my voice at the end and matched it with a downward sweep of my hand. This was done whilst making clear eye contact with the 4 influencing pupils and in full view of them. The desired effect was

almost immediate, the influencing pupils nudging the other pupils and instructing them about what I wanted them to do. As the lesson progressed I noticed that rather than just following the cues of the influencing pupils, the other members of the class were beginning to pay far more attention to me than they had previously, almost as if to try to see what information the other pupils were getting that they weren't. The lesson progressed well and the pupils attained all the learning objectives set (unheard of for this class!). I gave out far more merits than in previous lessons. Most striking was that one of the influencing pupils was someone I would generally have had to reprimand time and again, often leading to him being fed up, me being frazzled, and a rash of de-merits. Yet for this lesson, he remained on task throughout and gained merits.

LESSON 2
Seating remained as before and I continued with the use of lower tonality and the downward hand movement. I also introduced other visual and spatial anchoring to the class. Again, use of any visual technique is problematic in the Food Room because of its layout, so once more I made use of the influencing pupils to disseminate instructions to their peers. The visual and spatial anchors I introduced were always in clear view of the influencing pupils:

- **Anchor 1**: Standing to the left of my desk with my right hand on it – the signal to quieten down, the lesson is about to begin.
- **Anchor 2**: Standing at the back of the class facing the whiteboard – the signal to prepare to carry out a task.
- **Anchor 3**: In the centre of the room, right arm raised – the signal to stop talking following a discussion-led task. I carried out these anchors many times during the lesson, along with the corresponding verbal command and always ensuring I made clear eye contact with the influencing pupils. As I expected, these pupils watched me carefully and ensured their peers were aware of my expectations. By the end of the lesson I only had to walk to one of these three places and the pupils became quiet in seconds. Once more I noticed that the pupils all became far more attentive to both my verbal and non-verbal communication and the lesson was as successful as the one the previous week. The pupils seemed to

be calmer and happier and I wonder if this was also a reflection of my demeanor.

LESSON 3
A practical food lesson when I am the only member of staff with 30 pupils is often a recipe for disruption and raised voices. In the past, I found shouting was the only means to get the students' attention and after a while this loses its effect. Often during a practical lesson it is important to get the pupils' attention very quickly, yet often they are not listening to me or not within my line of vision. I wondered how well tonality, anchoring and use of the influencing pupils would work in a practical situation. Initially, I found I had to raise my voice slightly because all the pupils were so engrossed in their work and communicating with their peers. However, the influencing pupils and several others became very quickly clued in to where I was standing in the room and to my body positioning and responded by becoming quiet and listening to instructions. During the practical lesson the anchor I found most pupils responded to best was a raised arm in the centre of the room. For a practical lesson last thing on a Friday, the whole experience was relatively calm. Compared with previous practicals for this class it was a revelation! We were tidied up on time and the pupils produced excellent products.

Impact
The impact of utilisation of my new learning has resulted in:

- Increased engagement with the class
- A more attentive class
- The reduction of low-level unwanted behaviours • A reduction in de-merits issued
- More suitable progression through learning materials
- A better quality relationship between teacher and pupils

My classroom practice has changed considerably because the NLP techniques are easily applied and have become natural behaviour very quickly. The impacts were quick, and plain to see.

CHAPTER 22

Post-compulsory education, 16 years and over

Education in the 16+ sector provides some helpful examples of learning in an adult environment.

NLP THROUGHOUT THE LESSON WITH 16-19-YEAR-OLD STUDENTS
Helen shows how to bring a range of NLP skills together for a successful and highly motivating lesson.

Helen Sweet teaches Level 3 Graphic Design to 16-19-year-olds and is also responsible for delivering group tutorials related to the 'Every Child Matters' themes

Research plan
Whilst the students are generally well motivated and engaged, and achieve the learning outcomes in lesson, I wanted to explore the use of various NLP skills and techniques to create a greater atmosphere of fun in the classroom to enhance the learning experience and further motivate the learners and build their confidence. In particular, I wanted to first explore this for a group tutorial preparing learners for Higher Education (HE) and job interviews. For the specific session I focused on for this project, (a session on interview skills), I wanted to ensure that they came away feeling confident about themselves and were able to manage nerves so that they perform well at their interviews, whilst emphasising the importance of preparation

ELEMENTS OF NLP
Initially I had planned to use animated storytelling / metaphor along with voice control and nested loops. However, during the session I also found myself using submodalities and anchoring as a means to build atmosphere and confidence in the learners, and also meta programs and some Milton language patterns.

Action

I planned a lesson in which we would explore the 'experience' of a job / HE interview, and the means by which we create first impressions.

I opened the session by 'acting' the story of one of my most 'nervous' experiences – my driving test! I expressed the build up to the event, from my driving lessons right up to the morning of my test... and I stopped there (opening the first loop). I did this through using character voices (driving instructor, test instructor, and a younger version of myself!). Some poetic licence was given and I somewhat exaggerated some of the experience for greater effect, though essentially the story was true. I used facial expressions and changed voice tonality as well as moving about the front of the room (sitting on chairs, changing directions etc.) to in order to fully act out the story.

Next we had a discussion about what creates a first impression, and how they could prepare themselves for interview. I began this by using spatial anchoring, facial expressions, body language, voice control and Milton patterns to inoculate against common fears and arguments (i.e. *'what you wear doesn't matter', 'I'll stuff up because I'm too nervous', 'I'm not good at interviews'* etc.), and install more positive beliefs. For example, *'some people think that they can't be successful at interview because they find that they get nervous, however... what they don't realise is that they can learn to remain calm at interview, and that a little nervousness in fact shows the interviewer that you care'*.

I also expressed the importance of preparing through practising mock interviews. I appealed to both 'towards' and 'away from' meta programs by expressing what impact it would have to practise, and what wouldn't happen as a result of practice. I used spatial anchoring when referring to this, placing the desired actions in one area in which I would use facial expressions and happy voice tones to suggest success.

Next I gave them some very simple tips on rapport building and body language, which I demonstrated with a volunteer through role-play. Following this, I instructed them the get into groups of three and gave them a set of interview questions and observation sheets, and placed each of them in a specific role (naming the three learners 'Fantastic', '

Amazing ' and 'Brilliant' rather than 1, 2, 3) in order to allocate roles. I then simply observed the activity, and then afterward requested that each observer feedback the points to the rest of the class, and I added points of my own, ensuring that everything was made 'positive'.

After rotating this activity so that everyone had taken part in all three roles, I sat them down for a plenary, and had them recap the main points and learnings. Following this, I returned to the story of my driving test and again acted it out. Of course, I passed first time ;-) And the moral was that (a) practice is important, (b) there are ways to control/ harness nerves, (c) it's common to be successful, despite being nervous (nerves are ok).

I had planned to end the session there, only I found that I had time to spare, and so off the hoof, I gave them the option of trying out an anchor they could use to access a resourceful state before an interview. (They know a little about this area of NLP as I've spoken to them about it previously). They were really keen to do it (not one of them asked if they could just go to lunch early!). They chose the 'states' (self-confidence, calmness, happiness) and I had them stand in a circle. I used voice control to make them calm, and embedded commands to put them in the right state to begin with. I had them recall their own memories of the states they wanted and simply built them up through asking them to spin the feelings, make the images bigger and brighter, turn up to volume on the sounds, breathe in the scents etc. When they were at the peak, I had them step into their 'space'. We ended the session with this.

Impact

The animated storytelling had a surprising impact on the learners – they were keen to listen, and were leaning in to watch and hear my experience. They asked questions afterwards, showing curiosity, and were fully engaged. They were also frustrated when I would not tell them what happened in the actual test and insisted I'd leave that part until the end of the lesson. Following the story the learners were energetic though also frustrated, but this soon passed and they got on with the discussions and activities I prompted with energy.

In the second portion (discussing interview nerves and practice), learners were nodding along in agreement with me. And following this, they were keen to practise the interviews through role play. Previously the suggestion of role play would have invited moans and groans, but I was pleasantly surprised to find that they were all very keen and got straight to it! The energy in the room was lovely. The students were fully engaged in the role play and I was surprised to find that they were all happy and pleased to take part. The feedback session which followed showed that the learners had all gained a great deal from the activities. At the end of the lesson they even requested more of "this type of thing".

When I closed the loop on the driving test story, they appeared happy to hear that I had passed, and again were full of questions, giving me the opportunity to further express the learning points. It was clear from their body language and eye contact that they found it interesting and engaging.

Creating the calm, confident, happy state was perhaps the most successful part of the session. They all had their eyes closed and I noticed the atmosphere in the room change, the smiles creep up into their faces, their posture change, skin tone change. It was exhilarating even for me, as I watched the state of the whole room change – breathtaking. Afterwards, when I asked them to open their eyes again, they were all smiling, and thanked me as they quietly picked up their things and left the class. I was quite simply 'buzzing' at the success of the session. I have continued to use these techniques in my lessons, and find them very successful. I've not since explicitly used submodalities and anchoring (only covertly) as it hasn't been appropriate to do so again, but other subtle means of doing so have proved useful in a number of sessions. It's been difficult to explain what I have been doing in this report, as so many aspects of NLP come in to my everyday teaching now. It's had a great impact on my enjoyment and at work, and the enjoyment of the learners I have the pleasure to teach.

MEMORY PEGS STRATEGY

Here is an extract from Marian's report highlighting the results of her Memory strategy project.

> *Marian Bradley was a Practitioner in NLP when she completed this project. She went on to complete her Master Practitioner and Teaching Excellence the following year.*

Research plan

The Learning Mentor Programme in Omagh, Northern Ireland, was developed in response to the consistent underachievement of children from the ONRAs (Omagh Neighbourhood Renewal Areas). Approximately 67% of Year 12 (age 15-16) students attending Omagh Secondary schools achieve 5 A*-C grades in GCSEs including English and Maths. Only 23% of ONRA students achieve 5 A*-C grades in GCSEs including English and Maths, highlighting the disparity between ONRA children and the general population.

My job as a mentor is to work with children from the ONRAs, helping them to build confidence and self-esteem and develop skills and coping mechanisms so that they are in a better position to achieve their potential. The students are selected for mentoring for a variety of reasons, including academic under-achievement, negative behavioural referrals and poor attendance at school. At the time of writing, there are 35 students on the mentoring programme.

The group for this research comprised 10 students who had all been recently selected for mentoring and were presenting with the most difficulties. The young people were mentored individually during May and June 2013 and were invited to take part in the research at the first group meeting in September 2013.

Action

A significant number of the students are referred to me because they have poor coping mechanisms and a limited or distorted view of emotional intelligence. Their model of the world may include the notions that *'all the teachers hate me', 'I'm stupid'* and/or *'everything always goes wrong for me'*. The Meta Model was great for challenging these negative beliefs in a gentle way and helping the young people to become aware of their own mental maps and where these maps were distorted. Practising using the Meta Model and becoming familiar with the use of the responses of *'how?'/ 'who says?/ 'everyone?'* when challenging a negative belief produced very powerful results.

During NLP Module 2, I was fortunate in that I was used to demonstrate the Memory Peg system. As a result of this and the positive glow I felt when I remembered the 10 random objects 'pegged' onto my body, I decided that this might be useful for my young people.

The Memory Peg system was explained to the young people as a 'Gift' that they nurtured, developed and presented to themselves; a gift that they would have for the rest of their lives, a gift that they could carry with them and use again and again. The fantastic thing about this gift was the more they used this gift the better and more powerful it became.

The research started during the second week of September with a plan to have it finished by the Hallowe'en break at the end of October.
The children were interested in this 'gift' and agreed to take part in the research.

Scheduled Timetable
WEEK BEGINNING
- 9th Sept - introduce research, 'Memory Peg GIFT'
- 16th Sept - learn 10 pegs
- 23rd Sept - pin 10 pieces of information from agreed subject/s on to pegs
- 30th Sept - pin 10 more pieces of information from agreed subject/son to pegs
- 7th Oct - pin 10 more pieces of information from agreed subject/s on to pegs
- 14th Oct - pin 10 more pieces of information from agreed subject/son to pegs
- 21st Oct - record 40 pieces of information plus 10 pegs, giving a total of 50

The timetable did not go according to plan because individuals in the control group were not always available and with no uniformity of school holidays the young people did not get the opportunity to gather the 40 pieces of information. The young people I work with have a poor record of attendance and as a result were not always available to meet. The actual recording of the memory pegs was completed during the week beginning 11th November 2013 and the evaluations were recorded during week beginning 18th November 2013. This extension I felt was necessary as the exercise was designed to help each child realise what an amazing brain they had and to rush the ending and the gathering of the results would, I felt, have defeated this purpose.

Impact

The Memory Peg Gift generated a huge amount of interest with the mentees and this resulted in students asking to be included. One 12-year-old student who is outside the group remit asked to join the group, and while his scores are not included, he did learn the system. This student has difficulty sitting in class and tends to walk out of lessons after about 10 minutes, so you can imagine the effect he had on staff when he asked to stay in an English lesson because he didn't have the 10 memory pegs to tell Marian!

The students whom I spent more time with and had built a relationship with prior to the test scored greater results. The research, which aimed to help the young people with issues of self-esteem and self-worth, has been successful. 90% of the control group gave very positive feedback and have successfully used the Memory Peg Gift for class tests and GCSE exams. One student out of 10 recorded that he did not like the Memory Peg Gift, but he has since informed me that he has used it to remember information for an exam.

The versatility of the Memory Peg Gift meant that it was easy to tailor it to meet the needs of individuals. Presupposing success in learning enhanced the delivery of the Memory Peg Gift research. Anchoring positive states in the mentees has become a very important element in my mentoring because the highest percentage of my work is one-to-one, where students have a time set aside where they can talk to me without interruptions. NLP has given me the tools to have a greater understanding of what I am doing, learn new skills and hone the skills I already have.

SELECTION OF STUDENTS' EVALUATIONS :
- 'I really enjoyed the Memory Peg Gift because it was a bit of a challenge but I feel it has benefited me quite a bit and will be a great learning tool coming up to revision time for my exams. The pictures chosen were very well selected and easy to pin things onto for subjects such as Religion and English. I found it a great success for myself. I don't have a great memory but found it really easy memorising them due to the pictures chosen. I'll definitely use this technique in the upcoming exams for GCSE I'll have this year and next.'
- 'I now know that I have a great memory. I am going to use this to study for my exams.'
- 'I scored 40 out of 40 plus the 10 Memory Peg Gifts.'
- 'I remembered the lists but I thought it was difficult to use.'

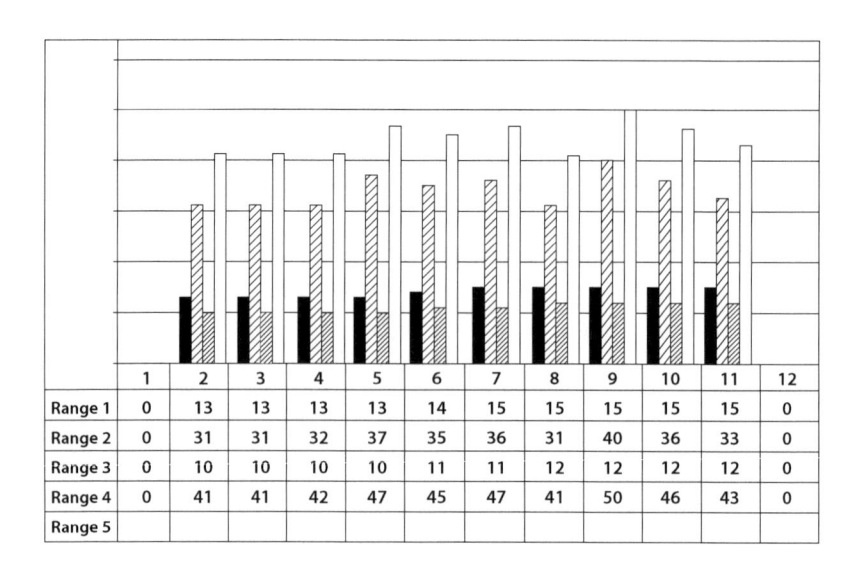

	1	2	3	4	5	6	7	8	9	10	11	12
Range 1	0	13	13	13	13	14	15	15	15	15	15	0
Range 2	0	31	31	32	37	35	36	31	40	36	33	0
Range 3	0	10	10	10	10	11	11	12	12	12	12	0
Range 4	0	41	41	42	47	45	47	41	50	46	43	0
Range 5												

Age	Scores	School Year	Scores +peg
13	31	10	41
13	31	10	41
13	32	10	42
13	37	10	47
14	35	11	45
15	36	11	47
15	31	12	41
15	40	12	50
15	36	12	46
15	33	12	43

STATES FOR LEARNING EXCELLENCE, OBSERVATION AND LEADERSHIP FOR UNDERGRADUATES

Here is an abridged version of Nancy's thorough research project.

Nancy Ault teaches in an Australian university

Research plan

Since 2003, students on the Developing Community Leadership course have been introduced to the idea that their beliefs about learning and about themselves as learners will impact on their behaviour and their learning outcomes. Thus, at the beginning of each intensive unit, students learn to create and anchor a state of learning excellence.

The aim of this research project was to enable students to make a connection between their personal state and their performance. In order to achieve, students needed to be able to:

- Become aware of their personal internal states; that is, their own internal representations and the submodalities
- Create a desired state
- Anchor and fire this state

In addition, an exercise was required to allow the students to evaluate and measure their performance in different states. In this way, they would be able to test the relationship (or not) between their states and their performance. More specifically, the focus of the project was upon the relationship between the students' states and their perception of their leadership capabilities.

Action
ELEMENTS OF NLP
Building, anchoring and accessing a state were used in the project. Attention was paid to the language patterns used in guiding the students. For example, using Milton language, the students were asked to *'imagine a time when everything flowed and learning was easily excellent'*. Artfully vague Milton language was used so that students could create their own states from their personal maps of the world. For students who might not be able to imagine such a time, they were also asked to imagine what this might be like or think of a person who they thought demonstrated this state of learning excellence. To help the students access this time and state, all the senses were used, ie., *what did you... see/hear/sense/smell/and taste* (different submodalities suggested for each representation). Once this state was created and easily accessed, the students were guided in anchoring the state on some accessible part of their bodies.

In addition to elements of NLP, a questionnaire on leadership motivation - the Leadership Motivation Assessment - was used as a measurement assessment. Three times during the intensive unit the students were asked to create particular states in which they answered the questionnaire. Two class tests were given during the period in which the States and Motivation for Leadership exercise was conducted. Responses to the overall exercise were collected in a Feedback and Recommendations questionnaire at the end of the intensive part of the unit.

To begin this project, it was necessary to establish a benchmark state and performance against which future states and performances could be measured. In the first workshop, after an exercise used to introduce students to each other prior to establishing the benchmark, the students were taught to create a state of learning excellence, anchor this state and then access it. The purpose of the exercise in building and assessing states was explained to the students. The first state created was one where learning was easily excellent. The purpose of creating this state was to enable the students to be able to access a state of learning excellence throughout the intensive unit. In an outdoor area close to the classroom, the following steps were taken: First, the students were led through building a 'Learning excellence state' using a script such as the following:

BUILDING A STATE OF LEARNING EXCELLENCE

In your imagination draw a circle on the grass in front of you... Now imagine a time with learning flowed easily... A time when learning was easy. Excellent easy... Like a sponge soaking up water... Sense this time... See how ever you see learning easily excellent

Notice the Images...

Close, far, still, moving, bright, dark, framed, an open vista, however you see learning easily...

Hear how you hear learning easily excellent

Notice the Sounds... Loud, soft, high, low, long, clipped, your own voice, another's, however you hear learning easily...

Feel however you feel learning easily excellent Notice the sensations...

Strong, weak, hot, cold, moist, dry, heavy, light, however you feel learning easily...

Smell how ever you smell learning easily excellent

Smells... Sweet, pungent, flowery, earthy, bland, spicy, however you smell learning easily...

Taste how ever you taste learning easily excellent Tastes... Salty, bitter, smooth, sour, sweet, how ever you taste learning easily...Sensing inwardly outwardly learning easily

Excellent...

Easily...

When you are ready, in your own time...

Step into your circle. Enter into, associate with and re-live your experience...

Learning... easily excellent... As your experience reaches its peak, step out of

your circle, shaking off the experience of learning easily, leaving it in your

Learning excellence circle.

The second step was testing the state of excellence. When all the students had stepped out of their circles, they were asked to step back into the circle to test if they accessed the state. The students were given time to build and strengthen their circles. They were told that they could add resources to this state of learning excellence through remembering a time when they had the resource that they wanted to add (or alternatively, imagining the resource or remembering a person who had the resource) and using the same process, add the resource to their state of learning excellence. The third step in the initial exercise involved anchoring the state. The students were asked to select a point on their upper body which they could easily and unobtrusively touch, such as an ear lobe or a knuckle. They were asked to create their state of excellence and step into the state and allow it to intensify. When they sensed that the experience was just about to peak in intensity, they were asked step out of the circle and pick it up and place it on the point of their body they had chosen. They were led through this process several times and then they were asked to fire off the anchor by touching the point they had chosen to see if the state came back.

BUILDING A STATE FOR AN EFFECTIVE OBSERVER
The class continued with another learning exercise related to their understanding of leadership and leaders. The students were guided, using Milton language, to imagine a time when they excelled at

observing something. After this imaginative exercise, they were invited to share what they thought was important in an effective observer. This step was taken to widen the students' perceptions of what might contribute to an effective observer state. While they were in this state, the students were asked to answer the questions on the Leadership Motivation Assessment.

LOW PERFORMANCE STATE
Midway through the unit, the States and Motivation for Leadership exercise was repeated. This time, however, the state created was one of low performance. The students were first led in an imaginative exercise of remembering a time when they had experienced a low or poor performance. This was followed by a general sharing of characteristics that might be found in such a state. Next the students were led through a process of building a poor performance state. This state was not reinforced as they sat down in order not to intentionally anchor the state to the chairs. Once the students accessed the poor performance state, they completed the Leadership Motivation Assessment a second time. Once the questionnaire was completed, the students were led through breaking the state, including tipping the chairs, grounding their experience and re-entering the class in a peak performance state.

HIGH PERFORMANCE STATE
The third time the States and Motivation for Leadership exercise was used was towards the end of the unit. The same procedure to build a state was used except for one difference. During the intensive component of the unit, the students were given 2 class tests. Each test was comprised of video clips about which the students were asked questions which linked their observations to theory. Some modelling of showing a video clip and analysing it had occurred prior to the first quiz, so that the concept was not entirely new. The first test was given on a day when the States and Motivation for Leadership exercise was not done. Prior to the test, the students were not primed to get into a high performance state. The second class test occurred directly after the students were asked to create a state of high performance excellence. Instead of breaking the state, it was suggested that the students increase their high performance state for the test. The test followed a similar pattern to the earlier test

with video clips and questions. After the test, the students were asked to break their state, go outside to the green, ground their experience and re-enter the class refreshed and ready to carry on with work.

EVALUATION AND FEEDBACK

At the end of the unit, the States and Motivation for Leadership exercise was evaluated as part of a Feedback and Recommendations questionnaire given to the students in class prior to a general review of the unit. The questions asked were: • What did you observe from doing this exercise? • What are you taking away from this exercise? • On a scale of 1 to 7, where 1 is 'Not Confident', 4 is 'Neutral' and 7 is 'Extremely Confident', how confident are you in your ability to now change your state to suit the situation? • Would you recommend this exercise to future classes? This feedback was anonymous so that students had the freedom to provide negative feedback. For each student, the answers to the Leadership Motivation Assessment for the three states were recorded and analysed both individually and for the class as a whole.

Impact

In Figure 1: Average Class Motivation to Lead, all the answers for each student questionnaire were summed and an average calculated. As it can be seen, there was an overall decrease in the motivation to lead when the students answered the questions in a state of low performance. There was an increase in motivation to lead when the students answered the questionnaire in a state of high performance. Because the sample number was low (24), the results were not tested for significance. Therefore, the results only indicate a trend for this particular population of students.

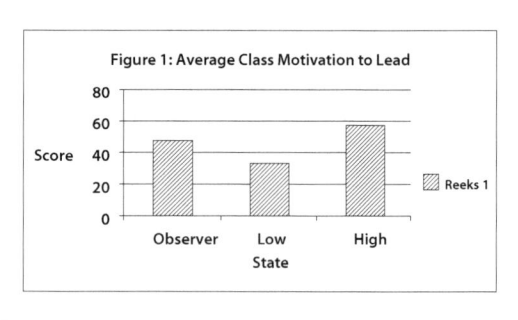

The observer state was used as a baseline benchmark against which the low and high performance states could be mapped. When the average answers to each question were graphed, the scores for a low motivation state were less than the average for the observer state (Figure 2: Breakdown by Question of the Average Class Motivation to Lead). The averages for the questions in the high performance state were higher than the observer state.

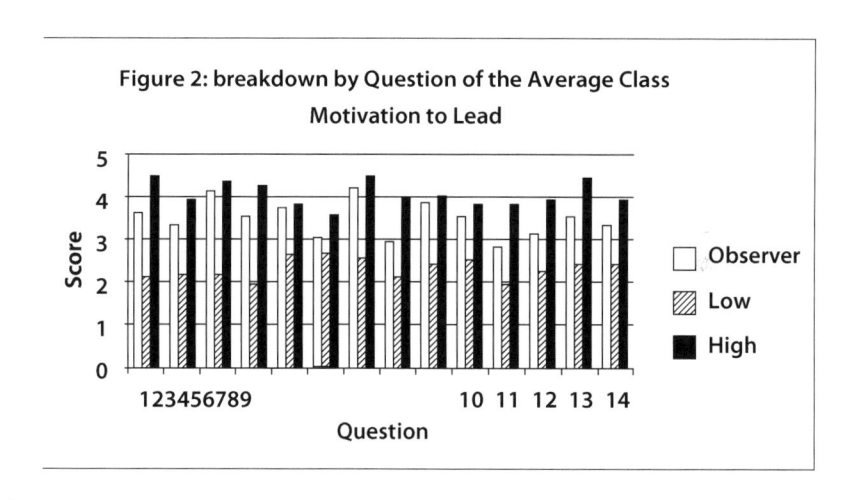

Figure 2: breakdown by Question of the Average Class Motivation to Lead

NOTE FROM THE AUTHORS:
Nancy's very thorough project runs to 40 pages, so only a sample is reproduced here. For a copy of the full report contact Meta on the details at the back of the book.

THE USE OF NLP IN AN ACADEMIC COACHING AND MENTORING ROLE
This case study highlights how practising NLP is so valuable in gaining skills.

Name withheld

Project plan
My intention was to study the use of NLP as an aid in my role as an academic mentor and coach to Sixth Form (age 16-18) students.
The question was how NLP could be used to address issues that were hampering the students' ability to reach their academic targets.

Three students presented with academic issues where I felt NLP might be helpful. The plan of action was to address these issues purely with

NLP, rather than the traditional system of coaching/mentoring, which I would previously have used.

Student A presented with problems with underperforming in recent examinations. This was believed to be a hard-working student who it was felt may have been inefficient in his revision techniques.

Student B presented with stress-related symptoms. Student B was again believed to be a hard-working student who was thought to be putting himself under undue academic pressure and thus causing physical symptoms.

Student C presented with confidence issues in his academic work. This student was again believed to be an able and hard-working student who lacked confidence in his own abilities.

Action
STUDENT A :
I used a deep learning strategy we had been taught on the NLP Practitioner course to teach the student a new method of revision. We used 10 words, turned them into visual images and anchored them to 10 different parts of the body. The student found that he could easily remember these terms and he was going to use this principle to anchor revision topics in different areas of his bedroom.

I also used the TOTE model to investigate the student's revision technique. I used elicitation questions to analyse the steps that he used in his revision for his summer examinations. We found that his revision technique consisted of first making revision notes and then making mind maps based on these. He would then complete practice papers based on these topics.

I was surprised that as we worked through these questions the student was automatically evaluating the effectiveness of his own system. He felt that he should have incorporated more breaks into his revision schedule, as his temptation had been to stick at a topic until he had finished it. He also felt that his revision would have been more productive if he had asked someone to test him at the end of each topic, as he had done in previous exam periods. He concluded that he had not always focused on areas of weakness in his practice papers and that in future he needed to make a list of questions or topics that had caused him difficulty. He also felt that he needed to ensure that he always followed up on asking for help on these topics as he had not always done this.

Although I am writing this several weeks after this session took place, I can still remember the 'road to Damascus' moment that this student seemed to experience when I asked the elicitation questions. Looking back at our course manual now, I see that I should have been looking for visual cues in the student's responses and I cannot remember doing this. However, he seemed to think that his responses were valuable and asked if I would write them up for him as he wanted to use them to prompt him in his revision for his next exam.

Student B had been seeing a psychologist to treat his stress during the summer holidays and asked if there were any NLP techniques that might help him. I used a Swish pattern to replace his tense and anxious state with a more positive one. This seemed to work well and the student reported that he had been using this technique between sessions and felt that it had helped him.

I have also used the Meta Model to drill down and find out what is causing his fear of failing. This has proved a challenge as I do not feel that I have yet got to the root of the problem. He has never failed any examinations before and questioning reveals that the pressure is self-imposed. The one positive outcome of the Meta Model is that we found an exception to the panic attacks this student experiences around exams. The exception proved to be when he used sport as an outlet for his stress. I suspect that the lack of progress in this particular area is due to my own lack of expertise. The limited experience I have had in using the Meta Model has made me realise that although I thought I was a good listener, I don't really listen to what people are actually saying. Moreover, the process of listening intently while thinking about what they are saying, is very much a work in progress. At the moment I still often reflect after a session on what the student has said and then revisit that the next time I see them. I have also realised the value of 'Columbo-style' of questioning (like the detective from the 1970s TV series who would 'innocently' question suspects in a non-threatening way) as it is too easy for me to sound like an inquisitor.

STUDENT B :
The timeline technique proved to be particularly effective with Student B. This student had a major academic deadline 3 weeks away and he had a huge amount of work to complete in this time. I thought it was interesting that when asked where he saw this deadline on his timeline, he showed that it was right in front of his face. When I got him to map out his timeline for these 3 weeks and anchor deadlines, he said that he was surprised that the deadline was further away than he had thought. Breaking down the work into sections and anchoring these on his timeline seemed to be very effective in showing him that the deadline was achievable.

This student plays sport at a very high level and has another source of anxiety in the shape of an on-going sports injury which he is afraid may prevent him from becoming a professional sportsman. This week I have begun using the Meta Model to try to help the student find his own solutions to the problem he is most fearful of.

I feel that we have made some small progress here, as the student was able to identify that sports coaching may be an alternative option to playing sport professionally, and he is going to find out if he can work towards achieving some coaching qualifications through his sponsors whilst he is in rehabilitation with his injury. Coaching techniques also helped him find a possible solution to the problem of him not being able to attend swimming sessions which would have been an outlet for relieving some of his stress.

STUDENT C :
Student C is in an exceptionally vulnerable student experiencing a lack of confidence in his ability in one of his examination subjects. We found that this lack of confidence was affecting his lack of focus and approach to this subject. We have done some work on creating a positive and confident state which this student is going to use going into this lesson. Using the Meta Model, I was able to challenge his belief that the other

students were cleverer than him. This technique seemed to be more successful than with Student B, as Student C commented that he realised that there was no foundation for his beliefs. I also used reframing to attempt to show that not understanding an explanation didn't automatically mean that he was less able than the other students.

Impact

At the time of writing, we have only been back in school for a short time but already I feel that the techniques I have learned are beginning to make a difference. It is a daunting process and I have quickly realised that it will take considerable practice to become more proficient in the use of these techniques. The one-to-one sessions with students have required the application of these techniques in unfamiliar situations and each student has had different issues. However, it is an exciting and sometimes powerful feeling to have a toolkit which could possibly change students' lives.

CHAPTER 23

Education Management

Headteachers, middle managers and curriculum leaders can all contribute to the dissemination of NLP good practice in their schools. Here are some examples of managers who have taken up the gauntlet and spread the word.

USING THE META MODEL TO CHALLENGE SELF-LIMITING BELIEFS IN SCHOOL

Michelle explains how she is changing the attitudes and behaviour of all her staff to provide a consistent NLP-based approach in her school.

Michelle Sheehy is the Headteacher at Millfield Primary School, Walsall, West Midlands

Project plan The main reason I chose to do the NLP Practitioner training was to find a means of motivating the children in my school, promoting their self-worth and challenging their self-limiting beliefs. I am fortunate to have a committed and innovative staff open to new ideas. I knew that if I were to present an alternative means of addressing the difficulties we faced, they would immediately be on board.

Since becoming Headteacher 4 years ago, the background of the children has always been a barrier that I am keen to remove. The school is on a white council estate with high unemployment. Education is not valued by many of the parents and aspirations are extremely low. Many of the children in school have parents who are addicted to drugs or alcohol. Just before I attended the first 4 days of my NLP Practitioner training, there was a lunchtime incident with one of these children, who we will call 'Sam'. Sam has two younger brothers and two younger half-sisters. His mother's partner, who is not his father, is an extremely aggressive and violent person. His mother is also violent. They are both addicts and both the younger boys have spent time sleeping in my office because their mother had been having a "rave" (their word) the previous night.

Sam, being the eldest boy and seeing the vulnerable position his mother is in, is extremely protective towards her and, due to numerous referrals we have made to social services, is suspicious of authority and always guarded when speaking to adults. He is very intelligent and sensitive and likes to be the class clown. However, he has very low self-esteem and if another child appears to be more popular than him, or if he perceives others appearing to laugh at him or criticise him, he reacts aggressively. On this occasion he had lashed out at another child and shouted at the dinner ladies when they tried to sort out the situation. I brought him into my office and asked him why he had behaved in that way. He was clearly upset and told me that everybody hated him. In true headteacher fashion (although I am now ashamed to admit it) I told him he was being ridiculous and that nobody hated him. I then used our usual sanction – putting him on "amber" which meant he lost some privileges. I thought I had dealt with the problem.

Action

After the first 4 days NLP Practitioner training, when I was introduced to the Meta Model, I realised immediately that I had compounded his problems and had basically made him feel even more worthless than before. I therefore asked him to come back for a chat and I used the Meta Model questions to enable him to be more specific about his perceptions and to challenge his beliefs. This was extremely successful. I also used some NLP coaching techniques to enable him to come up with his own solution to his lunchtime behaviour. This involved removing himself from the situation and speaking to a designated member of staff.

I therefore needed to ensure that the teaching staff were trained appropriately so that they would handle him and others in the same way. My ultimate aim is to have NLP techniques embedded in school so that they become second nature. My first staff training session was on the Meta Model. I began by explaining briefly what NLP was and discussing the assumptions underpinning it. We then discussed deletion, distortion and generalisation and immediately members of staff recognised these types of behaviour in the children they taught. We went through different types of questions they could choose to challenge these beliefs and the session was lively and very well-received. Each teacher left with the list of questions and agreed to try to use the Meta Model in their everyday management of learning and behaviour.

Meanwhile, Sam was behaving very well at lunchtimes and encouraging his brothers to do the same. This had been the case from the beginning of June until the end of the school year and for the first weeks of the autumn term. I was therefore disappointed when the Head Lunchtime Supervisor brought him to me for "rudeness". Apparently, Sam had sought her out and told her that one of her lunchtime supervisors had "anger problems", that shouting and aggressive behaviour was inappropriate and would not solve anything. He suggested that she should spend some time talking to me! Although I then spent some time with Sam explaining why he should not talk to an adult in this way, I was secretly pleased about his new-found strategies for dealing with stress. When I related this anecdote to my Deputy, apart from finding it amusing, he felt that there was a lesson to be learned here and that there was no point in the teaching staff using some NLP methods effectively if their work was being undone at lunchtime. I then decided to do some training with teaching assistants and dinner ladies so that there was a consistency of approach.

They were extremely receptive and keen to try out the methods. Generalisations such as 'everyone hates me' were one of the reasons often given by children for bad lunchtime behaviour and they were pleased that the Meta Model gave them strategies for addressing these beliefs. I asked my teaching staff to feed back on any occasions where they had used the questioning techniques or any other aspects of the training.

Impact

Although it is early days and we have only completed a fraction of the training I intend to do this year, we have had some encouraging successes already with several children in addition to 'Sam'. The most effective questioning with regard to classwork relates to the teachers now being able to pinpoint the exact difficulty a child is experiencing by asking the question *'what's stopping you…?'* They then follow up the

child's response with other Meta Model questions so they can provide the correct support to enable the child to succeed. An HLTA (higher level teaching assistant) provided me with the following transcript she had, showing her success with a child on the autistic spectrum.
The child had been asked to work out a sum in Mathematics:

Child: *I hate school*
HLTA: *What do you hate?*
Child: *Everything at school.*
HLTA: *Do you hate playtime and lunchtime?*
Child: *No – I hate work.*
HLTA: *What sort of work? Which lesson?*
Child: *I hate Literacy. I hate writing.*
HLTA: *Do you write in every literacy lesson?*
Child: *No. We sometimes read.*
HLTA: *Do you like to read?*
Child: *Yes.*
HLTA: *What books do you like?*
Child: *Magic books and funny books.*
HLTA: *Do you like Art?*
Child: *Yes, especially painting.*
HLTA: *So you enjoy reading, painting and playtime at school.*
Child: *Yes.*

This conversation went on in the same way and eventually the HLTA was able to ascertain the specific aspects of his work that the child was struggling with and made his teacher aware so that she could plan his work more effectively.

Another successful use of the Meta Model could be seen in our nurture group, which is led by a teaching assistant. She uses stories to address certain issues identified by the class teachers of the children in the group. She has now begun to use the Meta Model in the discussions about the stories to get specific detail from the children. This has made the discussions more effective and efficient.

AREAS WHERE THE META MODEL HAS BEEN LESS SUCCESSFUL:
Generally, staff have found that the children who are too young to articulate their perceptions effectively, and those children who "shut down" and refuse to answer questions about their difficulties, prove more of a challenge. I feel that it may be useful to do some training with staff on building rapport with these children and encouraging them to manage their state effectively in order to try to overcome the barriers they face.

Next phase
RESEARCH PLAN
Whilst I was pleased with the initial successes, I felt it was important to equip the children with skills they could use themselves to help encourage and motivate them in the future. The problem with the Meta Model and the Milton Model (which will be the focus of the next few training sessions for staff) is that the children are still reliant on an experienced practitioner. One of the most important ways in which the children can challenge their self-limiting beliefs is to manage their state so that they are the most resourceful they can possibly be. I want to enable them to do this and teach them how to anchor that state so that they can access it when they need to.

Action
In order to establish how to approach this seemingly daunting task I decided to work with "Sam" again, due to the fact that the change in him had already been significant and that he was now much more receptive to different ways of looking at problems and thinking creatively. I was anxious to ensure that he did not think I was carrying out some strange psychological experiment though, and I did not want to lose the trust I had already gained. I therefore spent some time with him on his work – particularly his writing, which he found difficult. In addition to this, as always, I used humour constantly, which always appeals to him. After spending a few sessions working in this way and building rapport with him, I was then able to help him to remember how he feels in another subject, which he is particularly good at. We changed the submodalities of this state – which he enjoyed – and when he was in the state which would be most helpful to him, we anchored that in a particular seat in the classroom.

Impact

Sam clearly experienced an improvement in his attitude towards his work and certainly appeared to feel more "enabled". This session took place the week before half term and it will be interesting to see if it may be sustained and if Sam will be able to access this resourceful state again when it is necessary. I will then work with teaching staff on managing state and building rapport. It is my intention that NLP practices will become second nature to my school staff and that we will become a flagship NLP school. Michelle has now completed the Master Practitioner and Teaching Excellence programme.

DISSEMINATING NLP ACROSS THE WHOLE SCHOOL

Naina offered short training sessions to Teaching Assistants and Teachers to spread NLP good practice across her school.

Naina Chauhan is Deputy Head/SENCO at West Thornton Primary Academy, Croydon, London

Research plan

My first training session was held on a Friday afternoon and was with a group of 33 teaching assistants. Out of the 33, some were 'fresh blood' and raring to go, some were just glad to be out of the classroom on a wet Friday afternoon (it didn't matter what they were being subjected to!), some were counting their months down to retirement and made no secret of the fact that they did not want to be there, and others, well, they were just doing what they were being told and were happy to play ball!

Action
The Teaching Assistants' Training sessions

SESSION 1 - ' THE POWER OF LANGUAGE
'So what are you going to train us on Naina?' Marion asked.

'Language and Communication', was my answer to her.

'What, because we don't know how to communicate?' she asked boldly.

'No, because we can all learn to communicate more effectively, Marion,' I smiled at her positively.

She mumbled something and walked out of the ladies toilets, leaving me thinking, *'this is going to be fun!'*

I started with 3 Yes... *'It's Friday afternoon, you're all here and we have one hour and 45 minutes to go to the end of the day'*. That was my first go at the 3 Yes and have been using it since to get attention, whether I am in front of a class of 7-year-olds, in a meeting which I am leading, or wanting to get the attention of my kids at home!

I began with the importance of how we use language and the use of the Meta Model to challenge our own beliefs and those of others, in particular our children:

'How many of you believe that you're rubbish at something or you've heard someone make a generalisation which you know may not be true?' The majority of the hands went up.... and that was the beginning of a truly fun, engaging and positive couple of hours! I thought that our TAs would probably be quite shy and not so forthcoming, but it seemed that most of them wanted to come to the front and have their beliefs challenged!

We had all sorts such as, *'I am really rubbish at maths'*... *'I have no confidence'* ... *'It's always me who has to clean up'*... and of course for me the best one was... *'I never get picked'*. You can guess the response of the others when Marion (the TA who I had met earlier in the ladies) sat at the front of the room ready to be challenged on that one... she did not remain there for too long! She did however walk off with a huge grin on her face, having just been proven wrong! She **did** get picked!

The session progressed to cover:
- Language to send people in the right direction
- Using positive suggestions to focus on what you do want
- Rewiring our thinking and using the Meta Model to specify, clarify and change beliefs

There was a real buzz in the room when they left the session and some lovely comments made.

This was my most successful TA training to date! This I believe was because it was something different. It was not the usual run-of-the-mill training they were used to receiving on a Friday afternoon. The introduction to the subject of NLP came at the end. Only 3 out of the 33 TAs claimed to have previously heard of NLP. For me, it was far more important that each individual felt the impact of what they had just experienced and understood its worth as opposed to knowing that it was an NLP technique, (in the initial part of the session anyway). It made far more sense to mention NLP at the end, as I did not want to blind them with science. I hadn't even reached home that evening and I received a voicemail on my phone from one TA telling me that she had just used the Meta Model on her 5-year-old who came home from school and said, *'you never let me do what I want and you're never fair'*. She said by questioning him further and talking to him, what would have transpired into a huge tantrum and confrontation leading to bad mood, turned into a 'little giggle' and a complete change in state. (See TA's account below)

SESSION 2 –LEARNING STRATEGIES
Following the success of the first session, I felt confident that this next session was going to be just as fun, and it was! The whole session was engaging and quite anecdotal, based on my strategy for buying a handbag. There was, however, a confused look from one TA who struggled to see how knowing her strategy for certain things was going to help her on a day-to-day basis. This for me was perfect as I was able to talk about resourceful vs. un-resourceful strategies and about how when people become 'stuck' in their lives over certain matters and how maybe changing their strategy could make them become 'unstuck'.

My strategy for buying a bag:
- Trigger: Sho
- Straight to the Handbag section!
- Go through all the aisles
- Do I really need it? (Internal dialogue)
- Answers always NO!! (Internal dialogue)
- But I want it!! (ID)

- Visualise myself using it (V and K-feel good)
- Visualise my Handbag wardrobe and go through colours/shapes/styles…and convince myself I need it!
- Yes feels right!! (K)
- Walking to till (Guilt)- K and ID
- Buy!

Resourceful or Unresourceful?

1. That would look great on me (external visual)

2. Try it on (external kinaesthetic)

3. Looks good, feels good (external visual and external kinaesthetic)

4. Buy!

Eliciting strategies
What's your strategy for…?

    1. Find something you are really good at learning

    2. In pairs, elicit each other's strategy (use questions below to help)

What happened when?

Think of the time when?

What did you/do you do?

What steps did you go through?

How did you know you had been successful?

What lets you know when you have finished?

What was the first thing you did?

Before that what did you do?

My handbag example was very amusing for some and I found that by the end of the session some were advising me to keep away from House of Fraser and TKMaxx and to change my strategy and 'walk away!'. One of the deputies sitting in on the training was completely blown away by how simply changing our use of language could have such a big impact on behaviour. She has been adapting her language with her grandson who has emotional and behavioural difficulties and with whom she has struggled tremendously for a considerable time now. (See Deputy's account below)

THE STAFF MEETING
I was all prepared and had rehearsed the 'ammunition', which I was ready to fire, expecting resistance from some members of staff. Something along the lines of using Carol Dwecks' 'Fixed Mindset' to illustrate just that point... that a lot of us who claim to be of a 'growth mindset' were clearly not! The training was delivered in the same way as the TAs with a little tweaking here and there (additional information). Although it was a little slower to get going, this session also went very well. The teachers were clearly more sceptical and asked many questions, which I expected them to. One teacher did argue that she knew that she was **never** going to be able to play the piano and that she had no desire to. I explained that this was a choice that she was making, however, was she of the 'growth mindset' and if she so desired, then she would be able to play the piano. Being 'open' to possibilities and change in your life was something I kept making reference to. Reference was also made to our already 'oustanding' challenge curriculum and practice (as noted by OFSTED), and our whole school ethos of creating independent, life-long learners. Implementing NLP techniques was like 'adding another tool in our toolbox'. On reflection, I did feel like I was having to work very hard at 'convincing' people about NLP because of their preconceptions (or ignorance, should I say) on the subject. However, the meeting ended on a very positive note and with a round of applause, which I was not expecting!

Impact
To say that NLP has helped me enormously in my both my personal life and in the workplace would be an understatement! I can see differences in other people which I know for some in particular is having a huge impact on them.

Here, the staff speak of the impact in their own words.

IMPACTS OF NLP
Teacher
Last year I was not very confident in my teaching abilities. I was often very emotional and would take things personally. I often found observations and being observed a very stressful experience. Since doing some NLP sessions with Naina, I have been using techniques personally and with my class. I have also shared some techniques with other members of staff. When a child in my class says *'I can't do X'*, I have challenged the concept of 'can't' by saying *'what do you mean, can't? Can you never...what about when you...?'* The children have started to understand that this is not always the case and I work with them to build their confidence. I have generally felt a lot calmer, more positive and in control. I now believe I am a good teacher and I am making a positive impact on my children's learning and showing myself as a good role model to others.

Teaching Assistant
After attending an NLP training course delivered by Naina Chauhan, I found myself thinking about everything I was saying, and subconsciously questioning the accuracy of what I was saying. In fact, I have found myself using the Meta Model questions on many occasions and have always had positive outcomes. One example of how I have used the Meta Model was actually on the way home from the training course. I had just picked up my 5-year-old son from school, and on the drive home I told him that I wanted him to go straight upstairs when we got home and get changed out of his uniform before he came down and had a drink and a snack. Only then would he be allowed to play on the iPad.

As usual, he kicked up a fuss and accused me of not being fair and said *'You NEVER let me do what I want'* and *'You're NEVER fair'*. At this point, I immediately turned around and asked him. *'Yesterday, I let you come home and watch TV straight away without getting changed. So do I sometimes let you do what you want?'* He stopped and thought about it, and then sheepishly replied *'Yes'*. I then continued with *'If I sometimes let you do what you want, then you can't say that I never let you do what you want.*

Are you tricking me?' He then started laughing as he thought he had fooled me, and we ended up having a laugh on the rest of the journey home. We got home, and he immediately ran upstairs and did all the things I had originally asked him to do without complaint. On any other occasion (without using the Meta Model questions) my son would have continued his tantrum in the car and stomped into the house protesting against anything I asked him to do. The technique definitely changes negative thinking into positive thinking and leaves you feeling so much better about what you originally felt was a negative situation. From the feedback given by other teaching assistants who attended the course, it seems that everyone had a positive story to tell. Several people had used the technique with children in their class, and expressed how it had made the children feel good about themselves and what they were doing. It is a simple but very effective technique, which I look forward to learning more about.

Deputy Head

After attending Naina's NLP training sessions at school and after many discussions regarding the positive use of language with children, I decided to try it out on my grandson who has emotional and behavioural needs on our journey home in the evenings. He gets frustrated very easily and is prone to temper tantrums. He is extremely physical and very, very active and is always jumping across the furniture rather than walking into a room. I found I was constantly using the word *'don't'* and so, after the first training session, decided that this is the first thing I would change. Instead of telling him **not** to do something, I asked instead *'what are you doing?'*. When he replied *'jumping on the furniture'*, I asked what the furniture was for. Every time he jumped on the furniture after that I asked the same question. He would say *'it's for sitting on'*, and would stop. After a few times he got the idea and even if he forgot and jumped on the furniture I would say his name and he would say *'sorry Nan for jumping on the furniture'*. I then decided to concentrate on helping him to talk about the behaviour he was exhibiting rather than focus on the negative and reprimand him for it. He didn't understand what I meant at first as he could describe what he was doing physically, but not what he was doing emotionally. It is amazing the difference a change in the language we use can make. My grandson is much more able to verbalise his behaviour and is beginning to use language to express himself appropriately which leads to less frustration and aggression. I am building on this week-on-week as the use of positive language is having a really great effect on his self-image.

Behaviour Mentor

Given the intensive and sometimes challenging nature of the relationships built between myself and the children I work with, the development of rapport is all-important. I have used several techniques such as mirroring to engage more constructively with the children. Mirroring stance and assimilating idiosyncratic phrases the children use helps with the development of rapport. This reinforces the relationship and thus enables the facilitation of progressive change for the children. NLP has helped support the nurturing of trusting and proactive relationships with the children. I am more aware of the language I use around the children. Even though I believed I was considered and selective with my language to begin with, I am more aware of the importance of specific wording and the potential impact. A basic example being the substitution of *'if'* with *'when'*. I would often say, *'if you have a good lesson then you can…'*. Now I rephrase such sentences to, *'when you have a good lesson you can…'*. This is a simple change but is noticeably more positive and has a more beneficial impact. With NLP in mind I have started to apply positive challenges to negative comments, an example of this being a Year 6 girl who stated she was getting very anxious about her SATs in general and Maths specifically. She said, *'I am rubbish at Maths; I've never been good at it.'* A natural response could have been to dismiss this comment, offer empty positive affirmation and move on. I stopped her mid flow in order to analyse her statement. *'Rubbish in what way?'* She responded, *'I still don't know my times tables, I'm rubbish at them.'* I replied, *'so, you're "rubbish" at times tables. What are you good at in Maths?'* She listed several methods she could do and other elements of Maths that she felt confident with. *'Ok, so you're not "rubbish" at Maths then?'* She responded with, *'Well, no. I just find times tables hard to remember. My Nan is helping me with them.'* A simple interjection at the opportune moment helped revise the child's over-generalised statement. NLP has helped raise my awareness of the language I use, when I use it and how I use it. Naina has now completed her Master Practitioner and Teaching Excellence training and she continues to spread good practice across her school.

NLP SUPPORTS THE CHANGES NEEDED IN A SCHOOL IN SPECIAL MEASURES

*Max Vlahakis is Headteacher at Alumwell Primary School,
Walsall,
West Midlands*

Research plan

I saw the potential of using NLP to support the leadership and management of my school as I often encounter many difficult and challenging relationships with various stakeholders within the school community. Coincidentally, prior to commencing the course I was asked to take over a school that was in difficulties. The school had gone into Special Measures, which is the most serious of Ofsted categories, because of complete failure in leadership at every level within the school. A key factor in the failure was a breakdown in the interpersonal relationships between staff. I quickly became aware following the training that NLP, especially the Milton and Meta models, could be utilised to effect positive change. Initially, I felt that the presuppositions from the Milton Model could be used effectively to challenge the self-limiting beliefs of the staff, which were mainly to blame for the negative climate and ethos of the school.

I initially organised a series of staff meetings addressing the educational underperformance within the school. However, it occurred to me that a far more significant condition limiting the performance of the school were the extremely poor interpersonal relationships between staff members compounded by several complaints of bullying. The behaviours had split the staff into two factions separated along racial boundaries, and although the complaints, and in fact the issues, were not race-related, a schism had formed between a number of staff who were Asian and a small number of staff who were white. The accusation of bullying had been unresolved for a significant period of time, which had fuelled the negative belief that institutional racism was behind the lack of resolution. Initially, I addressed the issue of bullying using established local HR systems. However, the feelings ran too deeply and I felt that I was papering over the cracks. I therefore decided to use the Milton Model first to build good beliefs, therefore tackling several issues at the same time and to use Meta questioning at a later date to deal with perceived problems.

Action
A special staff meeting was arranged during an additional inset day for me to address issues regarding school ethos. I began the meeting by using the "yes sets" to presuppose success, as follows:

'We've just completed our buffet lunch. We've all managed to get here on time and AD gave us a lot to think about this morning during her presentation on guided reading and I am sure that we are all going to work together effectively now to address the issues we're facing.'

I then established a time anchor using May, when their Ofsted inspection took place, to highlight the negative patterns of behaviour that were occurring in the school when I arrived. For example, staff members gossiping about one another and numbers of HR complaints not addressed and unresolved. I then focused on the present (July) and reiterated the progress we had made to date and looked forward to the future, predicting the progress we were hoping to make by Christmas. I used the following key parts of speech from the Milton Model in order to direct the thinking of the staff members so that they felt empowered:

- Verbs to ensure awareness – 'I'm not sure if you realise yet that we have already come a long way to addressing our problems simply by recognising that they exist'
- Adverbs to assume that something is true – 'Fortunately, we already have in place everything we need to effect positive change'
- Adverbial time phrases so that I convinced staff that something was true by positioning it in time – 'when we achieve our goals, you will all think that this hard work has been worthwhile'
- The more the more – 'The more we work together, the more we will see how easily we can tackle the problems we are facing'

Impact
This meeting proved to be extremely effective. Attitudes visibly changed and although the staff still suffered from some historical negative feelings towards the situation they found themselves in, they

saw the light at the end of the tunnel with regards to their situation. One of the presuppositions that was at the heart of the session for myself as the leader was that the staff had come to school wanting to help every pupil to achieve, whether they realised it or not. It was my aim to remind them of that fact and help them to uncover their motivation.

Following the meeting, the majority of the staff threw themselves into their work with a renewed vigour that comes from believing in what you are doing and being part of a bigger picture.

Whenever the staff met as group it became important to use anchors to reinforce the positive visualisation. An example of this was getting the group into a positive state for brainstorming - the creation of a motivated state. The question was, how can the state be anchored so that the group could get back that same degree of motivation more quickly in the future? The strategy decided upon was the use of a key phrase as a means to draw the focus of the group. The phrase was 'no problems, just solutions'. This immediately focused the group and individuals to approach meetings they attended in a changed state. They were able to access their 'want to believe' state of mind and as a result began to bring forward real school improvement solutions instead of responding to the solutions and reality being imposed upon them by external sources.

The school's journey from its starting point to where it is now has been quite remarkable. The most difficult change to take place within the school has not been the structural changes, which are straightforward and fairly easy to introduce, but the changes in the beliefs through NLP approaches that have occurred in key staff throughout the school.

CONCLUSION

This book is not designed as a quick fix or little book of tips and hints. It is designed as a primer to give you the knowledge and skills of NLP that are essential to excellence in teaching and learning. It's a software update for the human brain for thinking, remembering, encoding and decoding learning to learn. As we continually strive to give teachers and learners the exquisite skills for voracious and tenacious learning, we hope that you will do so too.

We are hopeful for the future as a great many teachers are making an enormous difference to their students. In NLP we often say *'we change the world one person at a time'.* In education we can do more than this and change the world one class at a time! Over the past 15 years of working directly in schools and colleges we have seen many situations where one individual teacher has changed the system and thinking in a school. They haven't done this by evangelising, but by getting better results with their students than their peers. When you consistently improve the performance and behaviour of your students, it isn't long before people begin to ask you what it is that you are doing and want to learn for themselves.

The skills, behaviours and attitudes of NLP enable you to teach so much more effectively and with enjoyment and ease, so that before long you may find your colleagues and managers wanting to know how you do it and you may find yourself changing the system without much effort at all. 16 years ago, when we began this work in the UK, most people could not see the relevance of NLP in teaching. NLP was for therapy or business and was not perceived as useful in schools. How wrong they were! Now we have thousands of teachers, all over the world, using NLP to improve their lives and the lives of their students.

The advent of initiatives such as the 'flipped classroom', blended learning and mindfulness training in schools strongly suggest that times are beginning to change and the focus is changing from **what** to learn to **how** to learn. Some initiatives go even further and remove the teachers from the process completely, replacing them with a virtual Grandmother who focuses on asking really great questions for the learners to explore.[1] NLP is not a static field, and by its very nature it continually evolves; we have more to do to challenge out-dated concepts and integrate more of the Bandler Technologies into education. Just as the nature of therapy is change, so the nature of learning is change. A student who has learned a new skill or gained some insight into a new subject is not the same person as they were before they did so. They have changed irreversibly. If the teaching and learning is effective, by the very nature of learning the students will be different people. So NLP was an educational model from the outset. As we have said before, people are not broken so they do not need fixing. Rather, they are uneducated as to how to drive their own brains.

Take Mary for example. Mary is 60-years-old and works in a laundry which participated in an NLP project to teach numeracy in the workplace.[2] Upon receiving her certificate for her level 2 Numeracy she sat with tears in her eyes stroking the certificate. She said, *'Is this really mine? Can I take it home? I have never had a certificate before and thought I was stupid. Now I know I can learn anything I put my mind to'.*

NLP enables us to know what is useful to others in ways that allow them to achieve beyond what they could previously conceive. Mary did not merely learn some Maths during the 12 weeks we worked with her, she changed her perception of herself, who she was and what she could achieve.

So we want you to take this book and begin to inspire your students, design easier learning to make them smarter and faster. To make this more worthwhile you can do more and design hope. We all have more to do!

REFERENCES

1. The hole in the wall project www.hole-in-the-wall.com
2. The New Wave Project 2011 Meta Education Team, Funded by Cornwall Learning Partnership

APPENDIX A

Submodality checklist

Chart for comparing submodalities of two experiences:

	Experience 1	Experience 2
VISUAL		
Number of images		
Motion/still		
Colour / black and white		
Bright/dim		
Focused/unfocused		
Bordered/ borderless		
Associated/dissociated		
Narrow/wide angle		
Size		
Shape		
3D/flat		
Close/distant		
In one place/panoramic		
AUDITORY		
Number of sounds		
Volume		
Tone		
Tempo		
Pitch		

Pace		
Duration		
Intensity		
Direction		
Rhythm		
Harmony		
More in one ear		
KINAESTHETIC		
Location in body		
Breathing rate		
Pulse rate		
Skin temperature		
Weight		
Pressure		
Intensity		
Tactile sensations		
OLFACTORY/GUSTATORY		
Sweet		
Sour		
Salt		
Bitter		
Aroma		
Fragrance		
Essence		
Pungency		

APPENDIX B

Questions to calibrate eye-accessing cues

What colour is your front door?

- What would you look like with green hair?

- When was the last time you saw your signature?

- What is the last line of your National Anthem?

- What does your answer phone message sound like?

- What would a room full of cats and dogs sound like?

- Say your name backwards

- What temperature is your big toe?

- What does cotton wool feel like?

- Which way do you turn a key to unlock a door?

- How do you feel when someone compliments you?

- What do you say to yourself when you wake up?

- Now over to you to create more questions

APPENDIX C

The Meta Model and Blooms Taxonomy

Benjamin Bloom created this taxonomy for categorising levels of abstraction of questions that commonly occur in educational settings. The taxonomy provides a useful structure in which to categorise formative and summative questions.

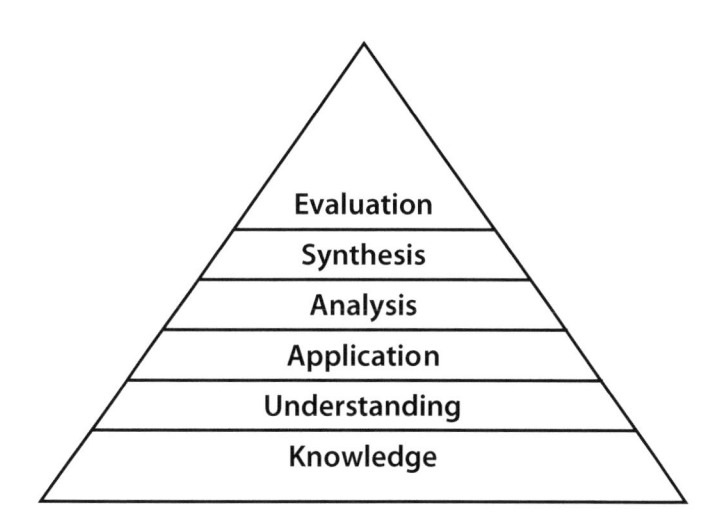

- Evaluation
- Synthesis
- Analysis
- Application
- Understanding
- Knowledge

Competence	Skills Demonstrated	Question Cues:	Examples of Meta Model questions to use at each level to promote even more thinking and learning at that level: 'Digging deeper'
Knowledge	• observation and recall of information • knowledge of dates, events, places • knowledge of major ideas • mastery of subject matter	• who, when, where, etc. • list • **define** • tell • describe • identify • show • label • collect • examine • tabulate • quote • name	• How do you know? • **Where did you find this out?** • What else? • What does that mean? • Always? • Is this true for every example? • **What, where etc. specifically?** • So what will that mean for..? • What other information might be useful?
Understanding/ Comprehension	• understanding information • grasp meaning • translate knowledge into new context • interpret facts, compare, contrast • order, group, infer causes • predict consequences	• summarise • describe • interpret • contrast • predict • associate • distinguish • estimate • **differentiate** • discuss • extend	
Application	• use information • use methods, concepts, theories in new situations • solve problems using required skills or knowledge	• apply • demonstrate • calculate • complete • illustrate • show • solve • examine • modify • relate • change • classify • experiment • discover	• What would happen if..? • How do you know that will work? • If that is true, what else could that mean? • How will you know when the solution is reached fully? • If we change x what will happen? • How does that happen? • What have you learned about this concept in previous topics? • What is this similar to? • **How is this different to..?** • What is the exception to this pattern? • Could you explain this bit by bit..? • What links can you make to ...?

Competence	Skills Demonstrated	Question Cues:	Examples of Meta Model questions to use at each level to promote even more thinking and learning at that level: 'Digging deeper'
Analysis	• seeing patterns • organisation of parts • recognition of hidden meanings • **identification of components**	• analyse • separate • order • explain • connect • classify • arrange • divide • compare • select • explain • infer	
Synthesis	• use old ideas to create new ones • generalise from given facts • relate knowledge from several areas • predict, draw conclusions	• combine • integrate • modify • rearrange • substitute • plan • create • design • invent • what if? • compose • formulate • preparing • generalise • rewrite	• How does this change what you know about x? • **If you were to do this differently, what different results might you get?** • What makes this a great answer? • …so what exactly have you learned? • Now you know the options, what will you decide next time? • How do you know the evidence is correct? • How did you reach these conclusions? • If you had more opportunity, what further research could you do? • How do you know this is correct? • What does all this tell you about..? • What would have made this easier from the start? • **What did you do that made the difference?** • How would you check this answer?
Evaluation	• compare and discriminate between ideas • assess value of theories, presentations • make choices based on reasoned argument • verify value of evidence • recognise subjectivity	• assess • decide • rank • grade • test • measure • recommend • convince • select • judge • explain • discriminate • support • conclude • compare	

APPENDIX D
Transcript to use with students

TIMELINE JOURNEY

Imagine yourself floating up above your timeline and travelling into the future to that moment of brilliant success. See yourself now, look at the delight on your face as you realise for the first time how well you have done – listen to what you say to yourself, congratulating yourself on how well you have done, knowing now that all that you wish for your future is now not just a possibility but a reality! Make this image big and bright so you can study every detail. Who are you with? Are you alone or with others? What are the sounds around you? Are you telling yourself how clever you are? Our imagination is a wonderful thing - the more we imagine your success, the more vividly you see your future the more you can manifest those things in our lives. Step into your body now and notice the good feelings in your body, I don't know if you have a sense of satisfaction, or excitement, joy, or some other wonderful feeling. As you step into your body just begin to notice those feelings begin to spin through your body so you feel it in every cell of your body. Spread that good feeling all the way to the top of your head and down to the tips of your toes. It's good that you can do this easily now.

Imagine now that you can turn around and look back at all the things that you have successfully achieved to get to this moment in time. See yourself planning and preparing to revise, watch yourself being determined and tenacious in your revision and review. Notice how you easily remember the facts and information as you discover new ways to use your brain to recall, review and learn, really learn easily. Enjoy the sense of satisfaction as you begin to drive your own brain in the direction you want it to go. Focus your attention on two points just beneath your eyes on your cheekbones, as you do this you can become aware of how determined you are to succeed. Feel that determination as you realise how easy this is once you make the decision to just go for it now. So take a moment now to run through the time you have for revision. Making the most of every moment, engaging with your learning, using your brain to maximum potential and really enjoying the discoveries you are making. See yourself taking the time out you deserve and being able to really relax in the knowledge that you have used each session really well and returning refreshed to the next session

See yourself on the day of the tests, relaxed and alert, arriving in good time, well prepared and ready to do your best. Notice yourself focusing on the questions and answering them easily with enthusiasm. Relaxed and alert, concentrating and calm, saying useful helpful things to yourself to encourage yourself to do your absolute best. Using each day as an unprecedented opportunity to show how good you are. See yourself relaxing after the test and preparing for any others. Letting go of any feelings about the last one and focusing your attention on the next one just imagining the time available to you as flowing smoothly and easily right up to the day you receive the results.

That's right. Now in a moment imagine I am going to ask you to float back out up above your timeline once more and begin to travel back to the time and place of this room. And now as you float gently and easily out above your timeline begin to gather all the learnings and experiences that you have noticed yourself doing in this time before your exams and bring together all the insights and useful thoughts and ideas, helpful behaviours and feelings and bring them back with you to the time and place of this room. Because as you imagine yourself successfully completing your revision it's almost as if you have done the work once before and it's always easier to do something for a second time isn't it?

APPENDIX E
Glossary of terms

Accessing cues
Subtle behaviours that indicate which representational system the person is using at the time. Accessing cues include eye movements, voice tone, body posture, gestures, skin tone and breathing rate

Anchoring
The process of associating an internal response with an external trigger, so that the response can be quickly re-accessed

Auditory
Relating to the sense of hearing Behaviour The specific actions and responses by which we interact with other people and the environment Behavioural flexibility the ability to vary one's own behaviour to elicit a response from another person

Calibration
The process of learning to read another person's unconscious, non-verbal responses, by observing their behaviour

Congruence
Full alignment of a person's beliefs, state and behaviour orientated towards a specific outcome

Conscious Mind
The part of your mind that is working when you are alert and aware

Criteria
The values a person uses to make decisions

Design Human Engineering®
A technology and evolutionary tool created by Dr Bandler in the late 1980s–early 1990s which focuses on using more of our brain to do more than was previously possible

Eye accessing cues
Eye movements that reveal which representational system the person is using to process information

Future pacing
Mentally rehearsing a future situation to help ensure that the desired behaviour will occur naturally and easily

Gustatory
Relating to the sense of taste Installation The process of helping the acquisition of a new strategy or behaviour

Kinaesthetic Related to body sensations
In NLP the term is used to encompass all feelings including tactile and emotional

Meta Model
A model developed by Richard Bandler and John Grinder that suggests questions which enable people to specify information and clarify information to open up and enrich the model of a person's world

Meta Program
A learned process for sorting and organising information and internal strategies

Metaphor
Stories and analogies

Milton Model
A model developed by Richard Bandler and John Grinder based on the patterns of hypnotic techniques used by Milton H. Erickson and other masters of communication

Neuro Linguistic Programming
The study of the structure of subjective experience. It is an attitude, methodology and technology which teaches people how to improve the quality of their lives. It is an educational tool designed to teach people how to communicate more effectively with themselves and with others. It is designed to help people to have choice in the way they think, feel and behave

Neuro-Hypnotic Repatterning®
A technology which uses the hypnotic process to restructure people at the level of cortical pathways

Olfactory
Relating to smell or sense of smel

Outcomes
Directions, goals or desired states that a person aspires to achieve

Overlapping
Expanding experience by moving from one representational system to another Pacing Matching or mirroring certain aspects of a person's behaviour to quickly establish rapport

Predicates
Process words such as verbs, adverbs and adjectives used in NLP to identify which representational system a person is using to process information

Rapport
The existence of trust and harmony and cooperation in a relationship

Representational Systems
The five senses: seeing, hearing feeling, smelling and tasting. Also known as visual Auditory, Kinaesthetic Olfactory and Gustatory (VAKOG)

Sensory acuity
Using all senses as fully as possible to gain maximum information from a given situation or encounter

State
The total ongoing mental and physical conditions from which a person is acting

Strategy
A set of mental and behavioural steps to achieve an outcome

Submodalities
The sensory qualities perceived by each of the five representational systems

Synaesthesia
The process of overlapping representational systems so that the person has a fuller sensory experience Timeline The internal representation of time

TOTE
The term stands for Test Operate Test Exit which describes the basic feedback loop used to guide all behaviour

Trance
A state commonly experienced as a result of hypnosis. It is also a state of mind that is characterised by a focus of thought

Unconscious Mind
The part of your mind that is working all the time. It runs the automatic programmes of thinking and behaving

Visual
Relating to sight or sense of sight

Well-Formed Outcomes
Goals that are set according to conditions which in NLP terms must be positive, specific, sensory based, ecological and maintainable by the individual themselves

Bibliography

Here are some books for those of you who wish to pursue NLP further.

Bandler, Richard
Using your Brain for a Change, Durango, CO 1985
Magic in Action, Capitola, CA, 1985
Time for a Change, Capitola, CA, 1993
Get the Life You Want, Harper Element, London 2008
Make your Life Great, Harper Element, London, 2010

Bandler, Richard, Delozier Judith and Grinder, John
Patterns of the Hypnotic Techniques of Milton H. Erickson, Volume 1, Capitola, CA 1975

Bandler, Richard and Grinder, John
The Structure of Magic, Capitola, CA 1975
The Structure of Magic, Volume 2, Capitola, CA 1975
Transformations, Durango, CO, 1980
Frogs into Princes, Capitola, CA 1979

Bandler, Richard and Fitzpatrick, Owen
Conversations with Richard Bandler, Health Communications, Deerfield Beach, FL 2009
Memories, Hope is the Question, Mysterious Publications, Dublin, 2014

Bandler, Richard and La Valle, John,
Persuasion Engineering®, Capitola, CA 1996

Bandler, Richard, Benson, Kate and La Valle, John, Fitzpatrick, Owen, Roberti, Alessio, Thomson, Garner, Mora, Alessandro, Piper, Anders
Seven Practical Applications of NLP, Attrakt, Niewveen, 2012
Bandler, Richard and Thomson, Garner

The Secrets of Being Happy, IM press, 2011

BOOKS FOR CHILDREN AND ADULTS TO SHARE

Bandler, Richard
The adventures of Anybody, Capitola, CA 1993

Van der Leij, Joost
Joost is Happy, discussing feelings with young children, Attrakt, Neiwveen, 2009

Joost being bullied, Helping teenage kids deal with bullying, Attrakt, Niewveen, 2010

RESOURCES FOR TEACHERS

Benson, Kate, Skelton, Arnie
Our top 96 Tutorial Activities, Matrix Essential Training 2006, A Resource manual for teachers.

CD AND DVD

Kate Benson
The Revision Coach, CD

Richard Bandler
Getting Smarter Series, Mental Clarity and More Mathematical Mind, CD

Richard Bandler
The Art and Science of Nested Loops, DVD

Laura Spicer
Voice Power for Teachers, DVD, Available from www.meta-nlp.co.uk

WEBSITES

For information about the Society of NLP, Courses, Trainers and Products
www.purenlp.com

For information about NLP Education Courses, Products and resources
www.meta-nlp.co.uk
www.meta4education.co.uk

Richard Bandler
www.richardbandler.com

Kate Benson
www.kate-benson.co.uk

Index

A

Acknowledgements	x
Achievement	41, 137, 199
See Also Success	
Analogue Making	177, 284
Anchoring	81, 160
Creative use of Spatial Anchoring in the Classroom	266
How to create and anchor a great learning state	160
Spatial and classroom anchors for quiet attention	303
Using established Musical Anchors	265
Art	118
Assessment FOR learning not OF learning!	45
Attention Deficit Disorder (ADD)	248
Attention Deficit Hyperactivity Disorder (ADHD)	248
Attention-grabbers	196
Autistic Spectrum Disorder	250

B

Blooms Taxonomy	202, 367
Body Language	31, 140

C

Calibration	30, 160
Classroom management	
Creating lines of light	157
Keeping the lesson on track	186
Learning is an active process	158
Other variables	195
Setting up the group	156
Spinning the prayer wheel	189
Super-fast rapport is built through attention on others	158
Winning your class over	155
Comprehension	64, 67, 68, 73, 202
Counting	

Creative Writing	122
Curriculum	61
Confidence	
Building Confidence with Competence	191
How to praise effectively	191
Creative use of NLP for Creative Writing	287
Creativity and Talent	116
Art	118
Poetry and Creative Writing	122
Beyond the Arts	124
Music	121
The Picasso strategy	118, 119
The Chagall strategy	120

D

The Definitve Guide for NLP and Teaching and Learning	XI
Design Human Engineering® (DHE®)	XIX, 114, 373
Dyslexia	244
Dyspraxia	247

E

Early years: Under 5-years-old	259
Emotional State of Learning	32
Encoding and decoding learning	56, 75, 78, 83, 90
Enteric nervous system	XX, 149
Exams	
Exam preparation transcript	370
Preparing for exams and tests	231
Eye accessing cues	30, 58
Questions to calibrate eye accessing cues	366

F

Feedback	
Giving feedback for great results	193
Fundamentals of NLP	30

G

Generative Learning	204

H

How Learning works	24
How to drive learning with good feelings	37
How to use this book	XXII

L

Ready to Learn	305
Language	
Small changes in language to create a big impact	260
Language patterns with children with little English language	262
Learning difference	241, 252
Learning on Purpose	XIV, 28
A Learning revolution	XV
Learning environment	170
Building an Effective Learning Environment	170
How to speak to each student within the whole class	174
How to presuppose success	175
How to remove barriers and inoculate	19
Ready to Learn	305
Learning strategies	24, 26, 28, 40, 57
A step-by-step guide to Learning Strategies	
Literacy	87

M

Make the Difference	XVI
Mathematics	
Addition	92
Algebra	111
Counting	89
Division	104
Engineering successful strategies	109
Geometry	106
How to teach anyone to calculate: Strategies for Mathematics	86, 98
Multiplication	99
Skip Counting	90
Subtraction	96
Memory Strategies	
Learning names	76

Remembering lists	79
Memory Pegs	79, 80
The Memory Pegs Strategy	80, 332
How to learn the Memory Pegs Strategy	81
How to develop Memory Pegs Further	83
Meta Model	202, 214, 215, 216
Changing unhelpful beliefs and attitudes	214
Compared to what?	218
Mind reading	220
Modal operators	221
What has to be there?	221
What is 'deleted', or missing?	217
What's altered or distorted?	218
What's generalised?	220
What's the connection?	220
Where's the connection?	219
Where's the choice?	221
Who says?	218
The Meta Model and Blooms Taxonomy	367
Using the Meta Model to challenge self-limiting beliefs in school	348
Milton Model	172, 174, 284
Cause and effect	177
Generalisations	174, 217
I wonder...	302
Listen as you speak	187
More the more	192
Negatives	180
Put it in Quotes	192
Putting things in the Past	234
Yes sets	194
Motivation	182
Motivation and propulsion	41
How to ensure learners continue to be motivated	174
Timelines and other techniques for Motivation and Success	229
Music	27, 116, 121, 124

N

Nested loops	207

Storytelling and nesting learning	206
Ending with new beginnings	199
Neural pathways	XX, 149, 201
Neuro-Hypnotic Repatterning	XIX, 150
Spinning bad feelings into Good Feelings	235
Neuro Linguistic Programming	XI, XIX
The Study of Excellence	XVII
The building blocks of NLP applied to learning	23
Neurology	147, 149
Neurons	XX
Neuroscience	XX
Neurotransmitters	XX, 149
NLP	XI, XVI, XIX, 25, 32
Disseminating NLP across the whole school	351
NLP Fun in school	257
NLP is an Educational Model	XVI
NLP throughout the lesson with 16-19-year-old students	327
NLP supports the changes needed in a school in Special Measures	359
The use of NLP in and Academic Coaching and Mentoring role	341
Numeracy	XV, 87, 89, 138

O

Obsessive Compulsive Disorder	253

P

Phonics	64
Poetry	70, 75, 122, 128
Presuppose success	174, 175, 178
Propulsion	38, 41, 44, 192, 194
Primary and Elementary school: 5-to-11-year olds	270
Post-compulsory education: 16 years and over	327

Q

Questioning	200
Stretch and Challenge through questioning	202

R

Reading	36, 44

Comfort and fun to improve reading	280
How to teach anyone to read - the mechanics and beyond	61
A strategy for Speed Reading	69
A strategy to extract Information and Meaning	69
Learning to enjoy reading	62
Learning to Read	63
Reading to Learn	68
Teaching Reading - eye accessing study of different reading strategies	281
Representational system(s)	25, 26, 27, 40, 58, 79
Auditory	26, 43, 59, 68, 69, 77, 79, 89, 200
Visual	27, 56, 58, 59, 69|, 100
Kinaesthetic	27, 28, 29, 30, 56, 58, 70, 111, 160, 171, 208, 235
Representational systems and questions	200
Room Layout	70, 195

S

Secondary and High School: 11 to 15-year-olds	307
Self-esteem	191
Sensory acuity	31, 58, 68, 374
Spelling	
A whole class strategy for Spelling	270
How to be a great Spy!	57
How to teach anyone to spell	50
Improving poor spelling	54
Spelling success in the Netherlands	273
Teaching how to spell a word for the first time	53
Teaching Spelling from Scratch	53
Teaching spelling to the whole class	55
The Perfect Spelling Strategy	275
State	32, 37, 43, 54, 78
Creating happiness and harmony for a child with multiple challenge	293
Creating positive learning states and overcoming challenges	292
Driving learning with good feelings	36, 37
Emotional state for learning	32
Music and State Management	263
States for Learning Excellence, Observation and Leadership for undergraduates	335
Working with a child displaying severe anxiety	293

Resourceful states	136, 165
Storytelling	38, 206, 327
Subject-specific teaching strategies	270
Creating enthusiasm for French grammar	307, 309
It's good to talk in Science teaching	316
State and Language to build confidence in outdoor pursuits	321
Voice tone and body language in Food Technology lessons	323
Creativity and confidence in French Language whole class teaching	284
Subjective experience	71, 249
Strategies for Learning	
Building Strategies	36
Strategies for Learning Difference	241
Submodalities	26, 237, 250, 259, 284, 300, 336, 375
Changing submodalities to overcome anxiety and create happy states	259
Submodality checklist	364
Swish for Change	237
Synaesthesia	28, 66, 79, 375

T

Teaching	
Highly Effective Classroom Teaching	130
Teachers	
The Mind of a Highly Effective Teacher - The Art of the State	145
What makes a Highly Effective Teacher?	131
Highly Effective Teachers:	
Are flexible in their behaviour	139
Are proactive and outcome-focused	134
Are process rather than content orientated	137
Are systematic in their behaviours	133
Endeavour to like their students	141
See problems as challenges	134
Take notice, watch and listen	140
Temporal predicates	205
Test Operate Test Exit (TOTE)	40, 375
Thinking on Purpose	XIX, 25
Time predicates	205
Time verbs and adverbs	176, 193, 310
Timelines	229, 230, 274

Troubleshooting and Challenges 213

U
Universal quantifiers 178, 220

V
Visual Squash 237

W
Well Formed Outcomes 182, 231, 239, 252, 375
Moving from a child who 'does not write' to a
creative writing enthusiast 309

The authors

Dr. Richard Bandler, co-creator of NLP, has for over 45 years dedicated himself to developing new ideas, new tools, new techniques and models for the advancement of human evolution. Richard Bandler's 30 authored or co-authored books have sold millions of copies, and been translated into dozens of languages. Hundreds of thousands of people have studied with him to learn NLP, Design Human Engineering™, and Neuro-hypnotic Re-Patterning™. Richard Bandler has led the world into an era of behavioral technology. Richard has long taught that NLP is not a therapeutic model but an educational one. For the first time in this book he applies his technology directly to the field of Education.

Kate Benson, the International Director of Education for the Society of NLP™, has been at the leading edge of teaching and learning for many years. After training with Dr Bandler she dedicated her work to researching and teaching others the application of NLP to teaching and learning. Having a unique insight into the world of the teacher as result of her extensive experience of more than 30 years in the classroom and with Dr Bandler as her mentor, Kate has worked with thousands of teachers all over the world to create elegant and effective learning in their classrooms. She brings many practical examples, experience and knowledge to the text. She is the author of a number of guides for teachers and produces resources for teachers and students.

Testimonials

It is invigorating to read a book that requires the reader to question their preconceptions and review long held traditions that have underpinned so much practice. As teachers we constantly strive to invigorate our lessons, to polish and refine our strategies for learning but perhaps we do not spend enough time and thought considering and understanding the ways in which each individual learns. This book provides a wealth of ideas to move teaching away from the current obsession with observing teaching into a richer place focused on 'thinking', one which helps students learn to think and take responsibility for their own learning. Read it with an open mind, think and question, maybe there is much to gain and certainly little to lose.

Dr Beri Hare OBE

I truly believe this book can be a game-changer for teaching and the more widely these strategies are communicated in the world of education, the better. With the exception of some truly magical teachers, my own experience of the English state education system has been disappointing. As the mother of three sons, one of them with a diagnosis of ASD and Dyslexia, I have found the system to be largely unfit for purpose and terribly inhibiting for teachers who strive to enrich children's learning. I pray that this book, and the follow-on titles I look forward to seeing, will bring about a revolution in our education system and at last precipitate the step-change it so desperately needs.

Jane Pikett

Made in the USA
Columbia, SC
26 February 2020